# The International Political Sociology of Security

D1826379

This book builds a theoretical approach to the intractable problem of theory/practice in International Relations (IR) and develops tools to study how theory and practice 'hang together' in international security.

Drawing on Pierre Bourdieu's political sociology, the book argues that theory and practice take part in struggles over basic understandings (doxa) in international fields through what the book calls *doxic battles*. In these battles scientific facts, military hardware and social networks are mobilized as weapons in a fight for recognition. NATO's transformation and fight for survival and the rapidly growing number of think tanks in European security in the 1990s is taken as an example of these processes. The book studies a variety of sources such as funding to science programmes in Europe; think tanks and research centres in European security; NATO's relations with the EU, the WEU and the OSCE; and the mobilization of theory at crucial points in the transformation process.

*The International Political Sociology of Security* will be of interest to students and scholars of International Relations, Security Studies, Science Studies and Critical Theory.

**Trine Villumsen Berling** holds a postdoctoral position at the Centre for Advanced Security Theory, University of Copenhagen.

## New International Relations

Edited by Richard Little, University of Bristol, Iver B. Neumann, Norwegian Institute of International Affairs (NUPI), Norway and Jutta Weldes, University of Bristol.

The field of international relations has changed dramatically in recent years. This new series will cover the major issues that have emerged and reflect the latest academic thinking in this particular dynamic area.

# The International Political Sociology of Security

## Rethinking theory and practice

Trine Villumsen Berling

LONDON AND NEW YORK

First published 2015
by Routledge
2 Park Square, Milton Park, Abingdon, Oxfordshire OX14 4RN

and by Routledge
711 Third Avenue, New York, NY 10017

First issued in paperback 2016

*Routledge is an imprint of the Taylor & Francis Group, an informa business*

*British Library Cataloguing in Publication Data*
A catalogue record for this book is available from the British Library

*Library of Congress Cataloging in Publication Data*
A catalog record for this title has been requested

ISBN 13: 978-1-138-28942-0 (pbk)
ISBN 13: 978-0-415-59824-8 (hbk)

Typeset in Times New Roman
by Taylor & Francis Books

# Contents

# List of tables

# Acknowledgement

This book has travelled a long way before this final version. The work started at the Department of Political Science in Copenhagen more than ten years ago, proceeded at the European University Institute in Florence, materialized as an argument at the Graduate Institute of International Relations in Geneva, took new shape at the Centre for Advanced Security Theory (CAST) in Copenhagen, and finally found its current shape at the NATO Defense College in Rome. Along the way, I have benefited from numerous conversations with colleagues who have each left their mark on my work. Jens Bartelson, Asser Berling, Christian Bueger, Olaf Corry, Stefano Guzzini, Lene Hansen, Friedrich Kratochwil, Keith Krause, Anna Leander, Nicholas Onuf, Karen Lund Petersen, Mikkel Vedby Rasmussen, Vibeke Schou Tjalve and Ole Wæver have each in their way shaped my work. I am grateful for the time they put into our conversations and for their sharp and constructive engagement with my work.

Elements of this book have been published previously, albeit in revised versions. I would like to thank the editors of *Theory and Society* for permission to draw upon the article 'Bourdieu, International Relations, and European Security' (2012) 41: 451–478. I would also like to thank Routledge for the permission to draw upon the book chapter 'Knowledges' which appeared (pp. 59–77) in Rebecca Adler-Nissen's 2012 book *Bourdieu in International Relations. Rethinking Key Concepts in IR.*

# 1 Introduction

> Indeed, had we listened to theory, we would not have come half as far. Theory told us that NATO enlargement and a NATO-Russia relationship would be mutually exclusive goals. Practice proved otherwise.
>
> (Solana 1999b: Article V)

These words were stated by the then NATO Secretary General Javier Solana when he was confronted with predictions concerning the eastern enlargement of NATO in the late 1990s. Not only do these bold words signal a confident Secretary General proud of a strong Atlantic Alliance and a hope or belief in the fact that old enmities can be – perhaps even already had been – replaced with friendly relations and cooperation in new contexts. Importantly, the quote also frames a new and puzzling competitor – if not threat – in European security: Theory. Research and politics were apparently seen to be in conflict over European security decisions. This places science in a hitherto largely unexplored relationship with security practice that this book will seek to shed light on.

In order to capture this relationship, this book challenges the privileged and external position of the objective researcher with no influence on his or her object of study so prevalent in mainstream studies of International Relations (IR) (King *et al.* 1994). Instead, the researcher – or at least theory in some form – 'enters the game'. The relationship between theory and practice, as a theoretical and epistemological question, thus becomes the first important subject of the book. How has this relationship been understood in mainstream IR and Security Studies[1], and what are the recent developments in this debate? Is the relationship best defined by a 'gap' between different types of agents? Or is the Constructivist meta-point about the co-construction of social reality a more adequate point of departure for further research on the matter? The book argues for the construction of an approach to the relationship between theory and practice that takes its point of departure in IR Reflectivism. This means that the book applies an approach that is sensitive to discursive representations and challenges the privileged role of the theorist. However, I agree with Iver B. Neumann (Neumann 2002: 639) that 'what is needed … are empirical studies that specify exactly how IR practices contribute, or do not contribute to the status quo.' A Reflectivist/Constructivist understanding of discursive representations is merely a first step to understanding how the theory/practice relationship can be understood in general and how it functions in European security. Hence, the book argues that in order to get a full grasp of the status and depth of the theory/practice relationship, a turn to Bourdieusian sociology can strengthen IR discussions in general and studies of the science/policy nexus after the linguistic turn[2] in particular. Such a turn will address the question of whether there is more than a discursive link between theory and practice, and how this link can be analysed by zooming in on sociological patterns of practice in loosely structured fields.

## The case of European security and IR

European security in the 1990s remains one of the paradigmatic cases for understanding change in international relations (e.g. Behnke 2013; Kristensen 2011; Pouliot 2010). The area underwent such profound and unexpected transformations from before to after the end of the Cold War that it continues to be a source of wonder and contestation in IR and Security Studies. Overall, I would argue that the orthodox and heterodox positions within what this book will term the field of European security changed from mutual agreement on a militarily defined nature of threats, on states as the primary actors, and on a conception of change as one of recurring conflict. The difference in position lay in whether arms control, détente, dialogue or 'common security' was a strategy to be pursued (heterodoxy) or whether military balancing was seen as the only or most viable way forward (orthodoxy). Peace research occupied a position of heterodoxy whereas states, NATO and national foreign policy institutes occupied orthodox positions (Berling 2012a). After 1989 these positions gradually changed. An understanding of security broader than military threats came to structure the field and spurred new orthodox and heterodox positions. The orthodoxy focused on the possibility of qualitative change in IR and on a strategic environment constituted by civilized, democratic space (Rasmussen 2003), while Samuel P. Huntington's (1993, 1996) heterodoxy demarcated space culturally ('the West against the rest') and coupled it with an understanding of the impossibility of change and a return to recurring war. Both agreed, however, that security was about more than military capabilities and threats and that change could be brought about through active security politics (Buzan and Hansen 2009: Chapters 4–7; Guzzini and Jung 2004; Huysmans 2006; Krause and Williams 1997; Risse-Kappen 1994; Villumsen 2008; Wæver and Buzan 2007). While the new orthodox position grew out of a weak heterodox trend in the 1980s to focus on a broader concept of security (Buzan 1991 [1983]), the solidification and acceptance of the position only occurred after the end of the Cold War (see e.g. NATO's Strategic Concept 1991). The changes to European security thus took place on all levels: the nature of threats changed, the logic with which the strategic environment was understood to function was altered, and with it the means by which security could be obtained. Notably the role of NATO was put under pressure during this period of time. Having been the guarantor of military security in an environment of potentially recurring conflict, the Alliance had built a *modus operandi* of balance of power. But with the new understanding of threats, security and the strategic environment, novel practices and agents were called for.

Within IR, two broad approaches offered explanations of the situation of NATO after the demise of the Soviet Union: the Rationalists and the Reflectivists (Keohane 1988). The Rationalist model – often known as variants of (neo-)realism – emphasised rational state actors and an international system dominated by balance-of-power and alliance-building (see e.g. Walt 1987; Waltz 1993b, 2000). To this approach, the end of the Cold War came as a surprise: what seemed to be a stable, but delicate, balance of power situation in a bipolar structure suddenly ended. A (re)turn to a multipolar world was the only thinkable outcome (Mearsheimer 1990) and the dissolution of NATO was seen as a logical consequence of the lack of an external, balancing enemy to the Alliance (cp. Buzan and Hansen 2009: 166). Opposed to this explanation stood variants of Reflectivism. Generally, a distinction has been made within Reflectivism between what has been called 'Soft Constructivism' (or mainstream/modernist Constructivism) and 'Radical Constructivism' (Adler 2002, 1997b). Soft Constructivism lets norms play a role as an intervening variable in Rationalist-type arguments (Adler 1997a; Risse-Kappen 1996; Schimmelfennig 1998; Adler and Barnett 1998a, 1998b), whereas Radical Constructivism more explicitly focuses on the role of language as *constitutive* of social reality (Toews 1987: 881–882). Along these lines, the transformation of European security and the survival of NATO was understood as an example of the persistence of shared norms in security communities (Adler and Barnett 1998b; Pouliot 2006), or as the formation of a distinct NATO security discourse, narrative or identity which reconfigured international relations after bipolarity (Ciuta 2002; Fierke and Wiener 1999; Hansen 1995, 2006; Neumann 1999; Williams and Neumann 2000; Behnke 2013).

Neither of these approaches fully captured the symbolic power struggles that went into the transformation of NATO's role in European security. Notably, the role of social scientific agents and paradigms were important for understanding the transformation of what might be called – with Bourdieu – a European field of Security, understood as a relational field of struggle tied together by a central stake – the power to define European security – and a variety of forms of power to back up bids for legitimacy. Seen from such a Bourdieusian framework for analysis, a focus on the (re-)creation of specific types of capital and practices in a relatively autonomous field, constituted by both material and symbolic forms of power, will bring struggles to the fore which have been missed by Rationalists and Reflectivists alike. This book argues that the change in the struggles which took place in the European field of security went from a struggle over the distribution of a select number of capitals – notably military – between states or alliances, to a larger field of contest in which struggle occurred over definitions of capital bringing into play new actors, such as think tanks. States were no longer the primary actors. Military was no longer the primary source of power. And change in IR became thinkable. The Rationalist state/military prism did not capture this, and Reflectivism only grasped parts of the struggles by either remaining focused on states or overlooking the power practices behind norms and discourses (for an elaborate version of this argument, see Williams 2007). Indeed, theory itself became an important power practice in the European security field when looked at from a Bourdieusian point of view.

It should therefore have come as no surprise to the discipline of IR that Javier Solana made the statement that began this chapter. In addition to pointing to what was perceived as the inadequacy of Cold War theorizing in the post-Cold War world, this quote also epitomized central power struggles that took place in European security. A competitive relationship between the theory and practice of European security in which (social) science and politics struggled to define security anew revealed that science is not a detached, neutral practice, but indeed a power practice like any other social practice (Bourdieu 2004). For IR this means that 'science' has to be taken into account as a player – and not just as a detached observer – in European security.[3] Within the IR mainstream, this feature had been largely overlooked[4] or at least deemed unimportant for the changes that took place, whereas IR Reflectivism has argued from a meta-theoretical and philosophical point of view that science is not a detached activity that stands apart from its object of study, but instead co-constitutes it (see e.g. Smith 2004; Klein 1994; for discussion, see Berling 2012b). Bourdieu would of course agree (Bourdieu 2004). But the way science and security practice 'hung together' in a more practical sense has not been addressed in any systematic way in IR (but see Büger and Villumsen 2007; Berling 2012b). Important features of the power struggles that came to change European security were therefore missed.

## A practice approach to security

This book can be considered to belong to the *practice turn* still to be fully discovered by IR (Schatzki *et al.* 2001; Spiegel 2005; see also Reckwitz 2002; in an IR context, see Büger and Gadinger 2007; Neumann 2002; Hansen 2006; Adler and Pouliot 2011). In IR and Security Studies the turn to practices has recently entered debates to the extent where it might indeed be termed an intellectual fashion, not least with the influx of security studies scholars working with a theoretical starting point in the sociology of Pierre Bourdieu (e.g. Adler-Nissen 2012, 2014; Pouliot 2010; Mérand 2008; Berling 2012a, 2012b; Hamati-Ataya 2012, 2013; Leander 2002a). Adding to that debate, I emphasize how a reflexive, sociological dimension can be added to the Reflectivist debate, so that the largely linguistic analyses of IR Poststructuralism are complemented with a focus on a range of different types of resources and strategies. This makes an analysis of the relationship between NATO theory and practice possible, but also points in the direction of formulating a more general sociological approach to the study of international relations. With inspiration from Bourdieu, the Reflectivist point about the impossibility of detached knowledge production can be translated into a prerogative of always including the place and role of science in analyses of the social in a wider sense. The objectivist gaze of the scholar plays a significant role in structuring social reality and must be considered as a power practice. A broader focus on social struggles in *fields* follows.

In a sense, this book therefore also inscribes itself into a recent increase in the focus on the role of science in International Relations (Ish-Shalom 2006; Huysmans 2006; Guzzini and Jung 2004; Büger and Villumsen 2007). In fact, it has been argued that '[a]cademic literature and political statements are ... twin loci for the construction of NATO's identity that constantly feed off each other ...' (Ciuta 2002: footnote 26) and Steve Smith (2004) has famously claimed that 'IR has sung the world of 9/11 into existence'. In parallel, the book also inscribes itself into a trend towards a rise in the attention given to Science and Technology Studies (STS) within Security Studies. But while sharing an interest in the role of science in the co-production of the political[5] with these new approaches, many of them tend toward a focus on *emerging networks* with a limited history (notably Actor Network Theory (ANT), see Bueger and Bethke 2013, 2011; Strandsbjerg 2012). This book sides with a more classically sociologically oriented take on already existing structures and the limits to constructing entirely novel realities that these social structures may entail. In a sense, it shares baggage with a Luhmannian perspective, which studies different systems clashing and creating irritation in the codes that structure the systems (e.g. Petersen 2011). But while sharing similarities with such an approach, the present book insists on the specific value of Pierre Bourdieu's sociology.

Following from this, the theoretical challenge of the book falls in two parts: first, the book must address and reformulate the fundamental assumptions underpinning the orthodox understanding of the theory/practice relationship. The reformulation of the dominant view demands a close analysis of how the science/policy nexus has been understood in IR and security studies, but also an analysis of the fundamental assumptions that lie beneath distinguishing between science and politics in the first place. This leads me to a discussion of how *practice* has been understood in IR and Security Studies and how this has prevented analyses of how theory and practice 'hang together'. In addition to this first theoretical challenge, a second follows: how can theory and practice be studied beyond epistemology and philosophy in a way that carries IR Reflectivist insights further while taking sociological patterns of practice into account? In other words, how can the epistemologically formulated claims about the impossibility of detached knowledge production be translated into concrete analyses of *how* theory and practice hang together? The first part of the book addresses these challenges from a theoretical perspective and builds a new practice approach to security, while the second part of the book applies this approach to European security.

The empirical challenge for this book lies in showing how theory and practice in Europe 'hung together': what relation (if any) was there between theory and NATO practice in Europe in the 1990s, and how has this influenced the constitution of important issues? The answers to these questions follow from the discussion of how the link between theory and practice must be understood after a turn to reflexive sociology. The 'link' or 'hanging together' is thus conceptualized as being part of a wider power struggle in which 'theory' is both a specific type of *practice* connected to expertise and a specific type of *resource* (capital) that can be mobilized dynamically in struggles. The link between NATO and 'theory' thus becomes a question of changing relations with what we might call 'theory-type agency' (a range of think tanks and research institutions, including universities) *and* a question of how theory is mobilized as a weapon or resource in social struggles.

While attempting to answer the empirical research question, therefore, the NATO case will also serve as an important illustration of how to construct a sociological practice approach to the study of theory and practice in a concrete domain. The analysis will have a theoretical and methodological aim beyond the NATO case. Accordingly, the primary empirical focus of the book is on NATO and how NATO's relationship with 'theory' changed from the beginning of the 1990s to 2003. However, the theoretical framework developed in the book should be understood as applicable in IR more generally.

## Structure of the book

Chapter 2 sets out to discuss the basic features of knowledge production in the field of IR that has led to an oversight of the very basic interplay between theory and practice. The chapter argues that a set of distinctions have worked as ghosts in structuring our thinking. A double dichotomy of theory/reality and theory/practice have come to dominate. And whereas the first dichotomy has been intelligently opposed by the general trend toward Social Constructivism and Poststructuralism, the second dichotomy has survived critique and lives on as a structuring feature in our discipline. The chapter concludes that a turn to Pierre Bourdieu's sociology can help remedy this situation.

Chapter 3 goes on to constructing a sociological practice approach that can help shed light on the interplay between theory and practice. The chapter argues that the concepts of field-capital-agency-doxa can serve as the background for this approach. With such a discussion the contours of the relevant types of agency will appear, and the central resources that were in play will be illuminated. At the same time, the central battles in the field of European security are captured through a novel concept: *doxic battles*[6]. The chapter concludes that three types of analysis are required. First, an analysis of field-specific capital which works as agency-selecting and boundary-setting, while at the same time providing the agents with the central resources needed to obtain a position in the hierarchy in the field. Second, an analysis of the practical patterns of interaction in the field in order to determine the extent to which the field can be empirically supported and not just assumed a priori. Third, an analysis of the conversion and mobilization of capital in doxic battles.

Chapter 4 is the first empirical chapter in the book. It analyses the field-specific capital in the field and how these types set the boundaries around the field, selected agency, and determined the hierarchy. Three types of capital are discussed: Miliary, Social and Scientific .

Chapter 5 addresses the practical patterns of interaction. Bourdieu's research question was often how actors were related rather than if they were related – because the nationally defined fields were easier to define a priori than internationally constituted fields. In search of a way out of this, the chapter reviews the different types of contacts present in the field of European security in the 1990s.

Chapter 6 is the final empirical chapter of the book. It analyses the world-making *doxic battles* in European security which came to shape and change the field altogether. The chapter reveals that the balance between military, social and scientific capital changed and that military capital came to badly hinder NATO's position in the new structure in European security.

Chapter 7 concludes the book. It points to lessons learnt for IR and Security Studies and points to the enduring relevance of the analytical framework drawn from Bourdieu's sociology for NATO studies and beyond.

## Notes

1 I use the term Security Studies to refer to the broad debate about security, including the more narrow definition 'strategic studies' under the Security Studies label. See Wæver and Buzan (2007) and Wæver (2007) for an overview of the debate.
2 I use the term 'linguistic turn' to refer to general developments in the social sciences and humanities in which the role of language as a relatively transparent *medium* was replaced with an understanding of language as *constitutive* of social reality (Toews 1987: 881–882). For more details, see Chapter 2.
3 For a discussion of the role of science in security politics, see Berling (2011).
4 It is often discussed under the heading of a 'gap' (Eriksson and Sundelius 2005) which is ever widening and problematic (Kruzel 1994; George 1993; for discussion, see Büger and Villumsen 2007).
5 Co-production is often attributed to Sheila Jasanoff (Jasanoff 2004a, 2004b), but the thematic has a long history in social theory (see e.g. Haraway 1992; Shapin and Schaffer 2011). It holds that a constant negotiation and creation of new knowledge takes place across the science/policy divide, specifically with a focus on new technologies. Through these negotiations, the social world is constituted and transformed. The discussion of co-production has a mainstream variant in the division between Mode 1 and Mode 2 knowledge (Gibbons *et al.* 1994).
6 See also Berling (2011). Senn and Elhardt (2013) have picked up my concept of doxic battles in an analysis of the value of nuclear weapons.

# 2 When theory meets practice

Venturing into a study of the theory and practice in European security starts with fundamental concepts of knowledge. Concepts of knowledge have been extremely influential in the development of the discipline of IR over the past 25 years or so. When talking about knowledge in IR, the standard reference is often Keohane's seminal article 'International institutions: two approaches' (Keohane 1988), which set the scene for paradigmatic debates in the late 1980s and the 1990s. While debates in IR have certainly moved on since then, the basic distinctions that flowed from the juxtaposition between Rationalism and Reflectivism still seem to structure the discipline. Over the course of the 1990s, Ole Wæver's model of the IR debates drew a similar, helpful distinction between positivism and deconstruction. One end of the continuum was defined by a 'border of boredom' while the other was defined by a 'border of negativity' (Wæver 1996). According to Wæver, what lay between these two boundaries constituted (relevant) IR theory. Wæver's juxtaposition between positivism and deconstruction can be said to reflect Keohane's Rationalism vs. Reflectivism divide. Implicitly, therefore, both installed the possibility of occupying a 'middle ground' between boredom and negativity, Rationalism and reflectivity (Patomäki and Wight 2000). This position was filled by Adler (1997b), Katzenstein (1996) and others, who showed how a focus on norms, for example, paved a way to a synthesis of the discipline. With such a synthesis at hand, cumulative knowledge production seemed – to some – within reach.

But both Rationalism and Reflectivism have primarily focused on the *epistemological* features of the scientific vocation.[1] This led to insightful discussions about the (im)possibility of detached scientific knowledge (more on this below). But in addition to this, I will argue, a central feature of IR is constituted by the production and power of *practically generated* knowledge. Recall that e.g. the field of Security Studies grew out of the environment surrounding RAND in the aftermath of the Second World War and only later developed into an academic discipline (Wæver and Buzan 2007). Also, IR more generally evolved as a practical discipline before it became institutionalized as an academic field (Wallace 1996).[2] Focusing narrowly on scientific knowledge thus risks overlooking important knowledge dynamics. With the present case in mind, this would completely overlook important constitutive practices in European security in the 1990s. As a remedy, Bourdieu can draw our attention to the issue of practically generated knowledge by stressing the fact that many different types of knowledge-producing agency are important for understanding IR: when 'seeing as Bourdieu' the question of knowledge becomes one not only of epistemology, but also of sociology. Science is a socially situated activity that takes place in a context – a field – which is related to other fields in a dynamic struggle for power. This opens up new avenues for conducting research and lets IR see the plethora of knowledge-producing activities that go on between science and (political) practice. Further, Bourdieu reminds us of the potential power of science, which might bring about (unintended) practical consequences.

But how did IR overlook such a central feature of its own existence? In this chapter, I will argue that while nurturing insightful debate on the distinction between *theory* and *reality*, a central 'little brother' distinction between *theory* and *practice* has slipped unnoticed through the back door in IR – on both sides of the Rationalism/Reflectivism divide. It is by drawing attention to that very distinction that the work of Bourdieu[3] can be fruitful to IR and to the study of the transformations in European security in particular. From that perspective, Bourdieu can help carry the epistemological challenge to the theory/reality distinction over into a sociological challenge to the theory/practice distinction – thereby opening the door to studying the interplay between different types of knowledge and their practical manifestations. This carries with it a new perspective on how to conduct empirical research in IR. This book will apply this approach in Chapters 4–6.

The chapter will proceed in three sections. The first section sets the scene for understanding how the double distinction between theory/reality and theory/practice has shaped the IR discipline. It reviews mainstream IR and discusses the 'Reflectivist' challenge to it. The section concludes that the theory/practice distinction has not been adequately addressed. The second section turns to Bourdieu's practice approach to scientific knowledge and discusses how 'seeing as Bourdieu' might turn IR's attention to the practical relationship between science and its object of study. This puts the theory/practice relationship centre stage, while building on the epistemological dissolution of the theory/reality distinction as put forward by earlier Reflectivist discussions. The third section sums up the argument.

## Ghost distinctions

Bourdieu held that dichotomies 'haunt, like theoretic ghosts, the academic mind' (Bourdieu 1988; Swartz and Zolberg 2004: 3). IR seems to be no exception to this rule. If we take Keohane to be the paradigmatic starting point for a discussion of knowledge in IR, the juxtaposition between Rationalism and Reflectivism was based on a basic disagreement about the nature of the social world (what exists?) and what possibilities of obtaining knowledge are available to the researcher.[4] In other words, Keohane raised questions of both ontology and epistemology.[5] Philosophical questions of this nature were standard in the IR landscape during the late 1980s and the 1990s. Basically, as Patrick T. Jackson (2011) would argue, this debate was about how the 'mind/world hook-up' was conceptualized. Was knowledge seen as produced in a detached sphere independently of political practice (this we often call 'scientific knowledge')?; or was it understood as a constitutive discursive phenomenon which could be analysed on the same terms as e.g. political discourse? Or put differently, was the basic distinction between theory and reality a valid one?

Especially within Security Studies, Reflectivism (Constructivism and Post-structuralism) posed serious challenges to the theory/reality distinction by emphasising the contingency of knowledge through e.g. a critique of the concept of security (Wæver 1995a, 1995b, 1997; Krause and Williams 1997). Others cast light on the structuring dichotomies of the discipline (Walker 1993), and on how theory could be studied as discourse (J. George 1994). Keohane criticized the Reflectivist research programme for refraining from developing 'testable theories, and to be explicit about their scope' (Keohane 1988: 393) thus indicating that the Rationalist approach could be taken as a yardstick for evaluating the Reflectivist paradigm (see also Jackson 2011: 158). This yardstick implicitly entailed a perspective in which it is possible to distinguish the object of study from the subject studying it. From a philosophical point of view, this installed a Kantian 'view from nowhere' in which the subject and the object were clearly distinguished and distinguishable, and where the former did not affect the latter (cp. Kratochwil 2007).[6]

This (ghost) distinction is shared by most mainstream (primarily US based, e.g. King *et al.* 1994) methodologies in IR which rely on ontological realism and a correspondence theory of truth (for discussion, see Friedrichs and Kratochwil 2009). Friedrichs and Kratochwil argue in their usual ironic way that '[i]ndependent, intervening, and dependent variables are tossed around as if the social world resembled a bowling alley' (Friedrichs and Kratochwil 2009: 702) by social scientists who continue 'as if positivism had never been rocked' (ibid.).[7] But what implications does this mainstream position have for understanding knowledge in IR? As indicated in the introduction, I argue that it installs not only a distinction between theory/reality but also a distinction between theory/practice. When assuming that the social world can be observed by the social scientist without influencing the processes in the observed world, political practice becomes locked on one side of the theory/reality distinction: practice is exclusively placed on the right-hand side as a matter of behaviour in the real world. Scientific activity, on the other hand, is conceived of as an activity profoundly different from political practice. In other words, practice becomes an object of study for the scientist – from an external and elevated point of view. The separation of the scientific subject and the empirical object (theory/reality) thus carries with it a separation between a *sphere* in which scientific knowledge is produced in a detached setting from the sphere of practical politics (theory/practice) (Villumsen 2008).[8]

This central move has fertilized the ground for discussions of the *relation* between practical politics and scientific knowledge within mainstream IR: the most prevalent image of this relation consists of a 'gap' between ivory tower scientists/researchers and the world of practical politics. This gap – whatever it consists of[9] – is extremely hard to bridge, it is argued (A.L. George 1993, 1994; Jentleson 2002; Kruzel 1994; Lepgold and Nincic 2001; Wallace 1996) and is commonly held to be a problem for IR. More influence and closer ties are seen to be a good solution.[10] Articles often discuss the possibilities for adjusting research to the needs of the practitioners (Newsom 1995; A.L. George 1993; Zelikow 1994). Plato's philosopher-king ideal is taken as a starting point, rendering theorists the suppliers of knowledge for policy-makers (Whiting 1972)[11]. To some, the gap is widening dramatically and the policy relevance of research is waning. Kruzel (1994) stresses that the distance between IR and policy is a chasm-like widening: scientific subjects increasingly circulate their knowledge among themselves, while the objects being studied remain largely untouched by the (scientific) knowledge produced about them.

While interesting parallels to a Luhmanian understanding of differentiated social systems (Luhmann 1998) or (as we shall see below) a Bourdieusian perspective of practical reflexivity and fields could have developed from this understanding of separate spheres, the central problem in this debate is cast in common sense terms of how to convey research to politicians through simplifying communication and making complex conclusions understandable to the practitioner (Galvin 1994; A.L. George 1993; Gray 1992). The theorist is taken to possess a source of knowledge which can be communicated to practitioners if done correctly. However, the perspective has little faith in the prospects for knowledge bridging the gap. The image of the researcher in the ivory tower disconnected from the outside world is a popular variant (see discussion in Büger and Villumsen 2007; and Berling and Bueger 2015). The double distinction between theory/reality and theory/practice thus structures not only the epistemological basis for conducting IR research, but also the assessment of the impact and power of research. In other words, the 'gap approach' suffers from under-reflection regarding the 'truth value' of the knowledge produced in the scientific 'well of knowledge'. Knowledge is thought of as objective, of having a life of its own independent from actors and structures (Laffey and Weldes 1997). At the same time, the role of the practical/political group of agents in shaping research with the possible effect of researchers buying into a political agenda is underestimated. Following from these two features, a third follows: reflection on the own position of the researcher constitutes a blind spot in the IR mainstream. This can explain why analyses of the transformations in European security in the 1990s have largely overlooked the role of (social) science agency and theory.

Later in this chapter we shall see how a Bourdieusian perspective on knowledge can bring the relationship between theory and practice into focus while preserving a view of scientific knowledge production as distinct and valuable. Further, the position of the researcher will assume a central role in the knowledge production in the social sciences. First, however, I turn to the Reflectivist challenges in the field of IR posed by Reflectivism.[12]

## The Reflectivist challenges

Contemporary IR theorists under the general heading of 'Reflectivism' have stressed the impossibility of producing knowledge in an independent sphere (e.g. Walker 1993; J. George 1994; Klein 1988, 1994, 1998) A central – granted, provocative – quote holds that '[t]heories of international relations are more interesting as aspects of contemporary world politics that need to be explained than as explanations of contemporary world politics' (Walker 1993: 6) and that 'the theory of international relations should be read as a characteristic discourse of the modern state and as a constitutive practice whose effects can be traced in the remotest interstices of everyday life' (ibid.). In a more recent statement of the same point, Smith (2004) argued that IR has 'sung the world of 9/11 into existence' – placing IR knowledge in a potentially powerful position in the construction of how the world has come to understand the security situation after 9/11. Following from this, Poststructuralists such as Walker, J. George and Klein have focused on the limiting and structuring effects which theory exerts on how to think and speak about politics and have pointed to similarities in discursive constellations in science and policy.

This Reflectivist position therefore challenges the basic distinction between theory and reality as outlined above. Generally speaking, knowledge is considered performative and constitutive: the development of vocabularies and concepts has a structuring effect on the object of study. This not only means that the distinction between subject and object is put under pressure – the philosophical 'view from nowhere' is suddenly replaced by the *impossibility* of a nowhere. Instead, scientific knowledge can be studied alongside political practice as part of a wider discursive field (cp. Jackson 2011: 39).

The breaking down of the distinction between the subject and the object, and letting scientific knowledge production enter the analysis as a discourse (or a 'genre', see e.g. Hansen 2006) can arguably be seen to lead to yet another – more practical – question of the relationship between knowledge *producers* (academics) and political practice within the Reflectivist position. Here, mainstream IR created a literature on a 'gap'. Within Reflectivism, some analyses have stressed how realism has participated in upholding a doxic practice of sovereignty and anarchy in international relations. (e.g. Ashley 1988), and how experts participated in 'Making the Cold War Enemy' (Robin 2001). Others have argued that the end of the Cold War was directly related (if not caused) by the proliferation of new strategic thought by expert communities (Adler 1992; Risse-Kappen 1994), or that Democratic Peace Research led to a number of security practices following the end of the Cold War (Büger and Villumsen 2007).

This position differs markedly from seeing IR as a detached sphere of scientific knowledge production.[13] But only few have pushed the epistemological points about the impossibility of detached knowledge production over into studies of the role of the 'theorist' or 'expert' in IR – even though it seems a logical next step in the Reflectivist argumentation. And when it comes to situating the *critical* researcher it appears limited to some suggestions in introductions or concluding sections of monographs (Wyn Jones 2001; Campbell 1992; Buzan *et al.* 1998). Most often, however, scholars are only situated when they are labelled as belonging to the 'unreflective' mainstream (see Villumsen and Büger 2010). Following from this, a discussion of the *own* position of the researcher has been slim. As perhaps the most important contribution, Huysmans (2002a) formulated a normative dilemma (of writing security) that questioned the own *research practices* of the critical researchers.[14] This spurred a discussion about the responsibility of researchers in IR[15] and is now being translated into a discussion of dilemmas and coping strategies (Villumsen and Büger 2010; Berling and Bueger 2013). But even though including a reflection on the *practices and responsibility* of the researcher, a discussion of the own *position* as researcher is still underdeveloped. As we shall see below, when seen from a Bourdieusian perspective, the impossibility of a 'view from nowhere' can be replaced by a 'view from somewhere' in which researchers come into focus not just as 'factors' (discourse/genre) but also as 'actors'.[16] This can in fact explain the Reflectivist overemphasis on criticizing the mainstream, because it might be said to occupy a more powerful position in IR – if viewed as a player in a Bourdieusian field.

## A Bourdieusian perspective

If Keohane's distinction between Rationalism and Reflectivism and Wæver's argument about positivism and deconstruction created the opportunity for a 'middle ground' position, does Bourdieu then produce this? To my mind, no. Instead, his epistemological and sociological take on knowledge places him within the discussion of the dissolution of the theory/reality distinction within IR and helps push that debate further on the issue of theory/practice. In parallel, one might ask if Bourdieu's points are then similar to critical realism which is becoming ever more prevalent in IR? I would again say no. The 'depth realism' (Patomäki and Wight 2000: 218) of scientific realism involves a distinction between social construction and 'the real' (theory/reality) which is incompatible with Bourdieu's insistence on an epistemological and practical approach to knowledge. '[I]mportant as intersubjective meanings and relations are, they do not exhaust the social world', a recent scientific realist intervention argued (Patomäki and Wight 2000: 225). This would seem to rhyme with Bourdieu's use of terms such as 'objective relations' that would indicate something 'outside of' social construction. But this would be a misconception: Bourdieu did not conceptualize  objective relations as a pre-existing social construction. Instead, he talked about objectively holding a position of power or of subordination within the universe of the *field* and *habitus*[17], which are ultimately social. They may appear solid and unchangeable, but are always the product of social history.[18]

So, turning to Bourdieu's take on knowledge, three features of the concept of knowledge seem to capture how Bourdieu can push IR further. First, a confirmation of the dissolution of the theory/reality distinction and the extent to which it is possible to produce 'truth' or seek objective, universal mechanisms within the social sciences. Second, the attention directed to the position of science *vis-à-vis* practical politics, and third, the amount of practical reflexivity directed to the own position of the researcher. The answers consist in a *practice approach* which emphasizes the power of contextually produced knowledge, the basic involvedness of theory and practice, and a practical reflexivity about the position and habitus of the 'objectifying subject' – the researcher.[19]

## Knowledge and the practice of science

To Bourdieu, knowledge was formulated as part of his general sociology. On the truth value of research, Bourdieu argued that:

> [o]ne is entitled to undertake to give an 'account of accounts', so long as one does not put forward one's contribution to the science in a pre-scientific representation of the social world as if it were a science of the social world.
>
> (Bourdieu 1977: 21)

In other words, no conclusions could ever be presented without important caveats to the *scientificity* – or truth-value. To Bourdieu, social science was a practice about how to understand and explain (social) phenomena. The veil of scientific objectivism and distance was a historically constructed part of its habitus and not a statement of reality: 'Objectivity is a social product of the [scientific] field which depends on the presuppositions accepted in the field, particularly as regards the legitimate way of settling conflicts' (Bourdieu 2004: 71). On this basis it is possible to argue that the mainstream distance from the object of study can be understood as a dominant, orthodox practice in the field of IR, while the Reflectivist challenge can be understood as a subordinate practice.

But the objectivation of social phenomena was problematic: the regularities found would often not be structured by the same categories as those used by the agents under study. Instead, the analysis would (could) be a mirror image of the categories internalized in science. The scientists' view of the world was seen from the scientific field and with a scientific habitus. This created an 'altogether different vision' that 'risk[ed] destroying its object or creating pure artefacts whenever it [was] applied without critical reflection' (Bourdieu 1998a: 130). To Bourdieu, this created a responsibility of knowing that this fact was inevitable. The scientist should structure knowledge-production accordingly.

The scientist was an interlocutor in the formation of the habitus of practice-practice and could be responsible for creating a social reality not shared by practice-practice. Seen from a mainstream IR perspective, this would be a problem related to methodology in which reality was 'mis-perceived'. Seen from Reflectivism this would constitute a structuring effect on discourse. But seen from a Bourdieusian perspective, this in fact becomes a problem of epistemology and ontology alike. Not only would the categories be produced in the scientific field, science would also exercise *symbolic power* on the object of study:[20] 'Symbolic power allows dominant agents in a field to give their own beliefs a doxic aura of legitimacy, universality and naturalness' (Pouliot 2004: 13). This power was tied to the ability to define and categorize (Bigo 2002b) and was inextricably linked to the scientific habitus and field. The symbolic power of science could thus come to change the reality of international life (for an example of this process, see Büger and Villumsen 2007). This not only led to the 'impossibility of a nowhere' as argued above in relation to Reflectivism. It also created a *relationship of power* between theory and practice. This would not only mean the risk of reifying scientific categories, but also the risk of contributing to upholding relations of domination in society. For instance, the naming/definition of a social class risked naturalizing the economic inequality in a society, even if it was only used by social scientists to create clarity. In European security, the naming of certain types of (military) security runs the same risk of structuring social reality and upholding relational power structures.

> Visions of insecurity and their institutionalization do not only frame a functionally defined policy domain of security that is institutionally and conceptually differentiated from other policy domains ... They also imply visions of the nature of politics, i.e. of the political organization of social relations.
>
> (Huysmans 2006: 11)

Science/theory is an integral part of the ongoing power struggles in society. To use Bruno Latour's formulation, science was seen as 'a form of politics pursued by other means' (Latour 1983: 167)[21]. Science could exercise structuring effects because its standing ascribed it with the possibility – and recognized legitimacy – of speaking in the name of truth. This is profoundly different from perceiving science as a detached process with no bearing on the world it studies and it pushes the Reflectivist position in the direction of treating academic knowledge as more than a discourse/genre. Hence, to Bourdieu the challenge to the distinction between theory/reality also inevitably entailed a challenge to the theory/practice distinction. For IR, this implies that a study of the science-policy nexus should also include a study of a more general struggle for power in which science takes a position – a 'somewhere' – in the wider political field. This changes the epistemologically veiled concept of knowledge in IR into an empirical and sociological problematique of several 'knowledges'.

## The power and position of science-practice

Bourdieu used the terms science-practice and practice-practice to place knowledge production in a constitutive relationship with the reality it described (Swartz 1997: 58f).[22] As such, the Bourdieusian notion of knowledge shares features with the Reflectivist position in IR when it comes to the relationship between science and practice. But Bourdieu also took into account the *special status* of science – if not as a detached sphere of scientific knowledge production – then as a *field* with its own internal dynamics. This field belonged to the dominant field in society – albeit in a dominated role (Bourdieu 1988). Knowledge production and academic credentials were powerful resources in wider society, but far from arguing that science holds the most powerful position in society, Bourdieu called for empirical, sociological studies of exactly how science works in relation to political practice (for a discussion of science mechanisms in the field of security, see Berling 2011).[23] The philosophically formulated point about the impossibility of detached science thereby becomes not only an epistemological claim but also a *sociological research question*. The important point about the inevitable involvedness of science[24] can therefore be translated into an operationalizable framework for studying how theory and practice 'hang together', not only as discourses but also as *social agents*[25] in a field. This opens up for studying the space between the labels of science and practice in specific contexts. Research questions will include which types of capital (science) actors hold, which position they seem to speak from, and what central struggle the field revolves around. I specify this in Chapter 3.

As a reflection on positions, Bourdieu holds that *social* science occupies a different position than the *natural/technical* sciences:

> everyone feels entitled to have their say in sociology and to enter into the struggle over the legitimate view of the social world, in which the sociologist also intervenes, but with a quite special ambition ... to utter the truth or, worse, to define the conditions in which one can utter the truth.
>
> (Bourdieu 2004: 87)

The social scientist is therefore struggling with a range of 'experts' and other social agents over legitimate knowledge. Where natural scientists can more easily claim a special position (but remember Climategate!), the social scientist continuously struggles to obtain and maintain this position. Claims to accepted knowledge are thus also claims to power. Who enters the struggle – and with what means – therefore becomes an important empirical investigation for IR, in which IR and other knowledge practices need to be included. In the case of the transformation of NATO in the 1990s, think tanks and scientific arguments turned out to be struggling alongside important political actors such as NATO, the WEU and the EU in a European security field under profound change.

## Practical Reflexivity

Mapping and analysing struggles over accepted knowledge spills over into a call for what Bourdieu called 'Practical Reflexivity' (Bourdieu 2004: 90; see also Berling and Bueger 2013). With this, he zoomed in on our own dispositions as researchers. In the words of Schubert – 'Bourdieu is inviting us to join him in a rigorous scientific method in which our own positions as social scientists are foregrounded' (Schubert 1995: 1010). The researcher's own position was a blind spot in mainstream IR and had been largely overlooked by Reflectivism even though it seemed to follow logically from the epistemological claims about the impossibility of detached knowledge production. Bourdieu considered this issue to be of utmost importance. He not only considered – and studied – the sciences as practices alongside other practices in society with the power to intervene, to structure, to define and categorize. He also took a radical view on the inclusion of the researcher in the process of constructing the object of study. How was the researcher (he, himself) positioned in French sociology? How was he positioned in the wider social structures in France, and how might that influence how he saw the structures of domination in society? He called this process to "objectify the objectifying subject' (Bourdieu 2000: 10), meaning to turn the sociological tools onto the sociological observer (Leander 2010). Within IR, such a research strategy has yet to materialize. As argued above, an epistemologically informed discussion about the responsibility of the individual researcher has emerged within Reflectivism, but a focus on the social position, habitus, strategy and the biases and blindnesses inherent in these has not yet – to my knowledge – surfaced. Calls for it are, however, emerging (Leander 2010; Villumsen and Büger 2010; Berling and Bueger 2013, 2015).

Taken together, 'seeing as Bourdieu' can push the epistemological points made by IR Reflectivism in the direction of seeing science and knowledge as not just factors, but *actors*, in the co-constitution of social reality. And the point about the 'impossibility of a nowhere' can be pushed in the direction of placing responsibility on the shoulders of the researcher, while at the same time provoking reflection on their own position in the scientific field and the wider social setting. This requires reframing empirical analyses in IR. This book takes a step in that direction.

## Conclusion

Stating the question of knowledge in terms of epistemology had led IR, I have argued, into accepting a double distinction between theory/reality and theory/practice, which worked as a ghost in structuring IR analyses along certain lines. Whilst IR Reflectivists had insightful discussions about the impossibility of the detached production of scientific knowledge, a central feature of the IR landscape – the value attached to practically generated knowledge – had been overlooked by both Rationalism and Reflectivism. By stating the question of knowledge as one of epistemology and sociology alike, Bourdieu helped push IR out of this stalemate. The focus on the dissolution of the theory/reality distinction coupled with the focus on the epistemological and practical interconnections between theory and practice and the positionality of the researcher in wider society, spurred novel research questions. Turning to Bourdieu unavoidably meant thrusting the researcher into the foreground and turning to a focus on the theory/practice relationship as one imbued with power in specific contexts. Focusing on the relationship between theory and practice in meticulous, empirical ways did not, however, mean a return to an empiricist theory of knowledge, as was ascribed to by mainstream IR. Nor did it mean a position as a 'middle ground' between Rationalism and Reflectivism. Instead, I would argue, Bourdieu started from assumptions close to the Reflectivist dissolution of the distinction between theory/reality and pushed that epistemological standpoint further.

One aspect is worth stressing again, however, the role ascribed to science does not mean that Bourdieu perceived scientific endeavour as the most powerful type of practice in social life. To Bourdieu, social science formed part of the most powerful class in society, but as a dominated sphere (Fisher 1990; Bourdieu 1988). Political and cultural elites would hold different baskets of power (capital), which made them occupy different positions in the overall structure of society. The decision to foreground the scientist did, hence, not translate into perceiving scientists as 'holding the strings' in a 'puppet society'. Instead, it provided a means of emphasizing how science was embedded in social life and how the sociological vocation could (un)willingly be complicit in upholding patterns of domination.[26] To some extent, Bourdieu is thus following a line similar to Critical Theory in IR in which Cox famously held that '[t]heory is always *for* someone or *for* some purpose' and that the responsibility of the researcher lay in supporting the 'suppressed' (Cox 1981: 128). And after having 'thrust' the researcher into the foreground, Bourdieu distinguished between two positions for the intellectual sociologist: the *clinical* and *cynical* sociology. 'A cynical sociology makes use of its knowledge in order to make its own strategies more effective, while a clinical sociology uses its knowledge of social laws to challenge them effectively' (Schinkel 2003: 70; see also Bourdieu 1998b: 5–6; for a recent discussion, see Hamati-Ataya 2012). Bourdieu argued that the scientist could not 'keep aloof, far from the conflicts in which the future of the world is at stake' (Schinkel 2003: 70). He therefore argued that clinical sociology should form the basis of the craft of sociology.[27] Science could not be conceived of as a disinterested practice of objective knowledge production. On the contrary, Bourdieu attacked the self-image of objectivity, disinterestedness, purity and creativity of intellectuals (Swartz 1997). Science was an interested practice, which had to reflect on its own habitus and theoretical constructions of the world, while at the same time acknowledging its place in various social settings. In that way, 'reflexivity matters not only for good science but for progressive politics' (Leander 2002b: 606). This point will be carried forward in the chapters that follow. What does such an approach look like and how can we study European security from this starting point? Chapter 3 sets out to develop and approach capable of doing exactly that.

## Notes

1  For a thought-provoking analysis of the 'problem-field of IR' see Patomäki and Wight (2000).
2  The so-called 'Wallace debate' raised the issue of practical knowledge vs. scientific knowledge (Wallace 1996) and argued that IR has valued theoretical knowledge over practically applicable knowledge and criticized the discipline for being self-absorbed (for debate, see Booth 1997; Smith 1997). See also Guzzini (2001, 2004).
3  Bourdieu's thinking is far from covered in this chapter. I zoom in on the concepts helpful in discussing how IR might benefit from 'seeing knowledge as Bourdieu'. For a good discussion of Bourdieu's vast production, see Swartz (1997). See also Chapter 3 for an overview of Bourdieu studies in IR.
4  A related distinction is the classical one between problem-solving and critical theory made by Cox (1981).
5  In general terms, questions of ontology deal with what entities exist or can be said to exist, and, for example, how such entities can be grouped, related within a hierarchy, and subdivided according to similarities and differences. Epistemology, on the other hand, concerns the questions: What is knowledge? How is knowledge acquired? How do we know what we know?
6  The juxtaposition of the subject and the object stem, according to Latour (1993), from Kant's philosophy. See also Patomäki and Wight (2000) and Jackson (2011: 44f).
7  Patomäki and Wight (2000) argue that positivists and post-positivists ascribe to philosophical anti-realism because of their primarily epistemologically framed research programmes. I would argue that mainstream IR still holds firmly on to empiricist theories of knowledge which establish a clear distinction between theory and reality (see also Hollis 1996).
8  In fact, the distinction between theory and practice is a historical peculiarity. According to Lepgold and Nincic, the historical background for the so-called gap (and the clearly demarcated understanding of two spheres) is based on the behavioural revolution in the social sciences in the US from the 1960s onwards (Lepgold and Nincic 2001: 5, 12). Before that time, public intellectuals such as Morgenthau 'saw no sharp division between theory and practice in international relations' (Lepgold and Nincic 2001: 10). When the American Association of Political Science was established, it had the declared intention to help practical politics. With the behavioural revolution, the focus moved away from practice towards method (Lepgold and Nincic 2001: 13). Within the IR debate, this shift was reflected in the shift from political realism to more quantitative studies and theoretical neo-realism – a shift that deepened the gap between academia and practice. This contributed to the notion of the estranged academic working in his ivory tower.
9  Eriksson and Sundelius (2005: 53–55) divide this debate into three subcategories: the Bridge-building perspective claims that scholars have an obligation to bridge the gap; the Independence perspective argues that scholars should keep policy makers at a distance; and the Critical perspective argues that scholars should be critical of government power and seek relations with other (oppressed) actors.
10  Compare with the IR journal *International Security*'s demand for policy relevance and objectivity in submissions.

11  Nierenberg (2001: 363) holds that Archimedes was the first real scientific adviser. He advised King Hiero on military affairs.

12  Labels are powerful! I use the term as signifying general developments in the social sciences and humanities in which the role of language as a relatively transparent medium was replaced with an understanding of language as constitutive of social reality (Toews 1987: 881–882) and the ensuing dissolution of central distinctions such as that between representation and reality (ibid.: 885). In IR, a large and diverse group of thinkers has been given the label 'Reflectivist' (e.g. Ashley 1987; Der Derian 1992; Walker 1993; Bartelson 1995; Neumann 1999; Hansen 2006). Though important differences exist, they all stress the constitutive role of systems of meaning or discourses and challenge the possibility of representing reality as a detached activity.

13  Within the IR debate, Guzzini holds that 'stressing the reflexive relationship between the social construction of knowledge and the construction of social reality' (Guzzini 2005: 499) is a central feature of the Constructivist 'meta-theoretical commitment' (ibid.: 498).

14  The normative dilemma is defined thus: "how to write or speak about security, when security knowledge risks the production of what one tries to avoid, what one criticizes: that is, the securitization of migration, drugs, and so forth' (Huysmans 2002a: 43).

15  E.g. the so-called 'Eriksson debate' (Eriksson 1999a, 1999b; Wæver 1999; Williams 1999; Goldmann 1999).

16  I owe the formulation of factor/actor to Widmaier (2004).

17  The field is a conflictual, structured space which shares an implicit assumption about the stakes at stake, and works in relative autonomy from its surroundings. According to Calhoun (Calhoun *et al.* 2002: 262) 'a field is simply the terrain upon which the game is played. Broadly speaking, a field is a domain of social life that has its own rules of organization, generates a set of positions, and supports the practices associated with them'; the habitus was defined as 'systems of durable, transposable dispositions' (Bourdieu 1977: 72) and as 'determined by past conditions which have produced the principle of their production, that is, by the actual outcome of identical or interchangeable past practices' (ibid.: 72–73). It was conceptualised as a temporally situated social structure nested in social agents. Leander (2002a: 12) argues that 'it has the virtue of being both a social and an individual concept, which relates both levels'.

18  That Bourdieu tilted towards (re)production of fields rather than erratic change does not change this: 'fields capture struggle within the logic of reproduction' (Swartz 1997: 121).

19  As such, pragmatism and contributions to the growing practice debate can be said to belong to a position close to Bourdieu in IR. For a discussion of pragmatism and Bourdieu, see Leander (2010).

20  Compare with Giddens' 'double hermeneutic' (1984) and Hacking's 'looping effect' (1999).

21  Bourdieu strongly disagreed with Latour's understanding of scientists' interests and how they self-interestedly sought recognition (see Bourdieu 2004: 26–30). Instead, Bourdieu argued that objectivation was not a strategy for self-promotion but a historically produced practice of the scientific world. The formulation 'politics by other means' is of course a paraphrasing of Clausewitz's definition of war (Clausewitz 1982]).

22  This shares feature with sociologists of science such as Mannheim, Fleck and, notably, Giddens. Note also that similarities can be found between this understanding and Friedrichs and Kratochwil's insistence that ontological realism is a non-starter since the subject is deeply implicated in the constitution of the object (Friedrichs and Kratochwil 2009: 704).

23 This would meet the criticism of discourse analysis raised by Neumann: 'what is needed ... are empirical studies that specify exactly how IR practices contribute, or do not contribute to the status quo' (Neumann 2002: 639).

24 Note the resemblance with Cox's famous dictum that 'Theory is always for someone and for some purpose' (Cox 1981: 128).

25 Bourdieu argues that social agents can be 'isolated individuals, groups or institutions'. An agent is thus not only equivalent to a person – although it can be. Field positions can be occupied by individuals, social networks, social groups, institutions and formal organizations (Swartz 2008: 49).

26 Along similar lines, Huysmans has argued that 'security knowledge [does not] necessarily directly feed into policy-making and its political contestation. Academic institutions are not fully integrated in policy circles and political movements. They retain a certain level of institutional independence. But the competing claims to knowledge tend to reflect the politics of insecurity that is going on in a society ... academic debates are almost inevitably intertwined with governmental and wider political struggles' (Huysmans 2006: 10–11).

27 The cynical sociology would be closer to the work of Latour, who saw scientists entering a game of self-promotion (Bourdieu 2004: 26–30). For a recent use of cynical sociology, see Hamati-Ataya (2012).

# 3 A sociology of IR

## Doxic battles and the (re)configuration of a field

Despite promising attempts to apply the sociology of Pierre Bourdieu to International Relations (IR)[1], the field could still profit from the unexplored potential in his thinking for understanding pivotal theoretical and empirical puzzles. The failure to fully grasp the paradigmatic case of European security after the Cold War is an example of how IR would benefit from reformulating not only its empirical research questions, but also several of its central conceptual building blocks with the aid of Bourdieusian sociology. Bourdieu himself was reluctant to apply his conceptual apparatus beyond the nation state. I argue, however, that the work of Bourdieu, when viewed as a dynamic theoretical constellation of fields, capital, doxa and agents can make a significant contribution to understanding international processes.

The chapter argues that a Bourdieusian practice approach that focuses on the field-capital-agency-doxa nexus can serve as a framework for understanding the changes in European security and the under-explored connection between theory and practice in European security in the 1990s. I argue that social science think tanks and academic experts can be seen as players alongside practitioners such as heads of state and government and NATO Secretaries General in a power struggle over the legitimate definition of security in a European field of security. The practical field thus intersects with the field of IR/Security Studies. Moreover, this type of analysis can further serve as a guide for how to apply Bourdieu's tools to international relations in general. With such a discussion as background, the contours of the relevant types of agency in European security will appear, and the central resources with which struggles took place will be illuminated. Studies of the international are thereby translated into sociologically-conceptualized *power struggles* which can be studied empirically. Concretely, the chapter argues that the concept of *capital* can stand at the heart of such an approach.

But what is capital? Bourdieu defined capital as 'a weapon and a stake of struggle [which] allow the possessors of that capital to wield a power, an influence, and thus to *exist* in the field, instead of being considered a negligible quantity' (Bourdieu and Wacquant 1992: 98). As with Bourdieu's sociology in general, capital was understood relationally, not substantially (Swartz 2008: 48; Emirbayer and Johnson 2008: 3):[2] capital functions as a social relation of power because it needs to be recognized as authoritative in a specific field in order to be valuable. In other words, it has to become symbolic capital in order to be powerful.[3] Capital is put to work in three different ways in this chapter. First, instead of assuming the relevant agency and types of power in European security as has been done in IR up until now, the concept of capital can provide a discussion of *points of access* to a certain domain – a field – for different types of agency. When military capital was valued, states and alliances possessing military capital were allowed to participate. When social scientific capital became valued in the European security field, new scientific-type actors were able to gain access. In this way, I argue, sensitivity to capital helps *select agency and establish the boundary for participation* in a specific international domain. Secondly, capital also functions, following Bourdieu, as the most important criterion for defining an agent's *position in the hierarchy* in a field. Capital is a 'weapon' or a 'power-base' that can be used by agents in struggles in a particular field. Following from these points, the chapter discusses how social scientific types of capital became valued in the European security field alongside other types of capital. An exclusive focus on Bourdieu's concept of capital does not, however, easily allow for an explicit focus on the profound *changes* and instabilities that dominated European security after the demise of the Soviet Union and the fall of the bipolar world order. In order to fit better the framework to the international case of European security, I therefore stress, thirdly, the *strategic mobilization*[4] of capital in fields under profound change. I call these mobilizations *doxic battles*, drawing on Bourdieu's concept of *doxa*. The doxa involves the very basic structures of the field, the categories by which the field and the world are understood. It is the unspoken, common knowledge which constitutes social reality and which exercises a misrecognized structural power on the practices in a field (Bourdieu 1977; Ashley 1989: 259). Instead of focusing solely on *accumulation* and *possession* of capital, I argue for focusing on how agents use capital in the *(re)production process* of the basic structures of a given field. This brings the concepts of capital, field, doxa, and agency together in a dynamic 'action framework' for analysis. With this explicit focus on process and production, the chapter seeks to emphasize the practice element of Bourdieu's work for demonstrating how the paradigmatic case of European security in the 1990s was a case of power struggles involving hitherto overlooked agency and forms of power that came to change the very basic features of what European social reality consisted of. The discussion pulls IR away from substantive a priori assumptions and pushes it in the direction of process and empirically formulated research questions.

The chapter is structured as follows: in the next part, I briefly review promising attempts to adopt Bourdieusian concepts to the international realm within the IR and Security Studies debate. I conclude that while important Bourdieusian concepts have been used, a comprehensive discussion of how these can alter IR studies remains to be taken. In particular, the concept of capital has not yet been systematically thought through as an analytical device for understanding the international. Part II discusses the central Bourdieusian concepts that are needed for formulating a new Bourdieusian framework for analysis in IR: field, capital, agency, and doxa. Throughout the chapter, European security will illustrate the importance of the conceptual apparatus for asking new empirical question and for challenging basic assumptions. The conclusion sums up the framework for analysis laid out and highlights the added value of studying European security and other international phenomena through the prism of the Bourdieusian 'action framework'.

## Bourdieu in IR: a growing research programme

Within IR, Bourdieu has recently[5] provided inspiration to a growing number of (Reflectivist) scholars. The central lessons from Bourdieu have centred on how to include a practical, sociological dimension to IR and security analyses in a discipline prone to remaining detached from micro-practices and staying at the level of assumptions; how to see IR as comprised of more than just states as actors; and how to understand power in IR beyond material and military power. The debate so far demonstrates that Bourdieusian sociology can push the IR debate further on these points. But a comprehensive framework for analysis has yet to be developed from Bourdieusian concepts. In particular, the concept of capital holds largely unexplored potential as a significant contribution to understanding the international. I address the IR debate under three headlines: New Forms of Capital; Security Agents; and Doxic Practice.

### New forms of capital

In classical IR theory, the international system has been taken to be dominated by military and economic capabilities and balance of power practices (e.g. Waltz 1979). Several Bourdieusian inspired studies in IR, however, criticize this narrow understanding of power resources. For instance, Jef Huysmans (2002b) has argued that NATO had to attempt to convert its military capital into humanitarian capital[6] during the Kosovo crisis in 1998/1999 in order to be accepted as an important player in that crisis. Julian Go (2008) retains a focus on the nation state, but argues that historically speaking, states have struggled for both material/coercive power and international legitimacy, thus broadening the scope to include symbolic forms of power. Michael C. Williams (2007) emphasizes 'the 'cultural strategies' that have been powerfully at work in international security over the past decade and a half' (ibid.: 23) and argues that the 1990s was a period of extremely important power games, even though Constructivists seemed to overlook it: 'important elements of security politics from the late 1980s up to today have involved a reconfiguration of the 'field' of security. In this revaluation, military and material power has remained significant, but it has been repositioned within a broader field, what might be called the 'cultural field of security'' (ibid.: 39–40).

Cultural and symbolic forms of power existed alongside traditional power sources such as military capability. The focus on different and novel forms of power in IR constitutes the first contribution Bourdieusian sociology has added to IR.

### Security agents

States have long been considered the primary actors within IR (for discussion, see Bigo and Walker 2007)[7], or agency has been downplayed as an analytical category altogether in favour of structures or norms (Kauppi 2003: 777; Zehfuss 2001: 336). IR scholars have, however, used Bourdieusian insights to widen the focus on agents by including experts and private military companies. To take an example, Didier Bigo has focused on the practices of security experts and carried out analyses of security practices in Europe with a focus on intelligence and surveillance[8] (e.g. Bigo 2005; Bigo and Guild 2005; for a similar analysis, see Huysmans 2006; Bigo 2012). In so doing, he has shown how a field of European 'insecurity professionals' is in the making and is establishing a high degree of hegemony over European security knowledge especially in relation to immigration. The creation of a transnational field of 'professionals in the management of unease' (Bigo 2002b: 64) removes political control over what security means, installing in its place a security logic over a 'continuum of threats' (ibid.: 63) reaching beyond what was classically a matter of security: international and military questions.[9] The state is hence not seen as the primary actor as experts from different sectors take over the definition of security and threats on the subject of immigration.[10] These analyses highlight the value of using the Bourdieusian prism to study hitherto largely overlooked agents in IR. Instead of throwing out the usual net that only captures the role of state agents and alliances, or downplaying the role of agency, a Bourdieusian analysis can capture a far more detailed IR population of relevant players. This is a prerequisite for understanding European security in the 1990s.

### Doxic practice

Richard K. Ashley (Ashley 1984, 1987, 1988, 1989) was the first to draw on Bourdieu within IR. He presented a now classical argument that international relations in general can be studied as a field in which statesmen and 'the scholars who proclaim themselves realists' (Ashley 1987: 421; for a similar analysis, see J. George 1993) act according to a 'foundational practice' of sovereignty with which all actors agree. Sovereignty, Ashley argued, was a prerequisite for gaining acceptance in the field for practitioners and theorists alike: 'It is what one must *do* in order internationally to *be*' (Ashley 1989: 257). The distinction between inside the state and the international realm was thus a prerequisite for being heard in the field (see also Walker (1993) for a

Poststructuralist critique of the distinction between inside and outside). Ashley held that the Bourdieusian analysis enabled:

> [o]ne ... to see what the subjects of global life might not be disposed to see: that the recognizably objective structures of global life, far from being autonomous and pregiven conditions, are arbitrary and contingent *effects* that are imposed in history, through practice, and to the exclusion of other ways of structuring collective existence.
>
> (Ashley 1989: 253)

The realist, sovereignty-focused view of the world was therefore not necessarily synonymous with the 'truth' about the organization of international life. Instead it was just the dominant understanding, upheld by theorists and practitioners alike. '[T]hese rituals administer social time and space' (Ashley 1989: 261) in the sense that the international could only be grasped as a field consisting of states and in which war was a recurring phenomenon. This is what Bourdieu referred to as a *doxic practice*: a situation in which the arbitrariness of the structures in a field has been naturalized to such an extent that they become invisible to the actor (Bourdieu 1977: 164). To a large extent, the doxic practice described by Ashley has dominated the discipline of IR since and has prevented it, for example, from understanding the transformation of European security after the end of the Cold War. It has limited agency and focused on just the practices of sovereignty as the only relevant research question for IR to address.[11] And science and scientific agency have been excluded from the list of agents and power practices that have been considered important to IR.[12] My analysis reveals, however, that social science think tanks and models were very important in the restructuring of the field, and that technical science had backed up the doxic practice in the field before the end of the Cold War. Social and technical science came to shape the 'thinkable' in the field of European security.

All these studies demonstrate that inspiration from Bourdieu can provide insightful avenues for showing how certain practices uphold doxic understandings of the social world in large scale inter/transnational fields, how new types of agency can be brought into focus, and how concepts such as capital, social hierarchy and power struggles can form the basis for a reflexive study of the configuration of fields in IR. However, the discussion remains focused on individual Bourdieusian concepts. Instead, a comprehensive 'action framework' revolving around the concepts of field-capital-agency-doxa can help set boundaries around a field, focus on agency-selection, and understand the power struggles in a field which come to change basic features of a field (doxic battles). These dimensions have been left largely to assumptions and common sense research designs in the Rationalist and Reflectivist IR debates. Further, and hinted at by the work of Richard K. Ashley, a renewed focus on the power practices of international relations science and scientific agency can enter into IR debates as concrete, sociological analyses.

## An action framework for IR: the capital-field-agency-doxa

European security went from having been defined largely by military power and state actors during the bipolar world order, to being constituted by new actors and practices in the 1990s. These changes can be captured through a comprehensive discussion of fields, capital, agency and doxa.[13] With these concepts at hand, novel empirical questions will arise, and basic assumptions will be challenged. While not discussing the concept of habitus in detail, the concept of course remains important to the points I make as it points toward agency beyond rational actors.[14] The international field of European security does not, however, easily allow for an analysis of habitus due to the extremely divergent backgrounds of agents in the struggle. The focus here is therefore put on the doxa of the field and the mobilization of capital as the *analytical lens* that will capture struggles in international fields.

## The field

> [d]ifferent fields ... like magnetic forces, attract a multiplicity of agents, and polarise them around specific stakes.
>
> (Bigo and Walker 2007: 732)

A field is a less institutionalized social space than an institution: Bourdieu sought to develop a concept which could cover social worlds in which practices were weakly institutionalized and boundaries were not well established.[15] At least four features are central to understanding Bourdieu's concept of field and for distinguishing it from more common usages of the term (e.g. the 'field of international relations'). First, fields were seen as conceptual constructions based upon a relational mode of reasoning in which conflict and struggle played a major part. The term 'field of power' (*champs de luttes*) signals these competitive features. With the concept of a field in hand, the researcher can turn attention to practices of struggle and to latent as well as visible elements of conflict and competition in any arena regardless of the degree of institutionalization. Materialist causalities and naïve positivism are replaced with a potent prism for seeing how every practice is produced in systems of social and intellectual distinctions. 'Even the seemingly most neutral of ivory-tower cultural practices are, according to Bourdieu, embedded' in conflictual patterns (Swartz 1997: 119; see also Krais 1994: 112–115). The concept of a field of struggle thus potentially thrusts science into the foreground as a power practice in a relationally constituted field. As already argued, this holds promise for understanding the power struggles of European security in the 1990s. The struggle element in a field did, however, not mean that transformation was easily reached: 'fields capture struggle within the logic of reproduction' (Swartz 1997: 121). There is thus a conservative tendency in field struggles.

Secondly, a field is a structured space in which dominant and subordinate positions based on types of capitals and paradigmatic distinctions are pivotal.[16] A change in one position changes the boundary to other positions as if a field were a magnetic field (Bourdieu 1971; Swartz 1997: 123). Whereas the common sense or doxic practice of European security had been dominated by realism during the Cold War according to Ashley (1988), changes in this position occurred post-Cold War and changed the power relations in the field altogether. A tight fit between the conventional truth of realism and NATO's practices based on military capital, which had proven a viable and strong position during the 1980s, was suddenly a potential disadvantage in the field. NATO initially seemed at risk of withering away after the demise of the Soviet Union. Because NATO practices required a balancing enemy to remain relevant, most commentators agreed and expected that NATO would disintegrate (see e.g. Chalmers 1990; Hassner 1990; De Santis 1991; for debate, see Duffield 1994; for general statements, see Walt 1987; Waltz 1981, 1993a; Sagan and Waltz 1995). Some even argued that NATO was bound to disintegrate and that multipolarity was inevitable (Mearsheimer 1990). There was disagreement as to how long this would take, but disintegration was fully expected. An alliance had one purpose that kept it together: a common, external threat that needed to be balanced. In the event that this threat no longer existed, the members of the alliance would no longer see the need for upholding the costs of cooperation, since no obvious returns were envisioned (see also discussion in Buzan and Hansen 2009: 159–170). This understanding was the common sense of security in 1990. It built on the 'foundational practice' discovered by Ashley and the symbolic violence exerted by the structure of military and scientific capital in the field. NATO's powerful experience of the Cold War was therefore transformed into a new struggle for survival. This time the enemy was not a clearly defined military threat to be balanced, but instead a threat within the field of European security itself – involving scientific capital (see discussion later in the book). The doxic practice of the field came under attack as the realist common sense view of balancing power relations was challenged. NATO's dominance together with realist conceptions of security waned as other social science positions became powerful.

Thirdly, agents in a field share an underlying assumption that the struggle is worth engaging in and therefore (unknowingly, perhaps) accept that the field imposes certain ways of struggling. Both subordinate and dominant actors agree to this. 'Every field stimulates a certain interest, an *illusio*, in the shape of an implicit recognition of what is at stake in the field and how the actors in the field play the field power game' (Bourdieu and Wacquant 2004 [1996]: 103; Bourdieu 2005: 9). This *illusio* stimulates agents to think that 'the game is worth the candle, that it is worth playing' and creates a belief in the naturalness of the affairs in the field (Bourdieu 2004: 50). The field thus exerts symbolic power on agents in subordinate positions – they 'misrecognize' their position and uphold central distinctions in the field through practices of reproduction. In general terms, what is at stake in any field is 'the right to monopolize the exercise of 'symbolic violence'' (Swartz 1997: 123; Kauppi

2003: 779). I argue in this book that in the European security field, gaining authority over the definition of European security held the field together. The underlying logic to the game was thus a question of the power to define. Bigo found a similar stake in the field of (in)security professionals, where agents are 'in competition with each other for the monopoly of the legitimate knowledge on what constitutes a legitimate unease, a 'real' risk' (Bigo 2006: 111).[17]

Fourthly, fields are structured by their own internal mechanisms and are in Bourdieu's language 'relatively autonomous'. This means that Bourdieu often analysed the internal dynamic of a field as if it were a closed circuit even though he thought of fields as tied together with the broader 'field of power' and with other fields.[18] This point also means that a position of importance in one field does not translate directly into such a position in another field. Academic experts and think tanks may have gained a position in the European security field, but this does not mean that their power could be transferred smoothly to other fields, nor that the actions of individual states were made redundant.

So instead of seeing European security as a billiard table on which rational, unitary actors (states) seek survival with an exclusive focus on material capabilities (Neorealism), or studying the role of international norms in the reorganization of European security with only limited attention to agency and power (Constructivism), the focus of a field-approach orients the study of European security to the struggle over a central stake: the power to define the legitimate security logic in Europe. In this struggle, a range of different actors took part, and a variety of different resources were in play. Material capabilities and norms can therefore both be re-read as specific forms of capital in the European security field and the role of both 'theory-agency' and 'practitioner agency' in European security can be captured. The academic field of IR/security did not stand apart from the struggles in the field, but intersected with the field of European security.

For the researcher, this type of approach means turning studies of the social world solidly empirical:

> The theory of the field orients and governs empirical research. It forces the researcher to ask what people are 'playing at' in this field ... what are the stakes, the goods or properties sought and distributed or redistributed, and how they are distributed, what the instruments or weapons that one needs to have in order to play with some chance of winning.
>
> (Bourdieu 2004: 34)

Studying international fields thus involves studying what the main struggles are, and with what means they are supported. And contrary to common sense usage of the term, to talk about a European security field in a Bourdieusian sense means seeing European security as a field of struggle in which power is unevenly distributed. An agent may be deprived of the right to speak in the field of European security, if certain types of capital are not possessed or certain ways of playing the game are not followed. Because social identity is referential and oppositional, the agent needs to be recognized as a player in a field in order to become one. This constitutes the relational character of the struggle.

Former Secretary General to NATO, Willy Claes, can be taken as an example of an agent not possessing valued capital and not following the recognized rules of the game in the European security field in the 1990s. He tried to fill the void left by the Soviet Union with a new enemy: that of Islamic fundamentalism, in order to demonstrate the sustained centrality of NATO in European security. During the Cold War, NATO had become accustomed to a world split between it and a massive, material and political counterpart. This world had been understood through a tight fit between (realist) scientific and military capital. With the disappearance of the Soviet Union, NATO still held on to balancing the military capabilities of the former enemy for some time ('field struggles are captured within the logic of reproduction',) because the dominant logic of security remained one of balance of power and military capabilities. So when then Secretary General Willy Claes voiced his views in 1995 about the greatest threat in the future, he was still thinking in terms of a world split in two, organized by the presence of military capabilities and working according to strategic[19] balancing; NATO was defined by its counterpart. Claes is quoted for having stated: 'Muslim fundamentalism is at least as dangerous as Communism once was ... It represents terrorism, religious fanaticism' (Fisk 1999: 2; Droziak 1995; Behnke 2000: 3; Bilski 1995). In his thinking a new threat of the same magnitude as the Communist threat during the Cold War, which could be countered through military means, gave NATO a clear and legitimate purpose for remaining relevant in the post-Cold War European field of security. However, this attempt to define a new common threat created more problems than solutions for the Secretary General. It turned out not to be *comme il faut* in the changing European field of security to place religiously demarcated groups as a new counterpart to NATO. As we shall see in the following chapters, it was not recognized as a valid move in a field that increasingly believed – contra strategic balancing – that 'security is what we make of it' (Solana 1999a) and that military capital was part of the problem – not the solution. Following from this, he was either ignored or discredited in numerous ways by other agents in the field. Willy Claes felt a solid field effect.[20]

## Boundary-setting and agency selection

But how can a field be demarcated? In the IR literature, an priori drawing of boundaries prevail. Pouliot argues that 'only a few social agents are allowed to step in to partake in the social construction of international threats' (Pouliot 2004: 9),[21] while Buzan *et al.* (1998: 31) argue that 'security is ... very much a structured field in which some actors are placed in positions of power by virtue of being generally accepted voices of security, by having the power to define security.'[22] Powerful agents are defined thus:

In the contemporary era, security élites are the handful of individuals who gather at the highest level to make the ultimate arbitration regarding foreign and security policies: in addition to heads of state and government, security élites are comprised of senior ministers and top foreign policy officials and diplomats. Some high level officials from security-related international organisations should also be added.

(Pouliot 2004: 10)

But why are they powerful? By what standards are their voices considered powerful? I argue that these claims are based on an *assumption* about a powerful elite and not on an empirical investigation into the specific elites that actually operate in a specific field.

This type of argument has come to be the standard answer to the selection of agency in many Reflectivist analyses of the international and also remains central to Rationalist common sense approaches. Even though the answer is theoretically founded and carries weight, it is too static and exclusive for capturing the novel practices in the European security field after the fall of bipolarity. It is inattentive to historical variability and in fact takes the Cold War historical context as taken for granted rather than as historically contingent. This means that the default selection of actors hinges on a Cold War taken-for-granted assumed centrality of these actors. Centrally, it focuses almost exclusively on state actors and leaves out important scientific actors such as social science think tanks and academic university experts who also struggled for the power to define European security after the Cold War. Instead, I argue that a Bourdieusian approach with a special focus on the concept of capital can turn the question of powerful agency into an empirical analysis in which different types of *field-specific* capital serve not only as power bases in the struggles in a field, but also as *points of entry* to the field for different types of actors.[23] As capital can take a variety of forms, this multi-dimensional analysis of power allows for a range of newcomers and struggles over boundaries while retaining a central focus on the stakes. Capital thus helps set boundaries and select recognized agency in the course of the empirical analysis.

Within a Poststructuralist framework, the question of creating an inside and an outside has been central in critiques made by R.B.J. Walker (1993). Walker deconstructed the division of the world into the category of 'inside the state' and 'outside the state'. He argued that the binary opposition between inside and outside had created certain expectations as to what was possible in these two different spheres: 'Inside' was seen as occupying the positive side of a set of binary oppositions: peace, benevolence and order. 'Outside' was seen as the other, negative side of these binary oppositions and was associated with war, hostility and anarchy/disorder (Walker 1993). The most prevalent ways of addressing the question of boundaries in IR relevant to this book concerns levels of analysis, the geographical boundaries of Europe, and high/low politics.

*Levels of analysis*

Walker discussed which underlying assumptions the discipline of IR was structured by. These underlying assumptions were systematised in the levels-of-analysis scheme first coined by David J. Singer (1969). Singer divided the social world into two levels: the international system and the state.[24] To Singer, the levels were meant as an analytical tool: distinct features of the two levels were an empirical matter of fact – but not necessarily universally valid. Change in the way the levels worked was possible (for discussion, see Onuf 1995).

The distinction between system and state caused a number of problems. On the systems level, Singer argued that:

> this particular level of analysis almost inevitably requires that we postulate a high degree of uniformity in the foreign policy operational codes of our national actors. By definition, we allow very little room for divergence in the behaviour of our parts when we focus upon the whole.
>
> (Singer 1969: 23)

Morgenthau's famous statement that: 'All statesmen think and act in terms of interests defined as power' is a case in point (Morgenthau 1986 [1948]: 5–7). On the level of the state, the opposite problem could emerge. The focus on particular states might exaggerate the differences and tend to overlook the similarities.

Singer's analytical way of addressing the levels of analysis-problem was taken up by Waltz (1959).[25] However, Waltz postulated that not only were the two levels distinct, they were also practically and universally inhabited by different logics. The structural anarchy of the international system inevitably led to war, while order was only possible within the confines of the nation state. Waltz did not distinguish between the world and the way we see it (Onuf 1995: 44). The methodological approach to the concept of levels was thereby translated into an ontological statement.

In a critique and review of Waltz's conceptualization, Singer attempted to underline the possibility of change:

> It is just possible that this intellectual, literary and verbal effort, if applied to the problem in a more creative and imaginative fashion, might lead us to some way out of the dilemma of perpetual anarchy and its corollary of inevitable war.
>
> (Singer 1960: 459)

Singer's means of conceptualising the levels of analysis problem was over-hauled by Waltz when his *Theory of International Politics* laid the ground for thinking about levels in largely universal terms (Waltz 1979).[26]

Traditional studies of European security have often taken the distinction between state and system as their starting point. During the Cold War, it was common to refer to the structure of the system as the primary explanatory factor. Bipolarity was believed to have created an overlay over Europe, suppressing the security dynamics of the states and the region (Buzan 1991 [1983]). After the Cold War, the picture changed. States were often taken as the primary units in explaining the lack of cooperation in the EC/EU's foreign and security policy (CFSP). Cooperation was conceptualized as a two-level game in which interests were formed on the nation-state level and subsequently negotiated at the EU level (see e.g. Friis 1997; Moravscik 1998). The levels were understood as instances of reality, which theory could study from an external perspective.[27] Contrary to this, Bigo argues:

> We need indeed to set the constraints and opportunities that the field gives to the agents – effects which are visible – and to understand their less visible relations both inside and outside the field. These field effects will trace the limits of the field in rough contours – limits that are never given, but depend on the particular (con)figuration of a given moment of a struggle within the field.
>
> (2006: 141–142)

The limits of the field are thus not fixed, they are not given, and can only roughly be determined by studying the struggles in the field and the effects these struggles have on the agents. Boundaries are constantly under contestation and form part of the struggle to be analysed. However, discarding the levels-of-analysis scheme and the notion of boundaries as fixed does not mean that the states and international organizations inhabiting Singer's levels will be excluded from the analysis. On the contrary, states and international organizations continue to constitute an important part of the battle over European security. But no a priori assumptions about national interests or the weakness of international organizations would form the basis for including them.

### Europe as a geographical boundary?

Bourdieu's concept of a field was coined to fit the context of the territorial nation state. In order to counter the homologous notion of a field based on this fact, I hold that the emerging transnational social space of European security surrounding NATO is less stable and that the status of its boundaries are essentially contested. However, an important question of territoriality remains. How can we talk about a 'European' field? If all other core social science understandings are problematized, how does this affect the discipline of geography? Geography and territoriality are as much a result of a political and negotiated process as is the case with the conceptualizations of theory and practice or system and state. Hence, there is no ready-made conceptualization of Europe which can form the basis for drawing a line in this study. As has been so excellently documented by Neumann (1999), Europe has used different conceptualizations of 'the East' as a point of opposition in an identity/difference game. The boundary of difference has moved back and forth, territorially speaking: the debate after the end of the Cold War saw different conceptualizations of Europe: slogans like 'Europe to the Urals', 'Central Europe', and 'All-European security' demonstrate that Europe is not easily defined or conclusively a territorial concept (see e.g. Kundera 1984; Neumann 1999). For example, the then Romanian Foreign Minister Melescanu argued in 1993 that 'today's Europe is to be found where its democratic, liberal and humanist values and practices succeed in shutting the door on the nightmare of authoritarian regimes, command economies, and a disregard for human rights and fundamental freedoms' (Melescanu 1993: 13). A geographical boundary around 'Europe' is therefore not the correct place to draw a line when it comes to the study of the emerging field of European security surrounding NATO (for an excellent rendition of Europe as an identity rather than a territory, see Behnke 2013; for a debate on Europe as a concept and theoretical construct, see C.A.S.E. 2006, 2007; Walker 2007; Salter 2007; Sylvester 2007). The boundary should be allowed to remain fluid and tied to the stakes in the field: that of gaining recognition as a legitimate speaker and definer of European security. Like Bigo (2006: 13–14), I do not see the field as 'reducible neither to the national political field, nor to a level between two nations, or even to the European level.'

Europe becomes a matter of an *illusio* in the field: the struggles over the definition of European security hold the European field of security together. It is within this social space that an answer to the question of how NATO was related to theory in the 1990s emerges most visibly: the boundaries of European security were redefined after the Cold War when new actors entered the field and challenged the meaning of security in Europe. In the process, the field was remade. On this battleground, the theory and practice of European security fought over the right to remain central.

### High and low politics

One final distinction with relevance for my study is the distinction between high and low politics. This distinction is often made in the Security Studies debate in the United Sates between military and other subject areas. The traditional concept of security was exclusively defined as military security (see discussion between Art 1996, 1999; Baldwin 1999, 2002: and later in this Chapter), whereas the debate on the broad concept of security (Buzan 1991; Buzan *et al.* 1998) stressed that other sectors may also have implications for security or become 'securitized'. In this book, no initial selection of organizations, policies or academic work occupied with military security can be made. NATO is not necessarily a more important player in the field of European security because it is a military alliance. In fact, the opposite could be the case. As I will show below, Huysmans  directs our attention towards the possibility that military capital was becoming a problematic kind of capital in the field during the 1990s (Huysmans 2002b). NATO very actively pursued a strategy of conversion of military capital into humanitarian capital in order to retain a position of authority in the field. Military high politics versus low politics is therefore not a useful distinction for selecting agency and drawing boundaries in the European case. In fact, it seems as though defining battles were centred on challenging this very distinction.

The dissolution of the distinction between high and low politics was a general trend in the creation of a new doxa of the emerging European field of security (for a definition of doxa, see below). Different concepts of power and security underpinned different types of valued capital in the field and were employed by a diverse group of actors – many of whom possess no military capital. It would therefore be detrimental to this the study to exclude 'low politics' or 'soft power'[28] before venturing into the analysis of the field. Soft power may be the hard power of the future in European security. As Leander advises, 'an analysis of structural power needs to research which actor is authorised to speak (is empowered with authority) and how the actions of field-relevant actors reproduce and reshape such positions of authority' (Leander 2005a: 811–812). The hard power of the Cold War may no longer produce a powerful position in the field. New 'soft power' agents may be gaining ground in the field. This point involves a question of relations of recognition: 'these institutional loci of authoritative declaration must be recognized as legitimate both by the speaker and those to whom the declarations are addressed' (M.C. Williams 1997: 295).

According to Bourdieu, 'Any effort to establish precise boundaries between fields ... derives from a 'positivist vision' rather than the more compelling 'relational' view of the social world, for boundaries are themselves objects of struggle' (Swartz 1997: 121).[29] Instead, Bourdieu argued that boundary shifts and struggles over drawing boundaries around a field are key factors in social change:

> changes within a field are often determined by redefinitions of the frontiers between fields, linked (as cause and effect) to the sudden arrival of new entrants endowed with new power resources. This explains why the boundaries of the field are almost always at stake in the struggles within the field.
>
> (Bourdieu 2004: 36)

This is an important point. The default setting of boundaries – either by relying on the distinction between inside and outside, high and low politics, geographical areas, or by selecting powerful agency (e.g. states or security elites) before the empirical study – will risk overlooking important aspects of international power struggles (for discussion, see Bigo and Walker 2007). The massive changes European security underwent during the 1990s clearly indicate that the boundaries around the European security field were under fierce negotiation. This means that field boundaries and relevant agency should be posed as questions and not offered as definitions in an analysis of the field.

But if boundaries are fluid and newcomers are always a possibility, how can the concept of a field direct an empirical analysis? How can it help select agency? In a Bourdieusian analysis, the central issue in determining the relevant agents is keeping an eye on the central dynamic of the field: the struggle. The initial research question therefore becomes: struggle over what? In the case of European security in the 1990s, the struggle was over the right to define European security in the face of the loss of the central demarcating enemy, the Soviet Union.

## Hierarchy

Apart from setting boundaries and selecting agency, redefined and new types of capital also shifted the hierarchy of the European security field. Guzzini asks 'who is authorised to speak in the first place and which authority (roles, institutions and the taken-for-granted understandings) supports the claims?' (Guzzini 2005: 51). According to Bourdieu, the answer would be who has the symbolic capital, that is, a type of capital widely recognized as legitimate? I shall rephrase this question as: which types of capital authorize certain actors to participate in the field and hold a powerful position in it? As we shall see with regards to the European security field under study here, when military capital was valued, actors with great military capabilities such as heads of state and government and NATO Secretary Generals were recognized as speakers in the field and gained a high position in the hierarchy (such as NATO during the Cold War). When new forms of scientific capital became valued, a different type of agency was accepted as legitimate speaker in the field. The default selection of high-level officials, therefore, needed to be replaced by an analysis of whether actors actually held (or successfully mobilized, see below) the valued types of capital in the field. In subsequent chapters I will identify and discuss these types of capital by seeing who actually participated in the central struggle over 'who gets to define European security.' From this, the boundary-setting and selection of recognized agency will materialize. This will allow for an analysis of relations between recognized actors (what I call practical patterns of interaction), and thereby for a solidly empirical evaluation of the field.

The possession of capital is thus important for being accepted as a player in a field (capital is *boundary-setting*), but also for understanding the positions and power bases of agents and thus the *hierarchy* in a field: 'It is therefore not *what* you say but *where* you say it from that matters' (Leander 2005a: 612, 2006: 4).[30] 'Where you say it from' means with what capital – what resources or power – do you speak in the field? The hierarchization and existence of different types of capital are ultimately empirical questions related to the specific field under study. Where Bourdieu often focused on the interplay between economic and cultural capital in his analytical work and described economic capital as the 'dominant principle of hierarchy' and cultural capital as the 'second principle of hierarchy' (Swartz 1997: 192)[31], this dichotomy always needed adjustment and specification in concrete fields.[32] I argue that the European security field was traditionally structured by military capital (backed up by economic capital) and (realist) scientific capital, but that the valued types of capital were under reconfiguration in the 1990s. Other types of capital were becoming important: new forms of social scientific capital and social capital (in the form of the establishment of new networks) played an increasingly important role and reshuffled the hierarchy.

Thus, the concept of capital can analytically be used in IR as *points of entry* for different kinds of actors and for establishing boundaries around a field. Capital serves as an 'entry ticket' to the struggles and is thus boundary-setting. Further, capital helps structure the analysis of which sources of power are important in different fields and how this impacts on hierarchy/stratification in the field. Capital analysis is therefore also a means to knowing 'which voice will be likely to carry weight' in the struggles. But yet another – a third – dimension of the concept of capital will prove valuable when applying the field perspective to IR. Bourdieu's concepts have often pointed IR in the direction of conservation and stabilization of fields. After the Cold War, we have, however, come to accept the pivotal role of change – not least in European security. A central challenge for applying Bourdieu to IR therefore concerns the question of change. Given this, the concept of capital may become a straightjacket that favours stasis over process for IR. But by explicitly focusing on the strategic mobilization of capital – by getting closer to the practice element in Bourdieu's work – this peril may be avoided. This involves including a focus on how agents seek to optimize their position (or guarantee their survival as in the case of NATO) in moves involving specific forms of capital. I turn to that below.

## Conversion, redefinition and doxic battles

As Wacquant reminds us, we cannot limit the analysis 'to drawing an objectivist topology of distributions of capital'. An analysis is needed of how participants in various social worlds 'perceive and actualize (or not) the potentialities they harbor' (Wacquant 1998: xvi). I agree. And Bourdieu did point us in the direction of the strategic practices of agents. He argued that different types of capital could be *converted* into new power bases in the field and that struggles over *definitions* of what was to be considered the most valued resources in a field were central (Swartz 1997: 123). This underscores the value of zooming in on how agents mobilize capital in their quest for centrality in a specific field. Such a dynamic understanding of the capital-field-agency combination adds important insight to the stable and static image of Bourdieusian analysis by calling attention to process in field analysis.[33]

But the profundity of change in fields where the *basic structures* are under pressure and in which the limits of autonomy in classification struggles (Bourdieu 1986 [1979]: 483–484) are arguably less restraining than in stable fields calls for specific attention. The very assumptions underlying the

European security field were under reconfiguration in Europe in the 1990s. The strategic mobilizations that took place in this field, hence, had the effect of changing basic, taken-for-granted knowledge. I call this type of strategic practices in fields under profound change *doxic battles*. I shall discuss conversion and redefinition, before turning my attention to doxic battles.

### Conversion and redefinition of capital

An important aspect of the strategic mobilization of capital concerns the extent to which the different types of capital can be used in other settings than the obvious one: military capital can quite obviously be used for the purpose of deterring and fighting a war. But could military capital provide a powerful position in a situation in which the overarching threat had disappeared? Did a position at the top of the hierarchy in European security after the end of bipolarity follow from NATO's possession of military capital? Could military capital be converted into other forms of capital more appropriate to the new situation faced by NATO in the post-1989 period?[34]

Some types of resources will be more valuable for certain tasks than others and some will be more fungible than others. But the ranking and fungibility of resources must (in a Bourdieusian vocabulary) always be considered in the context of a field. No a priori ranking can be determined and no resources have inherent qualities that make them power assets (for discussion, see Baldwin 1999; Art 1999).[35] As Baldwin put it, 'what constitutes a 'good hand' in card games depends on whether one is playing poker or bridge' (Baldwin 2002: 179).[36] NATO had a good hand in balance-of-power and deterrence terms, but in the new risk society, it was less obvious how good the alliance's hand was. Determining whether an agent has a 'good hand' thus depends on the nature of the game being played and the fungibility of its capital. The game in the European security field remained one of 'security' (a type of politics) and the agents pursued the power to define security and security practice (cp. Calhoun 2003: 277). As we shall see, NATO was put on the defensive when military capital was devalued as a valuable asset in security after 1990. But some of the existing military capability remained an asset (and thus valued capital) for NATO: the structures already in place for decision-making in the field and the institutionalized links between the political and military branches of the Alliance remained a power resource, since they could rather easily be converted and function in the new security setting. This was NATO's strongest asset when the alliance attempted to convert its Cold War military capability to crisis management capabilities or to *humanitarian capital* during the Kosovo crisis (Huysmans 2002b) and later, when NATO and the EU fought over the leading position in European security (see Chapter 6).[37] But the EU became an important actor in security matters as well, through a strategy of first capital conversion and then redefinition. Spearheaded by the interventions made by the think tank the *Centre for European Reform* (CER) (see Chapter 6), economic capital was recast a new type of military capital, which was superior to the power of military capabilities (see Chapter 6 in this book). Strategically mobilizing the 'underwhelming power' (Everts 2004: 1) of the EU was thus an attempt to convert economic capital into a redefined type of military capital, while also clearly challenging the traditional type of military capital. According to CER, the EU was set on a course that would explain 'Why Europe will run the 21st century' as a CER publication was entitled (Leonard 2005).

### Doxic battles

A more deeply rooted dimension of an analysis of change in international fields concerns the concept of doxa: 'the doxa stands for the faith or belief in the presuppositions of a field' (Schinkel 2003: 77) or 'a 'strategic reserve' of self-evident yet ambiguous knowledge' (Ashley 1989: 256). In the world of doxa, things 'go without saying because they come without saying' (Bourdieu 1977: 89; cited in Ashley 1989: 262).[38]

What I term doxic battles are analysed as the mobilization of different types of capital in a field in which fundamental assumptions (doxa) have been/are called into question. While the doxa will of course always be undergoing incremental changes, the term doxic battles signifies a situation in which these changes are more abrupt and profound.

The European security field during the Cold War was structured by a belief that threats could be measured materially and ideologically, and that the 'nature' of the international system caused war to be a recurring phenomenon. In other words, the 'space'[39] of European security was largely defined by weapons and geographical distance, whereas 'time' was understood in cyclical terms. These were the deep, doxic structures of European security, which, as described earlier, also led Willy Claes to seek a new enemy in Islamic fundamentalism to replace the old enemy of the former Soviet Union. But as we shall see, the field no longer accepted moves that drew on these basic features in the mid-1990s. The taken-for-granted assumptions – the doxa – changed: I shall argue that the situation after the end of the Cold War exposed a doxa in the field of European security which could no longer be upheld. Military security and balance of power – the traditional objectives of the European security field, at least as seen through the eyes of realism – no longer captured the situation in which Europe found itself. This opened the possibility for newcomers[40] to the field and for new definitions to take over from old Cold War definitions. Ashley unknowingly foretold this situation:

> If this boundary [of the *doxa*] is not sustained in practice, if totalizing and formalizing discourses encroach upon and politicize the ambiguous zone of doxa, and if, therefore this zone of practice loses its natural, self-evident character, then the rituals of power constituted therein lose their capacities to orchestrate the enframing and discipline of collective possibility. Their arbitrariness exposed, they are deprived of instantaneous and

unquestioning recognition, and they are called upon to prove their legitimacy by appeal to universal grounds.

(Ashley 1989: 273)

Seen from the perspective of NATO, its role was uncertain after 1990. Having thrived on the space/time classifications of the Cold War, a new world with no clear enemy and where peace suddenly seemed to prevail made NATO seem obsolete. As subsequent chapters will show, the Alliance therefore threw itself into a battle over definitions of valued scientific capital, social capital, and the role of military capital after the Cold War, which, together with other agents' strategic moves, led to fundamental changes in the field of European security on the dimensions of space and time. Security practices were exposed as arbitrary and basic assumed classifications of space and time, which had exercised symbolic violence on actors and had guided NATO's military strategy, were questioned. By opposing NATO against 'theory', Solana, as the quotation which started this book suggests, was devaluing the scientific capital of the Cold War kind and with it the firm belief in the 'nature' of the international system as inherently cyclical and war-prone.[41] The wisdom that had guided NATO throughout the Cold War was called into question, as was its attempt to convert NATO's Cold War military power into a valuable resource in the new security situation. This involved devaluing the dominant theoretical understanding of what an alliance can do, but also implicitly the fundamental issues of time and space, which had limited the relevant actors and threats to states and military capability (space) and the inevitability of recurring conflict as the condition of the international system (time). Instead, a different type of scientific capital was mobilized: 'Security in the 21st century is what we make of it. The future can be shaped' (Solana 1999a), Solana wrote in 1999 before Lord Robertson took over as Secretary General of NATO. He thereby made it clear that security was no longer based on the doxic understanding of recurring conflict and that relations with relevant actors in security could be transformed. Put analytically, his understanding of *time* was not cyclical but Constructivist, and his understanding of the strategic environment of the alliance (*space*) was plastic rather than static.[42] But he also signalled in no uncertain terms that he was familiar with the vocabulary of the Social Constructivist paradigm, which was becoming ever more influential in Security Studies in Europe.[43] I argue that this was a central feature of the European security field in the 1990s: social science became a factor – a type of capital – which agents with no institutional, scientific backing sought to mobilize in their quest for domination in the field. This helped produce a new doxa in the field.[44] But in addition, social science also became an actor in European security.

As mentioned in Chapter 2, Bourdieu saw *social* science as intimately related to society. 'sociology, whether it wants to or not … is an actor in the struggles it describes' (Bourdieu 2004: 88). As we shall see, social scientific actors were indeed granted actor status in the European security field. This was underscored by changes in concrete practices of the NATO Secretary Generals such as Solana. He accumulated social capital by calling on scientific expertise provided by certain think tanks in order to back up the new valued scientific capital (on taste, see Bourdieu 1986 [1979]) and thereby helped a new type of actor gain access to the struggles in the field. In the process, doxic space/time structures of the European security field changed. The international system was now understood as transformable, and space was defined in terms of democratization and values rather than by external material threats. These were massive changes. But the stake in the field – and hence the magnetic force that held the field together – remained the same: the power to define European security. The definition had  been so stable during the Cold War that we ceased to reflect on it: strategic balancing and military capital were parts of a misrecognised structure in the field and the dominant scientific paradigm – realism – had contributed to upholding this state of affairs.

## Conclusion

The paradigmatic case of European security in the 1990s has not been adequately explained by the two dominant strands of thought within IR: Rationalism and Reflectivism. Through a discussion of fields, agency, capital and doxa, this chapter tried to formulate an 'action framework' which offers a more compelling explanation and set a new agenda for the study of international relations. This new agenda challenged IR to pose empirical questions in a new way.

Concretely, I argued that in an 'action framework' the concept of capital could be understood as working in three ways. First, different types of capital provided *points of access* to the field for different types of agency. If military capital is valued, states and alliances possessing military capital would be allowed to participate. If scientific capital became valued, scientific-type actors would be able to gain access. In this way, capital could be seen as an analytical lens for selecting agency and setting the boundary for participation in fields. This allowed for an analysis of practical patterns of interaction. Apart from serving as an entry point to the struggles in the field, capital functioned, secondly, as the most important criterion for defining an agent's position in the hierarchy in a field. Capital was a 'weapon' or 'power-base' which could be used in struggles in a particular field and determine the hierarchy in the field. Focusing on capital thus provides a prism through which to see the patterns of practice in a field and the boundaries surrounding it: the contours of the relevant types of agency appeared, and the central resources over which power struggles take place are brought to the fore. Thirdly, a discussion of the mobilization of capital in fields in which the taken-for-granted – the doxa - had been challenged, was added because of the pivotal role ascribed to change in IR. In this way, the production process of the doxa came into focus.

The framework developed in this chapter will let me shed light on processes in the European security field after the Cold War. Theory and practice have been reconceptualized as types of agents in a power struggle which help reshape doxic understandings in a field. Bourdieusian sociology thus helps redirect not only the empirical direction of research, but also poses the basic distinction between theory and practice as a research question: social scientific knowledge is recast as a type of capital in the hands of agents, and social science agents enter the struggles as agents in the European security field.

Apart from serving as an addendum to theorizing about theory and practice in IR, the discussion in the chapter also highlights the value of turning selection of agency and boundaries into empirical questions rather than offering them as a priori definitions. The default selection of states and security elites as practised within mainstream IR (and some Bourdieu-inspired studies) turned out to rely on doxic practices in European security prior to the end of the Cold War. The profound changes which that field underwent in the 1990s makes it an anachronism to take this as a starting point for understanding practices in the field after the Cold War. Bourdieusian sociology thus holds the promise of significantly challenging IR in ways that will lead to new knowledge about the international.

In sum, the practice approach developed in this chapter points to three different types of analysis with relevance for understanding the relationship between NATO theory and practice. First, an analysis of the valued types of capital in the field of European security, which work as agency-selecting and boundary-setting and at the same time provide agents with weapons in the fight for a position in the hierarchy in the field; second, an analysis of the practical patterns of interaction involving relevant agency in order to determine the extent to which the field can be empirically supported and not just assumed a priori; and third, an analysis of the conversion and mobilization of capital in doxic battles. The analysis of the field-specific types of capital is the topic of Chapter 4, while the practical patterns of interaction are the topic of Chapter 5. An analysis of doxic battles will be the topic of Chapter 6. In sum, these three types of analysis will help determine how NATO and theory 'hung together' after the Cold War. At the same time, they illustrate how a sociological practice approach to the question of the impossibility of detached knowledge production can be structured.

## Notes

1 Throughout the chapter, I use 'international relations' to mean the empirical subject matter beyond the nation state and 'International Relations' or 'IR' as signifying the academic debate.

2 For a discussion of the need for a relational perspective in sociology and a specification of Bourdieu as an exemplary voice, see Emirbayer (1997).

3 Bourdieu coined the concept as a way of distancing himself from Marxism, and even though the concept remained rooted in a kind of labour theory of value, labour was understood much more broadly than in Marxism. It could include e.g. social, cultural, political, religious and familial labour (Swartz 1997: 73–75). Under specific circumstances these could be converted into one another.

4 Bourdieu thinks of a strategy in terms quite different from the common sense usage within IR and rational choice theory: to him, a strategy is *social* in the sense that it is 'defined by its position in a system of strategies oriented towards the maximizing of material and symbolic profit' (Bourdieu 1990: 16). It is a 'more or less conscious pursuit of the accumulation of symbolic capital' (ibid.). Strategies are often concealed by a disinterested veil that makes claims to the pursuit of public goods rather than individual interests (Bourdieu 1990).

5 In 2004, Pouliot held that the influence of Bourdieu in IR remained 'thin' (Pouliot 2004: 8). Since then, the number of scholars and publications using Bourdieu in IR and Security Studies has been growing gradually. In December 2010, a workshop at the Department of Political Science at the University of Copenhagen even brought together a group of scholars dedicated to re-reading all major IR concepts from a Bourdieusian viewpoint. See e.g. (Adler-Nissen 2012; Berling 2012b).

6 As a definition, Huysmans offers the following: 'The humanitarian technologies are mechanisms of arranging assistance and/or protection (defined in terms of non-refoulement and asylum) of refugees' (Huysmans 2002b).

7 To some extent, this trend has been reproduced in Bourdieusian approaches to IR: Pouliot (2010) and Ashley (1987) centred their analyses on the primary role of states – indeed Ashley's point was exactly that states were the 'natural selection' of the doxic practice in IR (see below). Pop (2007: 398–400) also defines the international states system as a field in which the legitimate actors are states and intergovernmental organizations in her analysis of Romania's relationship with the IMF in the 1990s and Dezalay and Garth (2002) find that the state is still the key unit of analysis in their study of how neoliberal economics and international human rights law was received in Latin America.

8 In particular, the role of Europol and its competition with Interpol and 'some confidential circles of NATO' (Bigo 2002: 71). Bigo aptly talks about a 'stock exchange of security' in which European countries negotiate their different national understandings of the immigrants (Algerians to the French, Kurds to the German etc.) by using the label 'immigrant' as a common denominator (ibid.).

9 'The prism of security analysis is especially important for politicians, for national and local police organizations, the military police, customs officers, border patrols, secret services, armies, judges, some social services (health care, hospitals, schools), private corporations (bank analysts, providers of technology surveillance, private policing), many journalists (especially from television and the more sensationalist newspapers), and a significant fraction of general public opinion, especially but not only among those attracted to law and order' (Bigo 2002: 63).

10 Anna Leander suggested broadening IR analyses by including private military companies (PMCs) as a means to understanding recent developments in the field of security. Leander shows how 'PMCs contribute to the reproduction of a highly specialised security field in which 'experts' authorise an increasingly technical, managerial and military understanding of the field, which, in turn, empowers PMCs' (Leander 2005a: 805). According to Leander, the field of security is thereby both privatized and re-militarized – a process which places PMCs centrally in the security business: as agenda-setting, intelligence-gathering, and as lobbyists with close relations to governments. Other examples include Huysmans (2006: 154–155) who suggests including the security elite and security professionals (police, military and intelligence) in analyses of security (for such an approach, see also Bigo 2000, 2002b). He bases this on the assumption that the political process involves both a symbolic political struggle and technocratic processes. Williams adds a 'knowledge agent' to this: 'the institutions of knowledge and culture which constitute and structure specific knowledge claims and constructions … the institutions of education and accreditation which embody, produce and reproduce these knowledge structures and which produce 'legitimate speakers' who instantiate them' (Williams 1997: 289). He specifically

mentions 'security studies', think tanks, universities and ministries as examples of agents that create a 'realm of security' (ibid.: 299).

11  Vincent Pouliot has picked up Ashley's path-breaking work in a study of a Russian-Atlantic security community (Pouliot 2010). He builds 'on Bourdieu's notion of symbolic power to argue that misrecognised domination is what makes security communities possible in the first place' (Pouliot 2004: 9). Similar to Ashley's classical idea, Pouliot argues that the Russian-Atlantic security community can fruitfully be understood as a field in which peaceful means of action have become doxic practice (Pouliot calls it the 'logic of practicality', see Pouliot (2008)). In this setting, military means have become unthinkable in relations between Russia and the West (see discussion with Cox on this issue in Pouliot 2006; Cox 2005, 2006). Rebecca Adler-Nissen has also benefited from the concept of doxic practice in her study of British and Danish Opt-outs in the European Union. She argues that the *acquis communautaire* functions as a doxa that regulates practices in the EU (Adler-Nissen 2009, 2011).

12  Other Bourdieu-inspired studies should be mentioned: Guzzini has adopted the Bourdieusian framework in an attempt to come to terms with how power works in the international domain (Guzzini 1994, 2000) and how geo-political reasoning has shaped security in Europe after the Cold War (2003). Guilhot (2005) has studied the field of human rights and democracy and Dezalay and Garth have analysed the field of human rights. They reveal 'power relationships that are obscured in words like "the international community", "norms" and the "law"' (Dezalay and Garth 2006: 231). Niilo Kauppi (2003) has studied the dislocating effects of European integration on Finnish and French national political fields, Ted Hopf (2002) has used Bourdieu in a study of identities and foreign policy in Russia/the Soviet Union. Henrik Breitenbauch (2013) has studied the French intellectual field of IR from a Bourdieusian perspective, and David McCourt (2010) uses Bourdieusian field theory to study the interconnection between the fields of academia and politics in Britain's foreign policy establishment. Inanna Hamati-Ataya has called for a reflexive turn in IR building on Bourdieu's thought (Hamati-Ataya 2012, 2013). Matthew Eagleton-Pierce has used Bourdieu's concept to study symbolic power in the WTO (Eagleton-Pierce 2013).

13  Leander (2008) bases her discussion on fields, habitus and practices, Kauppi (2003) bases his discussion on field, capital, and habitus and Swartz (2008: 45) specifies habitus, capital and field as "Bourdieu's master concepts'.

14  Bourdieu defined habitus as 'systems of durable, transposable dispositions' (Bourdieu 1977: 72) and as 'determined by past conditions which have produced the principle of their production, that is, by the actual outcome of identical or interchangeable past practices' (ibid.: 72–73). The habitus 'links individual action and macro-structural settings within which future action is taken … and links past fields to present fields through individual actors who move from one to the next' (Emirbayer and Johnson 2008: 4). In general terms, practices 'flow from the intersection of habitus with capital and field positions' (ibid.: 48).

15  The concept was meant as a correction to three central debates in sociology at the time: positivism, materialism and idealism (Swartz 1997).

16  'The most important … modus operandi is the field's organization around two opposite poles: the protagonists of change and the apostles of law and order, the progressives and the conservatives, the heterodox and the orthodox, or the challengers and the incumbents.' (Kauppi 2003: 778). For instance, Bourdieu mentioned the distinction between orthodoxy and herecy in cultural fields and between 'curators of culture' and 'creators of culture' in intellectual fields (Swartz 1997: 124).

17  This type of stake follows Bourdieu's analysis of the cultural and literary field where the legitimate definition of literature and literary practice was identified as the *illusio* (Johnson 1993: 19; Bourdieu 1993: 42).

18 It goes beyond the scope of this chapter to discuss this issue in detail. Suffice to say that Bourdieu coined the central feature of this relationship as a 'homology' between fields and positions in fields.

19 Strategic is here understood as tied to the rational actor model adopted by Kenneth Waltz (1979) and his followers, and not as strategic practice in a Bourdieusian sense. Bourdieu did not invest his term with rational actor assumptions and eventually – in response to criticism – began replacing the term with the term *illusio*.

20 Willy Claes resigned soon after the statements for unrelated reasons. He was charged with corruption in Belgium (dating back to the time when he was member of the Belgian government) and chose to resign.

21 'In other words, social reality is constructed in such a way that only a very restricted group of individuals are legitimised to authoritatively define international threats: I call them "security élites"' (Pouliot 2004: 9–10).

22 The argument is tied to the concept of 'securitization' and how actors perform successful securitizations.

23 Though Williams (1997: 302) hints at the importance of a study of capital in IR, no such analysis has yet been carried out – nor has it been tied directly to boundary-drawing and the selection of agency. Bigo (2000) even rejects the study of capital in his bureaucratic field of security professionals.

24 Waltz (1959) also mentions a third level: 'Man'. This level has not been the subject of analyses of European security, although Booth (1991) tried to introduce it into the debate.

25 This is the most prevalent way of using the concept of levels within IR. See Onuf (1995) for alternative ways of conceptualising of levels in social theory.

26 Waltz did leave room for change. If the structural anarchy was substituted for structural hierarchy, international relations would function according to a different logic (Waltz 1979).

27 Onuf (1995: 38) argues that a distinction between 'what we see in the world and how we see it' has been prevalent in early debates about levels.

28 Lately, discussions of soft power have found a central fix point in Nye (2004). See also Wallace (2004). The discussion is, however, quite loose. Bourdieu's concept of capital will provide a practical way to address this: 'cultural and symbolic capital provide a degree of specificity beyond those approaches that reduce the processes to the operation of some amorphous form of 'soft power'' (Williams 2007: 90). The point stands, however: no delineation on the basis of hardpower /soft power arguments will hold in this thesis.

29 This also explains why Leander (2005a), Bigo (2006), Pouliot (2010), Williams (2007) and I can speak about a security field, an international security field, and a European security field. The fields are related and actors may take part in both, but all work according to their own *illusio* and value field-specific types of capital. This also means that actors will have different positions in the hierarchies in the different fields. By way of example, the EU figures prominently in the European security field in the 1990s, but is less powerful in the international security field.

30 In Bourdieu's words: 'While it is no doubt true that agents construct social reality and enter into struggles and transactions aimed at imposing their vision, they always do so with points of view, interests, and principles of vision determined by the position they occupy in the very world they intend to transform or preserve' (Bourdieu 1998b: 2).

31 This dualism was related to the analysis of the different fields in French society and was linked to an overarching analysis of the field of power (see for example Bourdieu 1986 [1979], 1993, 2005).

32 Swartz contends that Bourdieu himself did not have a clear hierarchization of types of capital. Economic capital, however, was often conceptualized as a 'root type of capital' (Swartz 1997: 78–80).

33  A sustained point of criticism often directed at Bourdieu within IR holds that his theory is too static and slides towards objectivism and reification (Pels 1995: 88).

34  In a similar sense, Baldwin talked about the *fungibility* of power resources, meaning whether a power resource could be used in different settings with few transitional costs (Baldwin 1989, 1999). He found it important to recognize that no political power resource begins to approach the degree of fungibility of money (Baldwin 2002). Military power was judged fungible to some extent, whereas political power was more easily used in different domains (Baldwin 1989).

35  For a general analysis of the concept of fungibility, see Guzzini (1994).

36  Leander talks about the existence of an 'exchange rate' for capital in an overarching field of power (Leander 2008: 16).

37  EU's move in the European security field concerning military capabilities was based on a strategy of accumulating military capabilities. The ESDP project was launched at the June 1999 European Council Meeting in Cologne and further specified at the Helsinki European council meeting the same year. The new institutions of the ESDP were laid out and the 'Headline Goal' involving the creation of a European armed force capable of humanitarian, crisis management and peace enforcement operations was formulated. This was a direct answer to NATO's attempt to gain a role in humanitarian crises and crisis management through the conversion of its military capabilities in connection with the Kosovo crisis (cp. Huysmans 2002b).

38  The concept of doxa is contested in the literature. Myles argues that there are at least two different versions of the concept of doxa in Bourdieu's work: first, the notion of the undiscussed, common sense which underlies all actors' way of acting in the world; and second, an epistemological concept of reflexivity. Most commonly in the literature, however, the doxa is associated with Myles' first reading of doxa (Myles 2004: 98). Nick Crossly equates the doxa with 'what we know without knowing that we know it' (Crossley 2004: 100), and Anna Leander argues that it is 'the inter-subjectively shared, taken for granted, values and discourses of a field' (Leander 2006: 9).

39  Behnke discusses how the definition of NATO's political and strategic space entered a time of crisis with the end of the Cold War. Behnke chooses to read this crisis through the friend/enemy dichotomy (Behnke 2013: 5–6).

40  Bourdieu often found that the distinction between the established, reproductive elite and the upcoming, younger agents who lack institutional distinctions stood at the centre of fields of struggle (see especially Bourdieu 1988; Fisher 1990). This distinction lay at the heart of Bourdieu's analysis of the boundary between scientific and ordinary knowledge in *Homo Academicus*.

41  Solana had previously made similar statements concerning the role of 'theory' or 'commentators', e.g.: 'Some commentators have predicted problems for NATO' (Solana 1997: 5). Admiral Norman Ray, Solana's Assistant Secretary General, also held that, 'Among some analysts, there is the view that somehow NATO has to 'choose' between NATO enlargement and good relations with Russia' (Ray 1997).

42  Reading through texts from 1990s security in Europe gives the impression that states were no longer the primary actors of security and that security could be achieved through peaceful, non-military means, e.g. democratization (Büger and Villumsen 2007).

43  His quote of course paraphrases Alexander Wendt who held that 'Anarchy is what states make of it' (Wendt 1992).

44  Behnke argues that Social Constructivism has put its theories forward as a 'view from nowhere', as an objective and neutral, scientific gaze (Behnke 2013: 11–12). I agree.

# 4 Field-specific capital and agency in the European field of security

> To represent the different kinds of power (or capital), one can use the metaphor of piles of tokens of different colours, which are the materialization both of the gains won in earlier phases of the game and weapons capable of being used in the subsequent rounds, in other words a kind of synthesis of the past and future of the game.
>
> (Bourdieu 2004: 62)

There are always multiple types of capital in play in a field, and the relative weight and definition of these types of capital will constantly be under negotiation. The constellation will at times be stable while at other times it will be defined by revisions. The purpose of this chapter is to define and discuss the historical development of the different types of capital in the European security field from before and until after the end of the Cold War. What was the state of the field in terms of capital and how did this change? Following from this discussion, the chapter reviews which types of agency the different types of capital allowed access to, and how this changed during the 1990s. The chapter argues that only military and scientific capital worked in a way that structured the boundaries around the field and thus functioned as boundary-setters or gatekeepers. I therefore focus on the agency which held military and scientific capital in the field. The chapter argues that the advent of a number of new think tanks during the 1990s challenged the theory/practice divide and created a new platform for entering the struggles in the field on the basis of scientific capital. Think tanks must therefore be included in the analysis of practical patterns of interaction in Chapter 5. Furthermore, the chapter argues for the inclusion of European security organizations and the EU.

The chapter discusses how different types of capital and the value attributed to them gradually started to change when bipolarity came to an end. During the Cold War, military capital, backed up by economic capital, had structured the field in a way that did not allow access to a diversity of actors. Due to its military capital, NATO was clearly placed at the top of a hierarchy which also included states and other international organizations such as the WEU and the OSCE. As NATO possessed the greatest amount of military capital, this position was difficult to challenge. What is less acknowledged, however, is that before the end of the Cold War, the NATO power base also consisted of other types of capital. Social and scientific capital supported the military standing of the alliance: being an actor comprising 16 states, NATO's social capital was high compared to other agents in the field based on member states alone. However, NATO also sought support very actively from a number of scientific-type agents during and after the Cold War. Networks with research centres augmented the social capital base of the alliance and formed an important aspect of the high standing of the alliance in the field. Moreover, the scientific agents also supported the alliance by producing scientific knowledge that consolidated the position of NATO at the top of the hierarchy. This added both scientific and social capital to the military standing of NATO and consolidated the hierarchy.

After the Cold War, NATO continued to bolster its position. However, the position and practices of the scientific-type actors began to change: to put it bluntly, the underdogs started challenging the top dog. Newcomers such as think tanks and policy research centres challenged the military dominance of NATO and the privileged position of esteemed research centres through moves including scientific capital and social capital, and challenges to the doxic understanding of military capital. These challenges were supported by changing funding practices in the EU. Williams suggests:

> that what took place in the 1990s was a reconfiguration of the 'field' of security where military and material power, while remaining significant, were repositioned within what might be called the 'cultural field of security' that privileged *cultural and symbolic forms of power.*
>
> (Williams 2007: 2)

At the centre of this process was a reconfiguration of the field of security away from a concentration on material and military factors towards cultural and symbolic forms of capital (Williams 2007: 40).[1] This meant that symbolic forms of capital such as scientific capital acquired greater relative weight in the course of the 1990s. Seen from my perspective, this in turn opened the floor for a range of different actors to challenge the position of NATO: the EU entered the struggles, and a number of think tanks were gradually accepted as players in the field. The dominance of military capital thus slowly started to wane as scientific and social capital were thrown into the battle in new ways. Nevertheless, this did not mean that military capital became unimportant; it merely had to be of a certain kind to be of any value in the field.

This is the situation in which the relationship between NATO and 'theory' played itself out in the European field of security when Solana stated that practice had proven theory wrong. A number of different types of field-specific capital were at work in and around the relationship. The most important types were military and scientific capital (because they were boundary-setters), though social capital also played a significant role. I turn to each type of capital below.

## Military capital

The obvious first type of capital that is valued in the field of European security is military capital. The military dimension of power 'has received more attention than any other means in international relations' (Baldwin 2002: 179). Military capital concerns: "… a capital of physical force, in the form of the military and the police" (Bourdieu 2005: 12). This type of capital is physical in the sense that it is relatively easy to detect whether an actor claiming to have it actually does have it. The classical example from European security is the rift between NATO and the EU in terms of military capability. NATO obviously possessed military capabilities – equipment and a command structure for carrying out military missions – whereas the European Community (EC) possessed no such capital.[2] Moreover, the discussion about burden-sharing between the North American allies and 'NATO Europe' has been a recurring theme involving military capital.[3]

Military capital consists of hardware (e.g. tanks, aircraft), personnel and organizational features such as command structure and logistics management, i.e. the ability to control and transport forces and equipment. Research and development capabilities tied to the military instrument also form part of how I define military capital here.[4] Military capital is thus not confined to hardware; it consists of a variety of features linked to the ability to plan and carry out military missions.

Debate about whether military power is rightly placed at the top of a power hierarchy is classic (see e.g. Art 1999; Baldwin 1999).[5] But military power – or capital – does not a priori to lead to a position of power in the hierarchy in the European field of security. Military capital was quite clearly an asset during Cold War bipolarity and it was a very important factor in placing NATO at the top of the hierarchy in the European field of security. NATO's role as the sole guarantor of European security was largely based on the fact that the alliance possessed a modern and visible amount of military capabilities, including a unified allied command structure. The Soviet Union backed up this narrow understanding of security as being tied to classic military capital: 'During the Cold War, the Soviet Union resisted those definitions of power whose stress on non-military factors would imply a decline in its status' (Guzzini 2005: 514–515). With a tight focus on military capital, NATO and the Soviet Union could remain the top dogs in European security.

The end of the Cold War changed this situation. Military capital was no longer the only important key to a high position in the hierarchy (cp. Buzan and Hansen 2009: 160). An outright rejection of the value of military capital did not follow, however: 'Indeed the power and persistence of NATO in the post-Cold War period derived in considerable part from the ability to maintain is military dimension' (Williams 2007: 91). But this had to be combined with other types of capital and a 'cultural and political narrative that overcame the challenges faced by a purely military representation of the alliance' (ibid.). The military dimension was therefore not unimportant, and as

Williams argues 'it is doubtful that NATO could have played the role it has without its capacity for military strength, its links to powerful economic capacities, and its reputation for both. But NATO's power cannot be reduced to this' (ibid.). Military capital played a role, though a role quite far from the one it played during the Cold War. The former, quite easily defined and quantifiable concept of military capital, was challenged by newcomers and 'the previous 'game' of military strategic calculation was downgraded' (ibid.: 4). A re-valorization of military capital followed.

The definition of security and threats and the ensuing valorization of military capital were important for understanding which actors were empowered in the field. Chapter 6 will show how military capital was challenged through a number of doxic battles that put NATO on the defensive.[6]

Below I focus on how the shifting value of military capital can be read in military budgets in order to provide empirical backing to the claim about changes in the relative value of military capital.

### *The changing value of military capital: an economic perspective*

From an empirical viewpoint, an indication of the development in military capital in the European field of security can be found in data on military expenditures. Focusing on the economic development does not translate into importance of economic capital in itself, but gives an idea of why Bourdieu argued that economic capital could be considered a 'root type of capital' (Swartz 1997: 78–80; see also Williams 2007) or the 'dominant principle of hierarchy' (Swartz 1997: 192). Economy sets the background for military capital, because it is generally expensive to uphold a large military apparatus. The money could also be used for other purposes, and the allocation of funding to military capital thus says something about the value attached to it. If spending falls, the value attached to military capital is likely to be decreasing. The conceptual changes in the value of military capital cannot be read from statistics, however. That dimension will be the topic of Chapter 6 on doxic battles.

Since 1963, NATO has published data on the military spending of the member states (NATO 2008). Since 2004, this practice has been extended to include Russia. Data on the development of spending on military capital is thus available and can provide a general idea of how this type of capital is placed in a larger setting.[7]

In 2002, NATO published an overview of military spending covering the period from 1980–2002 (NATO 2002a). The survey included data from all NATO member states.[8] In an overview of defence expenditures as a percentage of gross domestic product (GDP) divided into 'NATO-Europe' and 'North America', the development in the period 1980–2002 shows that NATO Europe countries spent 3.5 per cent of their GDP on defence in 1980–1984 and 3.2 per cent in 1985–1989.[9] In the period immediately after the end of the Cold War, the spending of NATO Europe as a percentage of GDP fell to 2.6 per cent, and further yet to 2.2 per cent in the second half of the 1990s – at which time NATO was in action in Bosnia. In 1998, 1999, 2000, 2001 and 2002, defence spending as a percentage of GDP lay at an average of 2.0–2.1 per cent, even though these years include the 1999 Kosovo air campaign (NATO 2002a: Table 3). Military expenditures in NATO Europe thus dropped relatively substantially after the Cold War. The value of military capital thus fell *from a strictly economic point of view.*

The same general picture goes for North America when considered from the economic angle. Two major changes come to view: decreases in military spending as percentage of GDP, from 5.6 per cent in 1985–1989 to 4.4 per cent in 1990–1994 and to 3.2 per cent in 1995–1999 (NATO 2002a: Table 3). In general, military spending therefore decreased when the Cold War ended. Even at a time when the alliance was actively involved in military action in the Balkans, the spending did not exceed the levels of the 1980s.[10] The role of the military dimension had changed in the field. Money was directed to other types of spending, and the military was allocated less over the 1990s. Gadea *et al.* find that 'most countries show a final break either before or at the beginning of the 1990s' (Gadea *et al.* 2004: 244), meaning that defence expenditures were significantly impacted by the events around the year 1990. This corresponds with the debate in the beginning of the 1990s centred on the concept of a 'Peace Dividend' – the possibility that countries could 'cash in' a surplus after the decrease in the relative importance of the military instrument in European security (for discussion, see Markusen 1992; Feldman 1993; Ullmann 1993; Chan 1995). Military capital thus underwent a declining value in terms of spending after the end of the Cold War.

Interesting extra features appear when we examine how the decreasing expenditures were distributed. The annual average strength of armed forces (number of soldiers) in particular changed over the period 1980–2002. The decrease in thousands of armed forces in NATO Europe shows a substantial change from 1990 onwards (see Table 4.1 below). Large standing armies were apparently less valued in the post-Cold War era. The numbers indicate that the classic military instrument was being downgraded and that the structure of military capital in the European field of security was decreasing in scope and changing in content.

To further underline the changing character and shrinking of the classic military in Europe, we can take a look at one of the countries which modernized its army quite substantially after the Cold War: the United Kingdom.

*Table 4.1* Armed forces, annual average strength, measured in thousands

|  | *1980* | *1985* | *1990* | *1995* | *1998* | *2000* | *2002* |
|---|---|---|---|---|---|---|---|
| NATO Europe | 3504 | 3603 | 3510 | 3010 | 2809 | 2967 | 2848 |
| North America | 2132 | 2327 | 2268 | 1690 | 1565 | 1542 | 1552 |

Source: NATO 2002a: Table 6.

British defence spending as a percentage of its GDP developed as shown in Table 4.2 below. The table shows that the UK defence expenditure was more than halved in the period 1980–2001.

In addition to this general decrease in military expenditure, the distribution between personnel expenditure, equipment expenditure, infrastructure expenditure and other expenditure for the UK shows decreasing expense on personnel (from 42.2 per cent in 1990–1994 to 39.3 per cent in 2002), a rise in equipment expenditures in the beginning of the 1990s (from 21 per cent in 1990–1994 to 26.5 per cent in 1998 and 26.8 per cent in 1999), and a rise in infrastructure expenditures throughout the 1990s (2.7 per cent in 1980–1984 to 5.2 per cent in 1990–1994 and again in 1995–1999 (NATO 2002a: Table 5). The picture emerging in Table 4.1 above is thus supported in the UK case. Personnel expenditure fell, while other expenses were upgraded. In large part, this had to do with the modernization of the armed forces and the changing definition of threats and risks.[11]

In sum, military spending fell and the role of the military instrument changed in the field. Economic resources were directed to other areas as countries attempted to cash in on the much-debated 'Peace Dividend'.

## *Agency*

What kind of agency did military capital allow to participate in the field of European security? If capital is a boundary-setting mechanism as argued in Chapter 3 then military capital can provide access for certain actors. The obvious first actor in this game would be NATO: the military alliance that had occupied a top position in the hierarchy in the field prior to the end of the Cold War. In addition, however, organizations such as the WEU and the OSCE could claim to have access to military capital and would be able to fight for access on these grounds.

The EU increasingly tried to establish a military capability – especially towards the end of the 1990s with the formulation of the Headline Goal (EU 1999). Throughout the 1990s, however, their efforts were not particularly successful. The EU budget for military capital was therefore not particularly large during the 1990s, and it was construed in a very inflexible manner (EU 2001a).[12] This meant that the EU military capital accumulation was low. After 1999, the EU witnessed a rise in the demand for further funding under CFSP and ESDP headings[13], and the EU military capital was accordingly on the rise. The EU vigorously attempted to redefine military capital throughout

*Table 4.2* Defence expenditures as % of GDP

|  | *1980–1984* | *1985–1989* | *1990–1994* | *1995–1999* | *2001* |
|---|---|---|---|---|---|
| UK | 5,2 | 4,5 | 3,7 | 2,7 | 2,5 |

Source: NATO 2002a: Table 3.

the 1990s and gained a stronger role in the field towards the turn of the millennium. From having been a 'nobody' in the security field, the EU played its hand wisely and gained a power base of field-specific capital by accumulating military, social and scientific capital and by challenging the existing definitions of capital. Think tanks supported the EU bid for centrality in the field. I shall return to this in subsequent chapters.

In addition to these European (security) organizations, *states* possessed military capital and could try to gain a standing in the field to varied degrees on this basis. Most Western European countries were allies, and the Central and East European Countries (CEECs) were lining up to join NATO. Military capital formed part of the background for being accepted into the alliance. But other types of capital were becoming important. Economic capital began to play an increasingly important role in the course of the 1990s: in the Membership Action Plan of 1999, the applicant countries were required to provide information on an annual basis regarding the state of their economy (NATO 1999: 3). This was primarily seen in relation to having an adequate amount of resources for defence, though it was also in relation to being able to share in the agreed costs of the alliance: this included the permanent facilities at the NATO HQ, the NATO command structure and other related costs (ibid.: 6). The reference to a requirement in terms of economic capital is interesting. Not only military capital was required in order to become a full member of NATO. Economic resources constituted a related type of capital, which formed a prerequisite for future membership. Whether military capital alone still provided states with a strong position in the field is therefore not entirely straightforward. Other types of capital may have overtaken military capital.

A number of other types of agency that can be related to military capital have already been studied. Leander has directed our attention towards private military companies (PMCs) (Leander 2005b). Bigo (2002a, 2002b, 2006) has studied what he refers to as a 'field of unease management professionals' (Bigo 2006: 109) and has argued that police and intelligence cooperation in Europe is a good starting point for understanding the emerging European security field. Huysmans has studied how the practices of border controls and immigration policies can serve as an empirical background from which to study the shifts in the European security landscape (Huysmans 2006). All of these types of agency are relevant and deserve attention. They can all be said to derive some of their power in the security field from military capital. But even though important insights can be gained from studying PMCs, border controls, intelligence agencies or the police, I have chosen not to include them in the analysis of the practical patterns of interaction surrounding NATO in Chapter 5, because their role in the security field has already been extensively studied by Leander, Bigo and Huysmans. Where appropriate, I include insight from their research.[14]

To sum up, the value of military capital decreased during the 1990s. Military spending fell and the role of the military instrument changed in the field. Economic resources were directed to other areas as countries tried to cash in on the 'Peace Dividend'. The European field of security came to question equating military might in any singular way with a powerful position in the field, and definitions of what the military capital should be used for became important for the value of different types of military capital. Furthermore, the section argued that the relevant agency selected on the basis of military capital as a boundary-setting mechanism would include European security organizations and states. All of them had military capital and could try and play that card as a means to acquiring a more important position in the field. But other types of capital were also needed in order to gain access to the field and to win a high position in it.

## Scientific capital

In Leander's words, Bourdieu's approach 'insists heavily on the role played by academia in the (re)production of social hierarchies' (Leander 2002a: 26). By focusing on scientific capital, theoretical *agents* and theoretical *arguments* can be studied as part of the power game in the European field of security. In the following, I pursue two lines of inquiry. First, a focus on the meaning of scientific capital, and how a specific 'common sense' had structured the field during the Cold War; and how challenges to this doxic practice were launched after 1990. Subsequently, the section investigates the changing funding structures in the field by zooming in on the research budgets of two important players in the field: NATO and the EU. The general picture emerging from this is an increase in EU funding and a decrease in NATO funding. In the third subsection, I discuss the types of agency that could gain access to the field on the grounds of scientific capital. I conclude that a range of knowledge-producing activities were accepted into the field and that think tanks had an important role in this process.

Scientific capital is a particular kind of symbolic capital, a capital based on knowledge and recognition. It is a power which functions as a form of credit, presupposing the trust or belief of those who undergo it because they are disposed (by their training and by the very fact of their belonging to the field) to give credit, belief (Bourdieu 2004: 34). In other words, scientific capital is vested in agents who are recognized as speaking in the name of science – of truth – and scientific capital is therefore tied to specific agents and specific knowledge-producing structures.

In Bourdieu (2004), scientific capital was tied to a discussion of the scientific field and the power an agent could obtain in that specific, autonomous field. Scientific capital referred to knowing the discipline in which the scientist participated and in being able to put that knowledge into practice (ibid.: 38). This could be translated into a narrow study of the scientific field of Security Studies. But scientific capital also has a broader dimension in which capital is tied to a larger field consisting of a variety of agents. This follows the ideas Bourdieu famously put forward in *The State Nobility* (Bourdieu 1998b), where the role of the education system is seen as linked to the overall power struggle in (French) society.[15] In a related way, theory-type agents and scientifically based arguments can be seen as linked to the field of European security comprising agents such as NATO, the WEU, the OSCE and the EU. Scientific capital played a role that structured this relationship and came to provide access to a range of new actors in the 1990s.

### The common sense of security: doxic practice in a changing field

Scientific capital was an important part of the configuration of the field of European security, both before and after the end of the Cold War. Schools of thought exercised an important type of symbolic violence on the entire field. As Wacquant argues, '[t]he instruments of knowledge and construction of social reality diffused and inculcated by the school are ... inescapably instruments of symbolic domination' (Wacquant 1998: xviii). This point is particularly true of the field of security. Scientific capital of a certain strategic-studies kind had held the struggles in the field in a tight grip during the Cold War and had dominated ideas about how to think and practice security. Agents in the field of European security had therefore to be able to recognize the structures of the debate in scientific Security Studies in order to understand and engage in the struggles in the field. Only then would they be able to understand and mobilize scientific capital to their own advantage and change the value and meaning of scientific capital from within. That grip loosened in the 1990s, however, as a new agency was allowed access to the power game, on the grounds of a changed understanding of scientific capital and new funding practices in the field. This challenged doxic understandings of security.

But what were the doxic categories in the European field of security? Perhaps the most sustained battle involving scientific capital and NATO concerns that which was held as 'common sense' in the field of security up until the end of the Cold War and for quite some time after: that alliances do not survive the demise of their counterparts. The concept of security within NATO and in security thinking in general had been dominated by the bipolar structure and strategic balancing which had divided the world into a clear 'here' and 'there' during the Cold War: the primary purpose of the alliance was collective defence against the Soviet Union.[16] The prevalent theory supporting this practice – the balance of threat theory of alliances – was formulated most fully by Stephen M. Walt (1987; for debate, see also Snyder 1984; Grieco 1988).

This type of valued scientific capital provided a powerful position for NATO during the Cold War: NATO had to survive, because security was found in a balance-of-power situation. Without NATO, the other side would win. The military capital and the valued scientific capital thus reinforced one another and created a powerful position for the alliance and strategic studies alike. This exerted symbolic violence in the field. In Bourdieu's phrasing:

> Symbolic violence is that particular form of constraint that can only be implemented with the active complicity – which does not mean that it is

conscious and voluntary – of those who submit to it and are determined only insofar as they deprive themselves of the possibility of freedom founded on the awakening of consciousness.

(Bourdieu 1988: 4)

The field submitted to the symbolic power of what was taken to be the common sense of security in Europe. NATO's position and the position of strategic studies agents were bolstered in the process.

When bipolarity broke down, however, the powerful positions of NATO and strategic studies were turned on their heads. The tight fit between the conventional truth in strategic studies about alliances and NATO's practices based on military capital, which had proven a viable and strong position during the 1980s, was suddenly a potential disadvantage in the field: NATO initially seemed at risk of withering away after the demise of the Soviet Union. In the immediate aftermath of the Cold War, most commentators agreed and expected this to happen (see e.g. Chalmers 1990; Hassner 1990; De Santis 1991; for debate, see Duffield 1994; for general statements, see Walt 1987; Waltz 1981, 1993b, Sagan and Waltz 1995), as could be expected from the symbolic violence exerted by this common sense version of how alliances and security operate. Some even argued that NATO was *bound* to disintegrate and that multipolarity was inevitable (Mearsheimer 1990). As mentioned before, there was disagreement as to how long this would take, but disintegration was a fact. An alliance had one purpose that kept it together: a common, external threat which needed to be balanced. In the event that this threat no longer existed, the members of the alliance stopped seeing the need for upholding the costs of cooperation, since no obvious returns were envisioned.

This understanding was the common sense of security in 1990. It built on the 'foundational practice' discovered by Ashley and the symbolic violence exerted by the structure of military and scientific capital in the field. NATO's powerful experience of the Cold War was therefore transformed into a new struggle for survival. This time, the enemy was not a clearly defined military threat to be balanced, but instead a threat within the field of European security itself – involving scientific capital. This was the background upon which the moves in the field involving scientific capital transpired. All of the mobilization of scientific capital in the field had to relate to it; and since it was so tightly tied to military capital, there were great changes in store for both types of capital in the field. The doxic practice of the field was under attack, and challenges to the common sense arose.

Looking back on developments in 2001, Waltz described the failure of NATO to disintegrate from this very perspective: 'The error of realist predictions that the end of the Cold War would mean the end of NATO arose not from a failure of realist theory to comprehend international politics, but from an underestimation of America's folly' (Waltz 2001: 34). If NATO did not disintegrate, the only reason could be plain stupidity! In 2001, this standpoint was no longer left unchallenged. At the beginning of the 1990s, however, it clearly remained the dominant version of the future of NATO in the European field of security. The grip of strategic studies on valued scientific capital coupled with military capital prescribed a certain future: and a future in which NATO no longer played a pivotal role.

NATO struggled with these predictions. The problem for NATO, however, was not only 'out there' in the field: NATO itself had worked and legitimized its existence on the basis of this type of argument during the Cold War: strategic balancing remained the central dynamic that made the NATO story work. NATO therefore fought a battle against this type of common sense, both on the outside and from within the alliance. Nevertheless, one could argue that NATO also used the strong predictions of its demise in a manner serving the alliance's own interests: threatening the inevitable demise of the alliance (and ensuing multipolarity – or just sheer chaos) could make member states and other related agents more interested in keeping the alliance alive. Outside of the alliance's membership category, the ground was ripe for this type of argument: the CEECs were interested in forging a strong and viable alliance with the West. Without NATO, there was no guarantee that Russia would not pose a risk to them. Scaring people into thinking that NATO was going down was therefore in part a strategy of power. NATO played the scientific capital card from the Cold War days in order to frighten member states into being in favour of its survival. The doxic practice that tied strategic studies scientific capital together with military capital and which seemed to cause the doom of NATO was therefore Janus-faced (to use one of Bourdieu's oft-used metaphors). In order to remain in the game after the Cold War, NATO required a new definition of what alliances can do and a new story of what the military instrument can be used for. At the same time, however, the strong doxic practice of the Cold War could work in favour of NATO's continued existence – at least in the short run. This duality still exists in discussions in the field today.

### Funding for research

Following Bourdieu's argument that economic capital is a root type of capital, a review of the changing economic resources allocated to research in Europe shows interesting features. Just as in the case of military capital, the economic resources could be used for other purposes, and research funding can therefore be taken as an indication of the importance attached to science.

In the following, I focus on NATO and EU research funding, because their share of funding was high and their role as competitors in the field of European security potentially made research funding part of their respective power strategies in the field. Interestingly, the overall picture emerging from these sources is an increase in funding for research activities from the EU and a decrease in research funding from NATO. Apparently, NATO did not attach as much value to scientific endeavours as did the EU.

NATO had invested in science since the report of the 'three wise men' was commissioned in 1956 (Nierenberg 2001: 365).[17] The Science Committee budget was 'a source of envy in the rest of the NATO bureaucracy' (ibid.: 368), while the Science Office enjoyed 'more than adequate funding' (ibid.: 367).[18] NATO was a 'force in science' (N. Williams 1997: 795). Today, the NATO science programme forms part of the civilian budget of the alliance (NATO 2001: 203).[19] Its budget is not large (roughly 30 million US Dollars), 'but is employed effectively' (Nierenberg 2001: 370).[20]

In the course of the 1990s, the NATO science programmes became increasingly directed towards Eastern Europe and participation from Partnership Countries under both the successful NATO Partnership for Peace (PfP) programme and later the Mediterranean dialogue. However, the funding was not increased proportionately (N. Williams 1997). The end of the Cold War had meant a decreased interest in supporting science among the NATO member states. Canada withdrew completely from the science programme in 1997 due to domestic budget problems, and many were worried whether the programme would even survive given the pressure on the NATO budget (ibid.). In 2001, the science programme consumed 26 per cent of the civilian budget (35 million US Dollars); in 2002, its budget was 23 million US dollars, while funding was cut in 2003 to 20 million US Dollars (Schiermeier 2003; see also, Stone 2002). This was the first substantial cut in the science budget, but funding had been stagnating since the end of the Cold War (Stone 2002: 946). In conclusion, the budget was limited towards the turn of the Millennium and, 'the dollar value of each activity [had been cut] to a less-than-useful amount' (Nierenberg 2001: 371).[21]

Turning to the EU research funding, a different trend becomes apparent. 'Scientific activities have always been on the front line of European integration' (Gusmao 2001: 383) and 'Europe has become a key actor' in research over the last decade (ibid.: 384). In the mid-1990s, the R&D budget of the EU reached approximately 2.8 billion ECU[22] per year.

The EU primarily funds research over the so-called Framework Programmes. The first Framework Programme of research and technological development (FWP) was launched in 1984 and ran until 1987. With the adoption of the European Single Act, science became a community responsibility (EU 2008d). The Second Framework Programme ran from 1987 to 1990, and the Third Framework Programme ran from 1990 to 1994. Budgets were increased in both periods. The Fourth Framework programme ran from 1994–1998 and allocated 13.215 million ECU to research (including nuclear research under EURATOM) (EU 2008c). This figure increased by 4.61 per cent to 14.960 million EURO[23] with the adoption of the Fifth Framework Programme, which ran from 1999 to 2002 (EU 2008b). With the Sixth Framework Programme, which ran from 2002 to 2006, the budget rose to 19.100 million EURO. This represented another significant increase in research funding. The EU thus upgraded research funding substantially. Eligible for support were researchers, companies, students, post-docs, institutions running research facilities, and others  (for a list, see EU 2008e). EU funding opportunities thus increased from the mid-1990s onwards, and the types of agency eligible for funding diversified.

So while the NATO science programmes experienced stagnation, cutbacks and a need to use funding more efficiently, the EU's research funding increased substantially. This provides an indication of the importance attached to science by two important players in the field of European security. The different funding strategies in NATO and the EU may have influenced the standing of the EU in the field of security. As the next section will show, however, it also supported a trend of multiplying the types of agency inhabiting the space between theory and practice. I turn to this below.

### *Agency*

What type of agency could gain access to the struggles in the field of European security on the basis of the possession of scientific capital? Because strategic studies had a tight grip on the definition of valued scientific capital during the Cold War and immediately after the end of bipolarity, this type of actor gained access more easily than other types of theory-agents. But other agents struggled to gain access on the grounds of scientific capital. This point is related to the status of the social sciences in contemporary Western societies. According to Bourdieu, a lack of monopoly over definitions of the truth is characteristic of the social sciences:

> The social sciences, especially sociology, have an object too important (it interests everyone, starting with the powerful), too controversial, for it to be left to their discretion, abandoned to their law alone, too important and too controversial in terms of social life, the social order and the symbolic order, for them to be granted the same degree of autonomy as is given to the other sciences and for them to be allowed the monopoly of the production of truth.
>
> (Bourdieu 2004: 86–87)

A range of agents thus claim knowledge, expert status and scientific capital when it comes to the social sciences. This influenced the type of agency that could gain access to the European security field on the grounds of scientific capital.

If we review which types of agency strive for expert status in IR and Security Studies, 'there is a far wider range of IR activities and groups than the simple theorist-practitioner dichotomy implies' (Lepgold 1998: 43).[24] Lepgold mentions four different types of activities and literature with relevance for the relationship between theory and practice in international relations (ibid.: 47, Table 1). First, general theory (typically university-based research); second, issue-oriented puzzles (typically more empirically oriented area studies); third, case-oriented explanations (primarily think tank studies); and finally fourth, policy making (ibid.: 47–50). The first and fourth groups are the ideal types of theory and practice, whereas groups 2 and 3 can be labelled 'in-betweens'. According to Milliken:

[m]ost expert knowledge of International Relations is created and circu-
lated not as the 'pure science' of ... International Relations theorists, but
as 'applied science' of scholars advising governments and international
organizations, working for think tanks and non-governmental organizations, and speaking publicly on issues of the day in institutional publications, magazine articles, editorials, television interviews and trade books.

(Milliken 1999: 238)

The agency that could gain access on the grounds of scientific capital in the
European field of security thus potentially consisted of a variety of actors
spanning the theory/practice divide.[25] Some agents – those that advocated the
valued type of scientific capital of the day – would more easily gain access to
the field. However, other types of agency that stressed different types of scientific capital and derived their standing from the plethora of knowledge-
producing activities going on between theory and practice could also gain
access on the basis of scientific capital.

A certain type of agent was central to this development: *think tanks and
research centres* flourished in Europe in the 1990s.[26] These agents somehow
stood between scientific and practical knowledge and not only challenged the
*content* of the valued scientific capital, they also challenged from where scientific statements would and could be mobilized and from where expert status
could be sought. This has important implications for this book: if knowledge
was produced and disseminated by agents inhabiting 'the gap', and if scientific capital thereby allowed a new type of agent access to the field, then
NATO's relationship with 'theory' was perhaps not tied to classical university
research or the scientific field of Security Studies in any direct manner.[27]
Instead, 'institutions and professional networks ... create a potential trans-
mission belt that runs from 'pure' theory to 'pure' policy making. The two
intermediate types of activities involve people who have mixes of theoretical
and applied interests' (Lepgold 1998: 47).

These mixed types of agency challenged the primary constellation of the
strategic studies type of scientific and military capital, which was understood
in strategic balancing terms. This led to struggles between NATO and
'theory' – but far from the struggles that any singular relation between theory
and practice would foresee. Instead:

today's world is a more competitive marketplace of ideas and expertise.
The think tank world has grown and deepened – there are more of them
dealing with a broader range of issues, and often doing so in ways that
contribute significantly to literature building as well as policy debate.

(Jentleson 2002: 181)

Theory-type actors who could gain access to the field on the grounds of scientific capital are therefore potentially found among think tanks, research
centres *and* classical scientific agents (universities).

But does Europe have many think tanks? It is quite well documented that the number of think tanks is far greater in the USA than in the rest of the world. To a large extent, however, this documentation is based on the fact that the definition of a think tank has been modelled on the Anglo-American experience, where think tanks are defined as economically and politically independent institutes with the explicit purpose of promoting certain ideas (Abelson 2002, 2004). This type of think tank is not present in many European countries outside of Great Britain (Stone *et al.* 1998; Stone and Denham 2004; Villumsen 2007).

Notably, Great Britain and Germany have developed a *tradition* of think tanks, while most other European countries do not have think tanks in any great number if Abelson's definition is taken as a starting point (with Poland as the exception). In Germany, think tanks are usually funded by political parties,[28] while British think tanks have changed over time from being research-oriented 'universities without students' (Weaver 1989: 564) towards becoming more ideologically oriented and eager to participate directly in the political process (Denham and Garnett 2004; Dahl Kelstrup 2007). In France, the idea of a think tank clashes with the political culture that sees interest organizations as illegitimate: the primary political relationship is between the individual citizen and the state; anything coming between that relationship is considered a distortion (Fieschi and Gaffney 2004). The think tank's function is therefore performed by so-called political clubs and cabinets within the administration.

A strictly Anglo-American definition of think tanks would exclude these kinds of organizations from study, thereby missing several *loci* for the reformulation of doxic practice and the value of scientific capital in the European field of security (see, e.g. Ullrich 2004). This might work in an American study. In Europe, however, the picture is too diverse for this to succeed. There are too many actors of a think tank-like nature not meeting the criteria of being economically and politically independent but nevertheless inhabiting the same middle ground occupied by think tanks: the ground where the distinction between the practical and the theoretical is challenged and where scientific capital is used as a power resource. A narrow definition of a think tank might contribute to the scientific rigour in studies such as Abelson's (2002, 2004), but in the case of the European field of security, the analysis would lack important agency.

The work carried out by Stone and Denham is instructive for a redefinition of the concept of a think tank which and is useful in the context of this book. Instead of basing their definition on an organizational *structure*, they argue for equating a think tank with a policy research *function* and a set of analytical and policy advisory *practices* (Stone and Denham 2004: 4). Furthermore, they argue against making a distinction between research institutes and think tanks because 'the style of 'informing' policy debates or 'educating' public opinion takes many forms' (ibid.). Arguments for distinguishing between the two types of actors often rely on an underlying assumption about the purity and rationality of science and the impurity of ideology. These arguments deny the inherently political nature of research.[29]

In order to understand the special European case of think tanks, it is not relevant to include or exclude certain research institutes or political clubs beforehand on the basis of clear-cut definitional boundaries. It is important to remain open to the fact that institutes, conferences and other actors may have sought access to the field of European security on the basis of scientific capital. The definition of what constitutes an important think tank in Europe should therefore not remain a question of money, organizational form or political orientation. It should focus on the *practices* and *functions* of actors occupying the ground somewhere between theory and practice. Are they linked to the field through practical patterns of interaction? Do they move in the doxic battles surrounding NATO in European security? Are they represented as 'experts' in the field and thus accepted and empowered in the field on the grounds of this expert status? Do they mobilize and accumulate scientific capital? A wide variety of actors are potential agents in the fabrication of the emerging social space of European security surrounding NATO. Think tanks, research centres and conferences such as the *Munich Conference on Security Policy* will accordingly be included in the analysis of practical patterns of interaction in Chapter 5. Important moves by think tanks will be included in Chapter 6 to illustrate the power process of doxic battles.

In order to make the selection of the relevant agency for this book, I have chosen to focus on those think tanks and research centres which NATO was linked with during the 1990s through *practical patterns of interaction*, rather than focusing on the total number of think tanks on security and international relations from a general standpoint.[30] Following from this, I shall leave the selection of specific think tanks until Chapter 5.[31]

One last thing remains important for the selection of agency on the basis of scientific capital. Scientific capital requires something of the receiver in the battles: 'Symbolic power of the scientific type can be exerted only on agents who possess the categories of perception necessary to know it and recognize it' (Bourdieu 2004: 55). The symbolic power of scientific capital thus requires that the agents in the field understand the categories with which the scientific capital is invoked. This is part of the boundary-setting mechanism of scientific capital: if categories are not understood and practiced, an agent will not be accepted as a legitimate speaker in the field. This requires some sort of common ground among agents. Bourdieu often sought this common ground in education, which he considered to be a fundamental and important reproductive mechanism of the social (most notably, Bourdieu 1998b). Through education, a naturalized (doxic) understanding of how the social works is learned, and the agent internalizes dominant scientific categories in their habitus. This means that 'the university system plays a role in (re)producing social hierarchies by its legitimation of specific forms and kinds of knowledge, problems and issues and delegitimizing other kinds' (Leander 2002a: 26).

Did agents in the European field of security share educational background – common ground? In the case of European think tanks, Stone has argued that:

> [b]oth policy-makers and think tank scholars are likely to have attended university and many of them would have studied the social sciences. Hence, they read the classics along with the textbooks. They may well be familiar with current debates in the discipline through personal contacts or an abiding interest in IR.
>
> (Stone 1996: 213)

Guzzini even argues that 'at least in some countries and in particular in the major international organisations, the elite is coming out of a relatively limited number of major schools and universities, sometimes moving back and forth to its faculty' (Guzzini 2006: 17). Following from this, Guzzini argues that 'international society ... starts increasingly to resemble Bourdieu's *Noblesse d'État*" (ibid.; see also Bourdieu 1998b). The shared background is thus increasingly becoming a reality among Western elites.

Certain international events support this finding. Guzzini speculates whether the annual meeting in Davos[32] could be taken to be the summit of the world elite (*la noblesse*) in international relations[33] (Guzzini 2006). I would argue that *The Munich Conference on Security Policy*, which is held annually each February and invites politicians (national and international), think tank members, researchers and media people to discuss the issue of European/Western security, can be seen as the meeting of the elite in European security. These meetings are snapshots of what type of agent is allowed into the field of (European) security. At the same time, the meetings reproduce the doxic practices of the field in question.

The basic educational background and internalized categories of science based on education were hence present among think tank members and practitioners in Europe according to Stone (1996) and Guzzini (2006). They had the prerequisites for engaging in the struggles *qua* their backgrounds in the social sciences. Not all types of background would wield the same kind of power, however. During the 1980s in particular, a very narrow strategic studies definition of background was required in order to be accepted and to be able hold a high position in the field (cp. Cohn 1987).[34] This had an impact on the hierarchy in the field.

## Social capital

The third type of capital important for structuring the hierarchy in the European field of security is social capital. Social capital concerns the formation of networks in the field and the power you gain from knowing and/or representing (the right) people in the field, 'to be able to represent reality effectively and authoritatively, and *to be able to represent people* (to speak from authority) are linked' (M.C. Williams 1997: 294, my emphasis). Social capital thus adds to the standing of an agent in the field: if you can claim to represent others, you add to your position as being able to speak authoritatively.[35]

Chapter 5 on practical patterns of interaction surrounding NATO will provide an important contribution to the study of social capital in the European field of security. While based on how different types of capital created points of access for a variety of actors in the field, the chapter analyses how NATO actively created an increasing number of links and networks with actors spanning the theory/practice divide. The alliance thereby 'piled up' social capital. So while the initial reason for carrying out the analysis in Chapter 5 was tied to an argument about the inadequacy of assuming the existence of a field beyond national boundaries a priori, the chapter therefore also concerns the distribution of social capital.

This section reviews the changing importance of social capital in the pre and post-Cold War periods. Furthermore, it discusses how networking also had potentially empowering consequences for new types of agency: when links were made with new actors, social capital was accumulated, but trust was also invested in the new actor. Social capital in itself did not work as an entry barrier to the field of European security in the manner that military and scientific capital did. Instead, social capital added to the power base of an agent already allowed to play the game.

### Networking as a new power strategy

During the Cold War, the social capital in the European field of security was largely tied to states. NATO was not linked in any systematic way to other organizations in Europe. In fact, the CSCE excluded NATO from participation, and NATO and the EC/EU lived rather separate lives during the Cold War. NATO focused predominantly on the ties *within* the alliance rather than ties with actors *outside* of the alliance, because the status of NATO as the guarantor of European security was largely unrivalled. The alliance did, however, create links with other types of actors during the Cold War: research environments were included in various activities, though the focus was primarily on technical types of research[36] of assistance to NATO in solving practical problems with hardware and developing new approaches to defence systems (Nierenberg 2001).[37] But faith in science was high: NATO's Assistant Secretary General was actually originally referred to as the 'Science Adviser' (ibid.: 366), testifying to the faith vested in the scientific endeavour's potential for serving as a bridge between conflicting interests.[38]

However, the web of relations in the field of security in Europe was rather confined during the Cold War. Some actors – such as peace researchers – tried to influence the field with varying degrees of success. Risse-Kappen (1994) argues that links between certain peace researchers, European left-wing political parties and arms control supporters in the United States joined by Western, liberal and internationalist values were influential in ending the Cold

War by influencing Soviet 'new thinkers' (Risse-Kappen 1994: 186; see also Guzzini 2004). Whether one agrees with Risse-Kappen's analysis or not, he documents the links that existed between peace research and political practice during the last stages of the Cold War. With reference to the high standing of NATO on the basis of military and scientific capital at the time, however, I would argue that peace researchers did not possess the right types of valued capital in the field to be seriously considered as legitimate speakers. Overall, NATO did not seek (or have to seek) networks during the Cold War. The status of the alliance was solid.

This changed during the 1990s: after the Cold War, the alliance needed to build new alliances. The social capital from the Cold War was not sufficient to uphold a position at the centre of the field. In the post-Cold War era, the web of relations surrounding NATO therefore grew denser. New actors entering the field on the basis of military and scientific capital were included in a range of different activities surrounding the alliance. As Chapter 5 will show, the alliance actively sought to create links with a variety of actors spanning the theory/practice divide, including think tanks, research centres and universities. This formed part of a new power strategy to compile valued types of capital in the field. This time, the 'theory actors' included the social sciences[39], and social science agency increasingly showed up in NATO publications and activities. 'With the dissolution of the East-West barrier in Europe, the NATO Science Program has recently been altered to more political goals' (Nierenberg 2001: 371).

Social capital involves being recognized as representing people. Representing people adds to your power base. NATO acted accordingly and pursued a strategy of maximising social capital through attempts to claim to be the representative of a large number of countries. The enlargements formed part of this strategy[40], though other programmes were initially more successful in accumulating social capital. For example, the alliance pursued a double strategy of being both the primary spokesperson *towards* Eastern European countries and Russia, while at the same time *including* these countries in practical patterns of interaction, which tied them close to the alliance and enabled NATO to speak *on behalf of these countries*. The primary programmes in this regard include the Partnership for Peace Programme (PfP) and the Euro-Atlantic Partnership Council (EAPC). This strategy was also pursued in relation to the WEU and the EU: NATO continuously attempted to maintain the lead role in relations with these organizations (see Chapter 5 for detail).

If we take a step back and consider the field as a whole, think tanks created links to one another and to practice-type agency to a great extent during the 1990s. It would appear as though this type of agency valued social capital highly. Nevertheless, while social capital accumulation added to the power base of NATO, the EU[41] and think tanks, this was not necessarily the case for all types of agency in the field. For some, primarily research agents, links to practical politics could be seen as compromising their independence and thus their objectivity. One could speculate as to whether research centres and universities actively pursued a strategy of downplaying institutional contacts with practical politics in order to uphold a scientific aura of objectivity (for dis-cussion, see Berling and Bueger 2013). Through such a strategy, scientific capital accumulation would rise. The potential problem, however, could be that universities and research centres were kept 'out of the loop' and possibly excluded from e.g. funding opportunities.[42] Social capital was thus a double-edged sword; it could prove a valuable type of capital for some while possibly undermining the position of others.

### Empowering new types of agency

NATO sought social capital accumulation through programmes such as the PfP. However, this programme not only added to NATO's total number of links to other actors in the field of European security and placed NATO at the centre of a number of networks; it also provided a powerful locus for 'setting the terms' in the field.[43] Gheciu describes how the PfP functioned as a means of teaching applicant countries how to 'do security', and what the nature of security was in Europe after the Cold War (Gheciu 2007). In other words, NATO could use the PfP to induce understandings of security and the (still important) role of NATO in the European security field. Social capital accumulation thus supported strategies related to military and scientific capital alike.

In the process of accumulating social capital, however, NATO also *empowered* other actors. Leander describes how private military companies (PMCs) assist in defining security through  teaching practices, consultancy and lobbyism (Leander 2005a: 817–818). The PfP process can be understood along similar lines: NATO  (through the PfP)  hired think tanks such as the *Geneva Centre for Security Policy* (GCSP) to teach bureaucrats and politi-cians from PfP countries how to adopt the 'spirit of PfP' (Gheciu 2007: 187; NATO 2007d). Think tanks were thereby potentially empowered through links with NATO. They were hired to teach applicant countries how to 'do security right' from NATO's perspective, but were at the same time placed in a position in which they could exert their own influence on that perspective. In the words of Huysmans:

> Producing knowledge and training people into a particular kind of knowledge can bear on the forms of knowledge that are available in the technocratic arena. It also can have an impact on the kind of security knowledge that can credibly legitimate political positions in the political spectacle.
>
> (Huysmans 2006: 155–156)

The position of the teacher is thus potentially powerful.

Through teaching practices, backed up by the social capital provided by being hired by NATO, think tanks became empowered in the field and helped legitimate the NATO version of how security should be practiced in Europe after the Cold War. Of course, this did not amount to the capacity to define security in the field authoritatively and exclusively. This required a 'feel for the game'. As in Leander's example of PMCs, however, it 'gives them a voice in how a variety of significant decision-makers in the state, the military, or non-state organisations ... at different levels understand security and hence judge and react to information that they get' (Leander 2005a: 818). NATO invested trust in think tanks by hiring them, thereby granting them a position to speak from in the field.[44]

With similar results of empowerment and access to the field, the alliance allowed a number of think tank employees and researchers to publish and comment on NATO affairs in *NATO Review*, the NATO flagship publication. Following Leander, I therefore argue that 'a new caste of private security 'experts' emerged; and the expert is of course privileged in the production of legitimate knowledge' (Leander 2005: 820). Social and scientific capital added to the standing of this new caste, and the financial resources invested in the PfP programme supported this trend.[45]

The focus on social capital thus brings a moral dilemma to the fore: 'This raises practical questions about who should be allowed to give what kind of training to whom', Leander (2005: 818) argues in the context of PMCs. The same moral and practical question applies here. From this follows a need to focus on how social capital (and the other types of capital specified in this chapter) granted different actors access to the security field and how it simultaneously provided them with a position from which they could speak legitimately about security. Empowering agency was a potential consequence of creating links to them and thus providing them with social capital in the field.

## Conclusion

Buzan *et al.* have argued that successful securitization is linked to the position of an agent in a field (Buzan *et al.* 1998: 31). With this chapter, I have specified that point as regards the European field of security: a strong position in this field was linked to the accumulation and mobilization of military, scientific, and social capital in the 1990s.

The chapter discussed the field-specific types of capital in the field of European security: military capital, scientific capital, and social capital. As argued in Chapter 3, the specification of these field-specific types of capital served several purposes: capital placed agents in a position in the hierarchy of the field, provided access to the struggles in the field for agents, and was mobilized in doxic battles. In the language developed in Chapter 3, capital was *agency-selecting* and *boundary-setting* in the field. Furthermore, the *hierarchy* in the field depended on capital.

Taken together, the field-specific types of capital were all under redefinition after the end of the Cold War. This affected both which types of agency were allowed into the field and the relative distribution of power in the field. NATO and the wisdom of strategic studies were put on the defensive, while the EU and a range of think tanks and research centres gained ground in the field. NATO even helped spur this effect by empowering agents through networks and programmes such as the Partnership for Peace. This discussion provokes the broader (Bourdieusian) question about what is 'happening to the weight different actors carry in defining legitimate knowledge' (Leander 2005a: 819). The weight of theory-type actors (such as think tanks and research centres) in the field of security appears to have shifted, as more and more 'in-between' type of actors gained access. I pick up this thread in the following two chapters.

As stated in the introduction to this chapter, the general theoretical lesson lies in understanding how the concept of capital can shed light on processes of change and struggles in a field of power (including 'theory'). A more specific lesson lies in acknowledging that theory and practice do not necessarily 'hang together' in the same way in all cases: in the case of this chapter, the concept of capital provided a lens through which to study the different forms of attachment and detachment in a specific context and found that a range of actors must be considered when the theory/practice nexus is studied in relation to NATO. On a methodological level, the lesson for the IR practice debate lies in accepting that these points require an empirical dimension of study using a number of different methods of inquiry. The chapter thus constituted the first step in the approach developed in Chapter 3. It provided insight on how claims about the impossibility of detached knowledge production can be translated into a theoretically informed empirical analysis of field-specific types of capital. But the approach does not limit itself to applications to the science/policy nexus. The chapter should thus be understood as an illustration of how IR analyses in general can approach the study of international fields. The following two chapters will further develop these points. First, by empirically confirming the place of NATO in a web of relations with the agency selected in this chapter (Chapter 5); and, second, by analysing the doxic battles involving field-specific types of capital (Chapter 6).

## Notes

1 Williams' (2007) field is broader than the field I occupy myself with here. He focuses on a field of security in a more general sense, whereas I focus on the processes in the European field of security surrounding NATO. The processes were parallel, but distinct. NATO was challenged by a diversity of actors in the European field of security. In contrast, Williams argues that: 'As a locus of accumulated cultural and symbolic capital and power, NATO was a key institutional site in the articulation of a new cultural logic of security' (ibid.: 2007: 41). In my analysis, this position was not given. NATO fought hard to retain a central position and has yet to win the fight once and for all.

2 The EU begun developing a military capability towards the end of the 1990s and early 2000s, thereby challenging the superior position of NATO with regard to military capital (see e.g. Chalmers 2001; Missiroli 2003). The EU Common Foreign and Security Policy (CFSP) was initiated with the Maastricht Treaty in 1992 and strengthened in the Amsterdam Treaty in 1998 by the creation of the High

Representative of CFSP (a position held by Javier Solana). The Helsinki Headline Goal from 1999 set the terms for a future EU Rapid Reaction Force (Lachowski 2002).

3  The US contribution to NATO defence expenditures has always been great, and debate about the lack of willingness among Europeans to contribute has been fierce. A report from the Congressional Research Service from 2004 draws on recent data from the *Military Balance* and the US State Department's *World Military Expenditures and Arms Transfers* (WMEAT) (Chamberlin 2004). The data shows that the US Defence spending as a percentage of NATO Defence spending ranged between 59.1 per cent (1999) and 64 per cent (2002) (ibid.: Figures 7 and 8). Ten years after the end of the Cold War, the US thus still contributed more than all of the European allies combined. Numbers show, however, that the total spending on military had decreased substantially.

4  It is standard to include R&D in military expenditures. NATO does so, as does the well-respected annual publication *Military Balance*.

5  Baldwin holds that this should be decided from domain to domain, from situation to situation. Art is concerned with grand strategy, which means that 'the goals a state posits and the ways that military power can (and cannot) be used to attain and preserve them' (Art. 1999: 187). Military power was central to both, as it has been to (neo-)realist researchers for a long time.

6  With respect to what she refers to as the 'field of security expertise', Leander ( has argued that 'If it can be shown that the actions of PMCs [Private Military Companies] reinforce a certain understanding of security expertise, or alter it, then they affect the habitus and dispositions of the actors in the security field. If such an effect, in turn, legitimates the type of expertise and services PMCs provide, then PMCs have been empowered' (Leander 2005a: 812). Likewise in the case of military capital: if certain actors could claim to have influenced the understanding of military capital, they were potentially empowered in the field.

7  Another source of information on this is the *Military Balance*, published annually by the London-based *International Institute for Strategic Studies* (IISS). Here, military expenditures are defined as the cash outlays of a central or federal government to meet the costs of national armed forces. The term 'armed forces' includes strategic, land, naval, air, command, administration and support forces. It also includes paramilitary forces such as the *gendarmerie*, as well as customs service and border guards if they are trained in military tactics, equipped as a military force and operate under military authority in the event of a war (IISS 2003: 10). The IISS follows the NATO definition of military expenditures. The *Military Balance* is alongside a similar publication from the Stockholm International Peace Research Institute (SIPRI Yearbook), widely considered the most detailed and accurate account of the state of military spending in the world. Other common sources for foreign military budget figures include the UN and the US Department of Defense (for allied military spending) (Chamberlin 2004). Gadea, Pardos and Pérez-Forniés (2004) use SIPRI data in their long-run analysis of the defence spending in NATO countries. The numbers I use in this section stem from SIPRI, NATO and IISS.

8  With the exception of France, which did not participate in the integrated military structure, and Iceland, which does not have armed forces (NATO 2002a).

9  Gadea, Pardos and Pérez-Forniés (2004) ascribe the fall in defence spending before the end of the Cold War to the changing political situation in the Soviet Union.

10  See Gadea, Pardos and Pérez-Forniés (2004) for an analysis of the changes in defence spending in 15 NATO countries in the period 1960–1999. The article uses an economic model to analyse which indicators may have influenced defence spending in a number of NATO countries. The authors identify several 'break

points', including decreasing threat, changing strategy in NATO and domestic variables.

11  The modernization of the armed forces is a process known as the 'Revolution in Military Affairs'. A revolution in military affairs signifies advances in technology or strategy that change the way war is conducted. The Gulf War in 1991 is often seen as an example of the RMA which was dominant throughout the 1990s (Ibrügger 1998).

12  The EU spending on military capital is divided into what is covered by the community budget and what is covered on an *ad hoc* basis. The CFSP budget, which includes civilian crisis management, conflict prevention etc, is charged on the community budget following Article 28 in the EU Treaty (EU 2001a: 3). Operations having military or defence implications are not covered by the Community Budget but are charged to member states (ibid.: 6). In budgetary terms, there are three possible categories of crisis management operations: 1) operations under a 'Community instrument' which are financed under the appropriate Community budget line; 2) CFSP operations not having military and defence implications, which are financed under the CFSP budget line; and 3) ESDP operations having military or defence implications, which fall outside the Community budget (ibid.: 4). The different funding possibilities fall under 1st pillar (civilian crisis management) and 2nd pillar operations (CFSP), and operations that fall outside of the budget (ESDP, 2nd pillar but no budget) (EU 2001a: Annex II). In comparison, NATO works from a 'costs lie where they fall'starting point, meaning that countries pay for the personnel and equipment they deploy (Missiroli 2003: 3).

13  The CFSP budget was increased quite substantially for the period 2007–2013 (to 250 million euros a year compared to 46 million euros in 2003, 62 million euros in 2004 and 2005 and 102 million euros in 2006) (EU 2008a: 1). The ESDP was not foreseen in the Treaty on European Union and therefore had no separate budget line (EU 2001a: Annex 2).

14  It is clear to me that the field of European security is not confined to the agents or the practices I select for analysis in this book. As in Bourdieu's analysis of the artistic field, many producers, gallery owners, buyers etc. are as much part of the field as are the artists, novelists etc. (Bourdieu 1993: 37). And as the analysis in Bourdieu (1988) indicates, a number of fields may exist within a larger field 'rather like a Ukrainian doll' (Fisher 1990: 583). The PMCs and border controls are therefore related to the field of security I study here.

15  The book analyses how the French 'nobility' (i.e. the elite) has come to be defined by the cultural capital which is tied to holding certificates from certain well-reputed schools in France (Bourdieu 1998b). Bourdieu eloquently shows how the success rate of students whose parents themselves hold certificates and belong to the economic/cultural elite is much higher than for students from other backgrounds because of the internalized, tacit knowledge these students have from home: they know the rules of the game better.

16  NATO papers had previously included more dimensions of security. See for example the 'Harmel Report' (NATO 1967). Even in the Détente period of NATO, however, when the focus was on the reduction of the number of nuclear and conventional weapons, the focus remained largely on military security.

17  The report was long under way and has become known as The Harmel Report (NATO 1967).

18  The Science Committee and the Office of the Science Adviser were created in Paris in 1957 after the Soviet success with Sputnik (Nierenberg 2001: 366; for background, see Krige 2000).

19  The science programme is the largest civil line item apart from salaries in the civilian budget of NATO (Stone 2002: 947).

20 Approximately 13,000 scientists are involved in aspects of the programme (Nierenberg 2001: 370).

21 Carvalho-Rodrigues (2001: 378) mentions two successful (in terms of funding) NATO science programmes: Science for Stability in which NATO invested 120 million US Dollars and local businesses added 250 million US Dollars. This programme was conceived to develop entrepreneurial capacities in a number of countries. Second, the Computer Networking Program in which NATO invested 1.5 million US Dollars and attracted 2.3 million US Dollars in supplementary investments.

22 The European Currency Unit (ECU) was a basket of currencies used by the European Community member states before being replaced by the EURO in 1999.

23 Note the difference in currency.

24 The dichotomy is based on the US context. The situation described by Lepgold (1998) and Jentleson (2002) cannot be applied directly to the European context. However, the tendency to view theory and practice as distinct spheres is also present in Europe, even if it does not depend on a scientific revolution of the kind seen in North America.

25 See Krause and Latham (1998) for an analysis of how a belt of experts surrounding practitioners may influence decisions.

26 Think tanks have been a much more widespread phenomenon in the US. The development of think tanks in European security was, however, largely a 1990s phenomenon (Notre Europe 2004; Stone 1996, 2000; Stone and Denham 2004; Villumsen 2007).

27 In support of this, Jørgensen (2000) argues that continental IR theory has been "the best kept secret" in debates. Theory emanating from Europe has been largely overlooked in both the theory debate and by practitioners. Wæver (2004, 2012) held that three schools were emerging in European Security Studies in the 1990s and the beginning of the 2000s: Aberystwyth, Paris and Copenhagen were the intellectual fix points.

28 There are seven political foundations in Germany: Friedrich-Ebert-Stiftung (FES) linked to the SPD, the Konrad-Adenauer-Stiftung (KAS) close to the CDU, the Hans-Seidel-Stiftung (HSS) close to the CSU, the Friedrich-Naumann-Stiftung (FNS) close to the FPD, the Hans-Böckler-Stiftung (HBS) close to the DGB, the Heinrich-Böll-Stiftung (HBS) linked to the Greens, and the Rosa-Luxemburg-Stiftung (RSL) affiliated to the PDS (NE 2004: 18).

29 Nonetheless, Stone and Denham's exclusion of *Centre d'Études et des Recherches Internationales* (CERI) in France demonstrates that potentially important *loci* for the formulation of ideas may still be overlooked when following their broad definition. The exclusion of CERI demonstrates how artificial a definitional framework can be. The premise in Stone and Denham (2004) is that the definition of 'think tank' has been too narrow. However, they still want to stick to some kind of definitional exclusion of some types of organizations – and hence exclude CERI while including the *Robert Schuman Centre* at the EUI in Florence. Of course this is partly because of a difference in interest between this book and Stone and Denham . They want to map the world of think tanks for the sake of understanding the concept of think tank. For me, on the other hand, the think tank represents an agent that mobilizes and accumulates scientific capital; it is not initially interesting because of organizational form. With their insistence on epistemic community approaches, however, it seems paradoxical to exclude the CERI from the definition.

30 For a discussion of European think tanks, please see Villumsen (2007) and Berling (forthcoming).

31 A study of all of the relations between all of the actors in European security is simply not practically feasible within the confines of this book. Moreover, the

result would answer a different – albeit interesting and larger – question than that which I intend. Such an analysis would say something more general about the emergence of a field of European security. My intention is more humble: I merely want to find out how NATO was linked to 'theory' in the 1990s. I therefore focus on the institutional ties between NATO and relevant agency in the next chapter. Even though the analysis centres on NATO, however, I argue that we will catch a glimpse of the processes in the larger field – something which provides me with research questions for the future.

32  The World Economic Forum (WEF) is an independent international organization that holds an annual meeting which gathers the business and political elite of the Western world in the Swiss town of Davos. The WEF was founded in 1971 and is based in Geneva.

33  The meeting of the counter-elite would be the World Social Forum (Guzzini 2006: 17). The World Social Forum tends to meet in January about the same time as the meeting in Davos in order to signal its opposition to that meeting. The first WSF meeting was held in 2001.

34  One thing is worth pointing out: the analysis I intend to carry out does not focus on the individual level. I will not carry out analysis resembling Bourdieu's own analysis of particular students at various French elite universities. Instead, the insights concerning common educational background will function as a way of understanding how the field was structured around (social science) categories shared by agents in the field. These categories structured how the struggles in the field were fought and enabled agents to relate to one another at a doxic level. An analysis of the backgrounds of specific individuals would be interesting and con-tribute to Bourdieusian research in international fields (see also Guzzini 2006 on this point). It could zoom in on how agents, while sharing the same general back-ground, could be divided into subgroups comprised people who have mainly received training in military schools, in contrast to agents who have been trained in civilian schools. Following this line of research goes beyond the scope of this book. My current research at the NATO Defense College in Rome goes in this direction.

35  This point is similar to Buzan *et al.*'s definition of how social power and the posi-tion of the agent in the field is a background condition for successful securitization (Buzan *et al.* 1998: 31).

36  The Group for Aeronautical Research and Development (AGARD) was estab-lished in Paris in 1950; the training centre for Experimental Aerodynamics was established in Brussels; the Air Defence Technical Centre was formed in The Hague and, (according to Nierenberg (2001: 364)), the most ambitious under-taking, was the Underwater Research Centre was created in La Spezia in Italy.

37  Nierenberg (2001: 365) argues, however, that the 'major scientific effort of the Alliance was conceived initially as an important part of a larger effort to weld the member nations into a stronger political, economic, and cultural union that went beyond the military goal of collective defence'. Science helped overcome divisions between the member states (e.g. the Greece-Turkey relationship and others) (ibid.: 367). Nevertheless, the focus was on the *inside* of the alliance.

38  When France withdrew from the integrated military structure in 1967, it main-tained its activities in civilian NATO, especially in scientific matters (Nierenberg 2001: 368).

39  Early in the history of NATO (in 1959), the Killian Working Group recommended the creation of networks including the social sciences and humanities. The Killian Working Group worked on plans to create a European MIT (Nierenberg 2001: 369 and footnote 8); however, the project never got off the ground.

40  The EU enlargement was more successful than the NATO enlargement in accu-mulating social capital. As regards the EU enlargement process, White holds that 'The end result of this process will be to expand the geographical boundaries of an

ostensibly unified Europe to include almost every European state, which cannot but reinforce Europe's 'clout' on the world stage' (White 2001: 3).

41  The EU has experienced great success in the field on the issue of social capital. It has, for example,virtually been a magnet for think tanks (Sherrington 2000; NE 2004; Villumsen 2007).

42  Carvalho-Rodrigues (2001: 376) adds that most scientists do not 'credit contributions to diplomacy as relevant to their careers or to the advancement of science' and holds that the absence of scientists in practice is caused by internal workings in the scientific community. This supports my suspicion that links to practice may be unwelcome for science (see discussion in Berling forthcoming). Compare also with Bourdieu's notion of the scientific field as dependent on being relatively autonomous from the field of power (Bourdieu 2004).

43  Along similar lines, Williams and Neumann use the concept of social power to shed light on how NATO had 'the power to define the roles which Russia could adopt in its evolving security relations with NATO' (Williams and Neumann 2000: 372). NATO could thereby drastically narrow the field of politically viable options available to Russian policy-makers. In light of recent Russian actions in Georgia (2008) and Ukraine (2014) this seems to have been accepted only reluctantly by Russia.

44  Michael C. Williams argues that '*trust* becomes essential, since the question of 'who knows' is answered in part by the judgement 'who can be trusted?' i.e., by asking who we believe, and who can be believed' (M.C. Williams 1997: 292).

45  Partnership for Peace is funded under the NATO Security Investment Programme (NSIP), which also covers the expenses incurred in relation to Peace Support Operations such as e.g. SFOR and KFOR (NATO 2001: 202). The NSIP forms part of the 'common costs', which also include the Civilian Budget and Military Budget. The costs are split between 18 or 19 states, depending on the participation of France (Homan 2006).

# 5   Practical patterns of interaction

Bourdieu's research question was often *how* actors were related – rather than *if* they were related – because the nationally formulated fields were easier to define a priori than internationally constituted fields. However, the empirical focus of this book does not lend itself to a priori contentions of that kind. I argue that the existence of relations between the actors in the field must be established for the claims of this book to be supported: are relations between the actors indeed present? has the number increased since the Cold War? and are the types of relations diversifying?

This type of analysis may seem tedious and descriptive. I argue, however, that it provides an important basis for importing Bourdieu into IR and building a practice approach sensitive to the question of how NATO was linked to theory in the 1990s. International Relations analysis after the linguistic turn largely assumes that relations between actors in the international realm are present: discourses are analysed, but agency is never really included. And 'Bourdieu in IR' approaches have not provided an adequate solution to this a priori problem, either. Williams offers a good example of this (Williams 2007). He analyses narratives and discourses when arguing that the field of security was re-valued and tied to a larger cultural and political field. Throughout the book, however, the limits of the field in question are fluid. The same critique can be made with regards to the pioneering work of Ashley (1987, 1988, 1989). I find an empirical dimension to be lacking. It is not sufficient in a sociological practice approach to assume a field's existence: links must be reviewed and changes established in order for the argument that an international field is in the making – or already exists – to be proven. This is how the philosophical claims about the impossibility of detached knowledge production gain an empirical standing. I therefore hold that an analysis of the *practical patterns of interaction* in the emerging field should constitute an important part of research. In an attempt to illuminate the emerging structure of the social space of European security, I have therefore chosen to review contacts between actors in the field. I will take a close look at how actors have established formal and informal relations with each other: how often they meet; how links between actors are sustained and built; and how this has developed from before the end of the Cold War and into the new millennium. Such an endeavour seems particularly necessary in an emerging and loosely structured field that is not bound by national boundaries and where the links are not self-evident.

It seems obvious to me that if there is no contact between the players in the supposed field, then it becomes a stretch to argue that it is in the making and has influence on the decisions about European security. I thus follow Leander's (2006: 11) claim that a Bourdieusian analysis does not demand a certain kind of operationalization:

> it does not and cannot – if it is to remain consistent with itself provide firm guidelines for what exactly should be studied, what kind of evidence is relevant and in what kind of quantities for a study. To be consistent with itself, it has to remain firm on the view that the answer to these questions is contextual and question related.
>
> (see also Leander 2002a: 11–12)

The practical patterns of interaction will provide contextually related indications of a European field of security under reconstruction and will provide an example of how philosophical and a priori assumptions can be replaced with empirical studies in IR in general.[1]

The previous chapter identified a number of actors who could gain access on the basis of the valued type of capital in the field. States, European security organizations and think tanks and research centres were identified as possibly being players in the field of European security. I turn to each of these categories in this chapter from the perspective of NATO: did the *number* and *character* of contacts between NATO and relevant agency in the field increase during the 1990s and into the new millennium? If so, what did this mean for the relationship between theory and practice in Europe?

In all three subcategories, a spectrum from *formal* to *informal* contacts is present. Some of these relations are represented by formal meetings, with decision-making capacity and formal documents spelling out rights and obligations. Other contacts are less formal: informal meetings with no power to make decisions or association programmes in which countries are invited to cooperate with NATO but have no right to vote for or against alliance decisions. And finally, some contacts are highly informal, such as the joint launch of a publication or presentations given in informal settings. The first (member states etc.) and second (European organizations) subcategories will tend towards the formal, while contacts with the third subcategory (think tanks, research centres) will tend to be more informal.

This chapter will also a further detail NATO's accumulation of social capital in the field. The links to other types of agency, the participation in networks, and the attempts to represent other actors all added to the social capital power base of the alliance. The analysis will therefore serve three ends at once: it will function as an empirical confirmation of the existence of a field in which NATO participated; it will contribute to our understanding of NATO's accumulation of social capital; and it provides an illustration of how the approach developed in this book can be translated into practical empirical work.

A central question immediately springs to mind: who and what is NATO, and how can 'it' have relations with anyone? At its very base, NATO is a set of relations between states and other actors; it does not act as a subject in the classical sense. Bourdieu even argues that international organizations can be considered fields unto themselves. NATO could thus be studied as a field in its own right rather than as an acting subject. I argue, nevertheless, that to study NATO alone as a field would miss the dynamics in which 'theory' played a role. This is why the field needs to be conceptualized in broader terms.

The *number* of contacts clearly does not amount to any conclusions about influence or which contacts were more important. However, the the fact that NATO did expand the number and intensity of relations with relevant agencies is an important part of the argument that NATO was engaged in a battle for relevance in Europe in the aftermath of the Cold War in which actors spanning the theory/practice divide were involved. If NATO did not interact with the selected agency, it would be a stretch to argue that a field existed and that a struggle for recognition was going on.

There are numerous ways of evaluating these practical patterns of interaction or links (see e.g. Daugbjerg and Marsh 1998; Peters 1998; Hay 1998). An approach which has been gaining prominence within Security Studies lately is the Actor-Network Theory (ANT) which argues that the focus of social studies should be on the networks which are weaved including both actors and things, and which spans long-held divisions between, for example, science and practical politics (for general statements, see Latour 1988; Callon and Latour 1981; Law 1992; for application to IR and Security Studies, see Bueger and Bethke 2013; Büger and Gadinger 2007). While I find this approach illuminating and inspiring, I think the focus is on the emergence of networks, with no real focus on the constraints posed by existing structures. Field analysis captures fields within the logic of reproduction, while ANT captures networks in their emergence. The types of analysis can be seen as complementary (Büger and Villumsen 2007). But in this chapter, I have chosen a way of addressing networks that fits the analytical framework set out in Chapters 2 and 3 in this book, which led me to an analysis of the field-specific capital in Chapter 4 and leads me to a mapping of concrete contacts in this chapter. I address networks in two ways here: first, I focus on the development of contacts from the perspective of the alliance as a whole; second, a focus on the contacts (speeches, press conferences etc.) given by the Secretaries General (SGs) of the alliance from 1990 onwards.[2] The changing institutional practices of the SGs show a marked change over the course of the decade when we turn our attention to where and to whom they gave speeches, the value they attached to media appearances, and where they travelled to.

In conclusion, the Alliance came out of the 1990s well-connected to think tanks and research centres and ended up creating formal links to the EU. On the level of states, the alliance carried out successful attempts to create links through programmes such as the PfP.

## Member states and other affiliated states

States were selected on the basis of possessing military capital, which had been a particularly valued type of capital during the Cold War and still had some clout in the 1990s. In the case of NATO, this category translates into member states and the states affiliated to NATO through various programmes.

### Member states

In 1990, NATO was an alliance of 16 member states. Belgium, Canada, Denmark, France, Italy, Iceland, Luxembourg, Netherlands, Norway, Portugal, the United Kingdom and the United States all became members when the alliance was established on April 4, 1949. Greece and Turkey became members on February 18, 1952, Germany on May 9, 1955[3], and Spain became the last member on May 30, 1982, before the end of the Cold War dramatically changed the situation for European security. Negotiations began in 1990 with a long list of countries applying for alliance membership. NATO thereby fought to retain a position as the primary security organization in Europe by accumulating social capital through – amongst other strategies – enlargements.[4] With more members, NATO could speak more legitimately on behalf of European security. In the words of then-Secretary General of NATO Solana: 'By enlarging in this way, we increase NATO's strength' (Solana 1997: 2). As early as 1990, the Democratic Republic of Germany entered the alliance after the peaceful merger of the two Germanies.[5] At the Brussels Summit in 1994, enlargement of the alliance was confirmed as an integral aspect of the new NATO (NAC 1994: para. 1). Decision was made to carry out a *Study of Enlargement* to clarify the political and institutional underpinnings of the enlargement process.[6] NATO insisted that '[i]n this process, which is already well under way, the alliance has played and will play a strong, active and essential role as one of the cornerstones of stability and security in Europe' (NATO 1995: para 1). The demise of the alliance, foretold by most commentators, was thus countered: NATO still had a powerful role to play in European security according to the plans for enlargement.[7]

On March 12, 1999, the Czech Republic, Poland and Hungary became new members of the alliance only days before the intervention in Kosovo. Bulgaria, Estonia, Latvia, Lithuania, Romania, Slovakia and Slovenia became members on March 29, 2004, at the NATO Madrid summit. With this, the alliance consisted of 26 countries. Formally, NATO thus went from having close and regular contacts with the heads of state and government, foreign ministers and defence ministers of 16 member states, to having contacts with 19 and then 26 member states. This in itself constitutes growth in the number and direction of contacts surrounding NATO. The number of European allies increased, and the formal institutional contacts multiplied on many levels. In addition to contacts with the Heads of State and Government, NATO membership also involved extensive diplomatic contacts between the member state missions at NATO HQ in Brussels and military-to-military contacts – both in the planning cell in Mons (SHAPE)[8] and between the military representations at the NATO HQ. NATO itself thus comprised a wide range of activities that fit the meaning of practical patterns of interaction. The formal member states met regularly at all levels, in negotiations and in concrete work on many different matters in the NATO committee structure. This ensured keeping cooperation practical and specific instead of limiting it to 'big issues'.[9] Permanent member state representations (or 'missions', as they are called) attend the meetings on behalf of their governments every week in NATO HQ, making NATO 'an organization of daily interactions and procedures' (Wallander 2000: 724). The formal relations – and the possibility for informal relations – are thus very present and dense in the NATO HQ and in the NATO structure more generally.

The slow pace of NATO enlargement did not make the attraction of membership any less attractive for the Central and Eastern European Countries (CEECs). They pushed hard to be accepted as aspirant member states. NATO's strategy became to lock the surrounding countries' attention to NATO and have them accept the alliance as their primary representative in European security – without promising full membership. In this manner, NATO created a number of contacts with non-members, thereby accumulating social capital. The important message from NATO was that 'NATO does not intend to be an exclusive club with slightly increased but closed membership, … a new line is not being drawn after the first admissions … Others can aspire to it and thus have an incentive to meet its standards' (Brzezinski 1995: 33). NATO used the prospect of membership as a strategy to remain at the centre of European security. It was not a classical, imperial strategy, but a strategy that sought to keep NATO high in the European security hierarchy, while at the same time refraining from promising access to NATO's structure.[10] NATO created links to a list of countries who were drawn into the logic of the alliance through the PfP and other programmes. The initial push for full membership by CEECs was thus 'stalled' using these programmes. But eventually the stalling mechanisms became very successful power strategies for NATO, which could support the strategies involving the mobilization of scientific and military capital. The alliance was placed in a position where it possessed:

> the power to include and exclude, legitimize and authorize, … [and where it could] wield power over those who stand outside them (who are excluded from their authorizing ability) and those inside them, who must work within the parameters of the prevailing institutional form.
>
> (Williams 2007: 65)

This powerful position was closely tied to the symbolic power of Democratic Peace and the broad concept of security (Büger and Villumsen 2007).

### Non-member states

Apart from the formal membership category, NATO developed measures to formalize contacts with other European states from 1990 onwards.

### NACC

The *North Atlantic Cooperation Council* (NACC) was established in 1991 and created a new forum for consultations between the former enemies – 'extending a hand of friendship across the East-West divide' (NATO 2002b: 3; NAC 1990b: para. 4; see also Bennett 2003).[11] In practice, this meant creating a formal setting for consulting with former enemies. The establishment of the NACC initially brought together the NATO member countries and nine Central and Eastern European Countries.[12] In March 1992, participation in the NACC was expanded to include all of the members of the Commonwealth of Independent States (CIS); by June 1992, Georgia and Albania had also become members. 'The NACC's creation was essentially the first step at the organisational level towards opening the Alliance's door to its former Cold War rivals' (Hendrickson 2004: 1). The creation of the NACC thus represents one of the first attempts to create formal relations beyond the full member states. As stated in the NATO Handbook, 'With the publication of the Rome Declaration in November 1991, the basis was laid for placing this evolving relationship on a more institutionalised footing' (NATO 2001: Chapter 2). However, Wallander (2000: 720) holds that the 'NACC's limitations were substantial and apparent very early in 1992'. Real political decision-making and coordination continued to be carried out in alliance structures, and non-members could see that alliance policy would first be worked out in the North Atlantic Council (NAC)[13] before being presented in the NACC. Moreover, having been designed to reconcile relations between former enemies, the NACC did not include important neutral European states.

### Partnership for Peace

One of NATO's major moves, which involved social capital accumulation and placed NATO centrally in practical patterns of interaction in the field, was the formulation and adoption of the Partnership for Peace programme (PfP). 'PfP was the most effective institutional innovation to come from NATO since the end of the Cold War' (Kay 1998: 496). This was possibly the most important step taken by NATO to foster relations with non-member states – a 'quantum leap' (NATO 2002: 3). Without promising membership, NATO tied new states to the alliance in an attempt to stabilize the region through strengthening the democratic control of the armed forces. NATO did not find it possible (or even desirable) to enlarge with full members in a rapid fashion, because the security guarantee of the Washington Treaty risked being compromised (Wallander 2000).[14] But outright rejection was not considered a viable option in the unstable situation in the aftermath of the Cold War. 'PfP was intended to offer a halfway house between exclusion and full membership to new democracies pressing to join NATO (as well as the EU)' (Forster and Wallace 2001: 116). NATO cast itself as the provider and guarantor of peaceful relations between former enemies, thereby attempting to move itself into a position in which it gained a natural and legitimate position as spokesperson for peaceful relations in Europe. One observer held that 'In just one year, this innovative idea has become an integral part of the European security scene' (Holbrooke 1995: 43). It placed NATO at the centre of a growing number of relations.

In terms of practical patterns of interaction, the PfP created a formal category of institutional contacts through which the Partners in Peace could discuss security-related questions with the full member states. The Partners were invited to set up offices at the NATO HQ 'in order to improve our working relationships and facilitate closer cooperation' (NATO 1994b: 2) and participate in the committee work in the alliance. This contributed to a growing number of formal contacts as well as the creation of more informal contacts between the partner staffs, the permanent missions and the International Staff at NATO HQ. Meeting daily in the long corridors in the NATO building, sitting around the same meeting tables and sharing the same canteen spurred informal contacts (Wallander 2000 reports that two senior defence officials of the US Administration support this finding).[15]

The practical measures were part of a strategy to accumulate social capital on the part of NATO that also included new consultation mechanisms, military diplomacy and joint peacekeeping exercises under the Partnership for Peace Umbrella (see, e.g. NATO 2007b). As one NATO representative put it:

> To the layman, all this activity must seem mundane. But that is just the point: PfP enables Partner countries to do most of the same daily work done by NATO Allies, directed toward the same end of promoting an increased sense of security in Europe.
>
> (Hunter 1995: 4)

Through everyday practical cooperation with countries that were not (yet) members of the alliance, NATO accumulated trust and placed itself in a dense network of countries relevant to European security.[16]

The practical arrangements underpinning the PfP could appear to indicate that NATO was planning for more than just a loose association of the countries in the programme. NATO gradually began sharing military planning, exercises and implementation procedures with the partners in order to facilitate joint exercises (Wallander 2000: 722). However, this did not easily translate into inviting new full members into the alliance: 'there is no timetable or list of nations that will be invited to join NATO' (Holbrooke 1995: 45). As the 1990s turned into the new millennium, this prediction seems to have been correct: 'the PFP will be a permanent part of the European security scene even as NATO expands to take in some, but not all, PFP members' (ibid.: 44). Some PfP countries did, however, join NATO in the two rounds of enlargement, and a senior US official reported to Wallander that 'Partners are de facto members: they plan, exercise, and consult' (Article 5 questions excluded) (Wallander 2000: 729).[17]

The Partnership for Peace was thus an important part of a strategy to build strong institutional ties with the former enemy countries and neutral during the 1990s:

> NATO has ... been important in extending the values and norms of the transatlantic security community beyond those who aspire to membership. Extension of the PfP participation to European neutrals has widened the NATO 'family', lessened the distinction between allies and neutral states, and strengthened NATO's position as the primary security organisation for the European region.
>
> (Forster and Wallace 2001: 116)

The practices through which this was accomplished included numerous activities: 'countless courses, seminars, and workshops for young civilians and military officers' were organized at the Partnership Training Centers, NATO's Defence College, the Geneva Center for Security Policy, the Marshall Center, the Partnership Coordination Cell, 'and various defence academies in Western countries' (Gheciu 2007: 186).[18] The 'NATO family' was thus extended through the PfP both by formal arrangements and by informal contacts between the new colleagues (see below for the initiative 'PfP Consortium', which was developed 'in the spirit of PfP' and tied think tanks and research centres to NATO).[19]

## European (security) organizations and the growing importance of the EU

The political ambition of creating 'a framework of interlocking and mutually reinforcing institutions; NATO, the CSCE, the European Community, the WEU' (NAC 1992: para 2) does not account for the many different formal and informal contacts that existed and developed over the 1990s between NATO and the other European organizations. In fact, some even argue that the concept of interlocking was quickly replaced by the 'interblocking' nature of relations (Croft 2000: 5).

The EU in particular emerged from the 1990s with closer contacts with NATO, after a period of rivalry in the 1990s. NATO and the OSCE lived rather separate lives in the beginning of the 1990s but cooperation and institutional contacts emerged from the mid-1990s. The WEU experienced sustained contacts with NATO in the beginning of the 1990s but ceased to be of importance when the decade drew to an end. I begin each subsection with a brief review of the contacts between the organizations and NATO *before* the Cold War in order to create a point of comparison for relations in the 1990s.

### *OSCE*

The OSCE has lived a parallel life alongside NATO throughout its history.[20] Initially, NATO had been opposed to a Soviet suggestion to hold a European conference that would focus on agreeing to essential issues such as the drawing of borders after the Second World War  and the status of Berlin. In the early 1970s, however, the Soviet Union agreed to allow Canada and the US to participate in a conference, and NATO allies agreed to participate in a cooperation conference.[21] The conference was to take place outside military alliances, and all states would participate as 'sovereign and independent States and in conditions of full equality' (CSCE 1973: Chapter 6, para. 65). This meant that NATO did not have a formal role in the negotiations.[22]

Throughout the 1970s and 1980s, the CSCE continued to work for the strengthening of ties across the East-West divide and for cooperation between aligned and non-aligned states.[23] The principle of the equality of all states pervaded the work. A Soviet proposal to establish a permanent structure for the CSCE was opposed by the NATO countries. The CSCE thus existed without a fixed address for almost two decades and without the formal participation of NATO or the Warsaw Pact as organizations.[24].

The CSCE provided a permanent channel of communication between the opposing poles but never formalized relations between NATO, the Warsaw Pact and the CSCE. As the principle of equality prescribed, the NATO allies were not participants in the CSCE process as *allies* but as member countries, equal to all other member countries in the process – whether aligned or non-aligned. This meant that the institutional tie with NATO was informal – or indirect – during the first two decades of the CSCE process.[25]

Following the end of the Cold War, the CSCE process picked up pace as interest in the organization increased (see, e.g. Glaser 1993). Many thought that the CSCE was the natural – and right – place to base security cooperation in a situation in which bipolarity no longer dominated the European security landscape. Russia especially held on to the importance of the OSCE throughout the 1990s (Pouliot 2007: 610). The countries participating in the CSCE process agreed upon a comprehensive set of issues at the Paris summit in November 1990.[26] In the years that followed, the CSCE was strengthened with the support of, amongst others, NATO. The Helsinki Document 'The Challenges of Change' was signed at a CSCE Summit Meeting in July 1992. The document described new initiatives for the creation of a CSCE forum for security cooperation and for CSCE peacekeeping activities, for which 'both the North Atlantic Council and the North Atlantic Cooperation Council expressed full support' (NATO 2001: Chapter 2).[27] At a meeting in December 1992, the position of CSCE Secretary General was created, and permanent facilities were set up in Vienna following the 1993 Rome Summit.[28] The CSCE changed its name to the OSCE after a process leading to a more coherent and strong political mandate following the December 1994 Budapest summit. The new OSCE was designed to assume a more important role in relations with Russia in particular and was now an organization with a spokesperson and a permanent structure; preconditions for establishing more formal links with NATO were in place.

The wars in the Balkans sped up the institutionalization of the OSCE and saw the organization in action. When the war in Bosnia and Herzegovina came to an end in 1995, the OSCE was entrusted the task of negotiating the detailed annexes of the *Dayton Accords.*[29] Some sort of division of labour between the OSCE and NATO was thus finding a balance. NATO had the military hardware to carry out military missions, while the OSCE had negotiating power due to its broad base of countries. The wars in the Balkans paved the way for regular contacts and increased the exchange of information between the OSCE and NATO (Bennett 2003); nevertheless, the OSCE did not come to occupy a central role vis-à-vis NATO in the 1990s. Regular, formal institutional contacts between the organizations were not present before 1996, and the formalization and nature of the contacts seem to be a point of contention. In general, therefore, the OSCE and NATO lived rather separate – or parallel – lives in the beginning of the 1990s, while close interaction in the field developed in the mid-1990s. In 1998, direct cooperation on the to-date most ambitious OSCE verification mission strengthened the bond between the two organizations.[30] Practical cooperation in the field between the OSCE and NATO thus existed towards the end of the 1990s. The roles of the two organizations were understood as complementary rather than competitive.[31]

In 1999 at a summit conference in Istanbul, the OSCE adopted the *Charter for European Security,* which includes the *Platform for Co-operative Security.* The Platform outlined how the organization would cooperate with other international organizations for the promotion of common security. NATO expressed willingness to contribute with institutional resources in support of the OSCE, especially in crisis management and conflict prevention in the Platform for Co-operative security (Bennett 2003: 4). However, the momentum from the early 1990s had been lost. The OSCE no longer occupied the central role many had previously ascribed to it. Pouliot holds that the 'OSCE is increasingly marginalised', but retains a number of specific and exclusive functions. NATO and the EU took over the central positions in European security (Pouliot 2007: 609).

## WEU

Almost since its creation, the history of the WEU has unfolded in the shadow of NATO.[32] It was not until the reactivation of the WEU in 1984 that the organization played an independent role in European security (WEU 2000: 39–42). Bailes even argues that the developments turned the WEU 'into a largely comatose organization' (Bailes 1999: 306) in the 1960s and that it did not revive until the policies of the Reagan Administration created dissent among European Allies. In the Rome Declaration of 1984, the WEU launched a series of joint WEU Foreign and Defence Ministers meetings, where the European contribution to NATO was to be addressed. In 1987, from 1985 the WEU adopted its Hague Platform following the introduction of the EC's Single European Act. For the first time, the WEU committed itself to also strengthening the EC (ibid.: 307).

The end of the Cold War saw a WEU that attempted to wrestle itself into a central position in European security. In 1991, the WEU was written into the

text of the Maastricht Treaty as an organization for implementing EU decisions: 'The Union requests the Western European Union (WEU), which is an
integral part of the development of the Union, to elaborate and implement
decisions and actions of the Union which have defence implications' (Maastricht Treaty 1991: Article J.4, 2). The WEU thus established formal contacts
with the EU in the early 1990s.

In 1992, the WEU adopted its *Petersberg Declaration,* which outlined a
role for the WEU in peacekeeping and humanitarian missions. This created tension
between NATO and the WEU/EU, until the roles for the organizations were
defined. 'An important milestone' (WEU 2000: 22) in the WEU–NATO
relationship in the 1990s was the 1994 NATO Summit declaration in which
the European Security and Defence Identity (ESDI) and a strengthening of
the WEU were agreed to. The NAC also agreed on the concept of 'Combined
Joint Task Forces' (CJTF), which was discussed between 1994 and the Berlin
summit in 1996.[33] In the Berlin Summit Declaration, the ESDI and the CJTF
concepts were combined: In future missions, 'operating under the political
control and strategic direction of the WEU' (NAC 1996b: para. 7) should be made
possible. This constituted NATO's most complete and advanced manifesto to date
on the subject of ESDI and the role of the WEU (Bailes 1999). The decision
was confirmed at the NAC Madrid summit in 1997 and represents a strong
formal tie between the two organizations.

After the 1996 Berlin decision to work towards missions politically and
strategically directed by the WEU, a series of practical measures strengthened
the institutional ties between the WEU and NATO. The goal of the cooperation between the WEU and NATO was to clarify consultation procedures
in crises in which the WEU sought alliance support, arrangements to transfer
NATO assets/capabilities to the WEU and monitor their use, and a review of
the necessary information-sharing arrangements (ibid.). It was decided that
joint sessions of the WEU and NATO councils should be held at least four
times annually; joint meetings of the relevant subordinate bodies should be
furthered; the Secretary General of the WEU should participate in Ministerial meetings in NATO and vice versa, and the respective Chairmen of the
NATO and WEU military committees were to attend each others meetings.
Moreover, a Security Agreement to enhance the exchange of classified information and practical cooperation was adopted, and the WEU was allowed to
use the NATO integrated telecommunications system. Classified information
being one of the cornerstones of NATO's functions, this meant a lot. The ties
between the two organizations were thus strengthened by this 'increased
mutual flow of papers' (ibid.: 313).

All of these decisions enhanced cooperation between the NATO and the WEU
and strengthened the institutional ties between them. Transactions were eased by
the fact that all  WEU civilian and military staff came from countries which
were full members of NATO. As an expression of the closer ties between the WEU
and NATO, the WEU was granted access for its military representatives to observe
NATO's planning work on Kosovo in May 1998 (ibid.; WEU 2000: 22–23).

On the issue of membership, the WEU increasingly linked the NATO member states and the EU during the 1990s. The organization's members included EU members, NATO allies, and some members that were both EU members and NATO allies. From being an organization with only seven members in 1984, the WEU grew to include all of the EC/EU and NATO members during the 1990s (Bailes 1999).[34] The NATO allies were therefore institutionally linked with several other states through the WEU membership structure.

The institutional links between the WEU and NATO climaxed in 1997–1998, and 'after a final spurt, hit all main targets established for the April 1999 Washington Summit' (ibid.: 312). The two organizations agreed to a long list of issues: consultation arrangements in the event of crises, guidelines for all detailed practicalities of cases in which NATO assets and/or capabilities were loaned to the WEU, common terminology on crisis management, information sharing, and the setting in motion of a process towards assessing the adequacy of national contributions to Petersberg missions (ibid.). Together, these decisions seemed to create strong, formal institutional links between the WEU and NATO. However, the WEU would eventually leave the scene, as the ties between the EU and NATO grew stronger.[35] At the same Washington summit in 1999, NATO decided to build on the existing WEU–NATO mechanisms in the creation of a direct EU-NATO relationship. The summit communiqué published on April 24 'dealt only briefly with the latest successes in the conventional NATO/WEU framework and went on directly to hail the St Malo initiative and its consequences' (ibid.: 315; for discussion of the St Malo Declaration, see below). The summit declaration held that 'We acknowledge the resolve of the European Union to have the capacity for autonomous action so that it can take decisions and approve military action where the Alliance as a whole is not engaged' (NAC 1999). The WEU was thereby effectively sidetracked, and relations with the organization no longer mattered as much to NATO as relations with the European Union.[36]

## *EU*

The EU-NATO relationship changed remarkably over the course of the 1990s. From being two organizations with almost no contact with each other in the beginning of the decade, the EU ended the decade with the adoption of the Headline Goal in Helsinki in 1999, which eventually led to regular meetings between the EU and NATO on security matters. By the beginning of the new century, 'Lord Robertson of NATO and Javier Solana on behalf of the EU often meet informally to coordinate the activities of the two organisations' (Moens 2003: 34).

During the 1990s, however, the 3.5 kilometres between the NATO HQ on the outskirts of Brussels and the EU institutions in the centre of Brussels had almost been comparable to the distance between planets. There was 'almost no contact', only 'occasional secret lunches between ambassadors', or 'extremely informal talks between wee members of the respective staffs' (Shea 2004). While Soviet officers were walking up and down the NATO corridors and partnerships with former enemies were being formed rapidly, there was no direct contact between the EU and NATO, even though they largely shared the same membership[37], were built on the same values, and generally held the same objective.

When considering the initiatives being forwarded during the 1990s by the two organizations, however, it appears as though some sort of dialogue was taking place. The EU and NATO adopted parallel declarations concerning the role of the European allies/the EU, thus engaging in a 'conversation' with each other. This conversation also included the WEU. The crux of the matter was that NATO wanted to keep security questions based in the alliance structure, while the EU debated having a security dimension of its own: first through the WEU, and later within the EU itself. The adoption of different documents throughout the 1990s can be summed up in a battle of 'ESDI versus ESDP'. The ESDI (European Security and Defence Identity) was the NATO solution to a European role in security. The ESDP (European Security and Defence Policy) was the EU concept which flagged European autonomy on security issues. I discuss what I call the 'ESDI/CFSP/ESDP letter game' and how it constituted a series of moves and mobilization of social capital in the field of European security in Chapter 6. Here, I will briefly sum up the 'conversation' taking place between the two organizations in order to illuminate how relations between the two evolved during the course of the 1990s.[38]

In the conversation between the EU and NATO, the first instance of an autonomous European role also involved the WEU, as discussed above. It carried a message to NATO: Europe wanted to assume a greater role in European security: 'The common foreign and security policy shall include all questions related to the security of the Union, including the eventual framing of a common defence policy, which might in time lead to a common defence' (Maastricht Treaty 1991: Article J.4, 1). The dialogue with NATO was explicitly mentioned in the Treaty: the policy of the Union in accordance with this Article shall not prejudice the specific character of the security and defence policy of certain Member States and shall respect the obligations of certain Member States under the North Atlantic Treaty and be compatible with the common security and defence policy established within that framework (ibid.: Article J.4, 4). A dialogue that would last more than a decade had been set in motion. The message about working towards a common defence initially spurred a reaction from NATO.

The wish for a stronger, more independent European role in security was debated in NATO in the years that followed. At a NAC meeting in Brussels in January 1994, the concept of the ESDI was unofficially adopted. This meant that the WEU would gain access to capabilities that the Europeans themselves did not possess. This move would effectively lock European autonomy into NATO command structures. At the 1996 Berlin Ministerial meeting in the beginning of June, the ESDI became official NATO policy: 'An essential part of this adaptation is to build a European Security and Defence Identity *within NATO*, which will enable all European Allies to make a more coherent and effective contribution to the missions and activities of the Alliance' (NAC 1996b: para. 1, my emphasis). The European role would remain within NATO, the Berlin Final Communiqué held.[39]

The situation in the Balkans – and especially the situation in Kosovo – fed into the NATO-EU dialogue. The Europeans wanted to be able to move faster in the region and without any alliance consensus (see, e.g. Lachowski 2002).[40]. In 1998, at a meeting in St Malo between French President Jacques Chirac and British Prime Minister Tony Blair, a document was prepared and agreed to (known as the St Malo Declaration). The document brought together the Europeanist and Atlanticist camps in a compromise, focusing on strengthening the European role in security. The purpose of the document was to 'make a 'reality' of the Amsterdam Treaty (which had not yet entered into force) through the full and rapid implementation of the provisions on CFSP' (Cornish and Edwards 2001: 588; Lachowski 2002). The document came as a shock to many (Atlanticist) allies[41], see Chapter 6 for details). Eventually, however, the language of the St Malo Declaration was carefully repeated in the NATO Washington summit Communiqué in April 1999 (EV 1999), and a compromise seemed within reach. The text left room for a reading that emphasized the central role of NATO in European security (the British position, see Bailes 1999) but could also be read as a rather clear argument for EU autonomy (the French position). This ambiguity was probably why the document could be agreed to in the first place.

By December 1999 in Helsinki, 'with the Kosovo experience clearly in mind' (Cornish and Edwards 2001: 588), EU leaders reached an unprecedented level of agreement. The 1999 Helsinki European Council adopted the 'Headline Goal' (together with a set of 'capability goals'), which held that 'member States must be able, by 2003, to deploy within 60 days and sustain for at least 1 year military forces of up to 50,000–60,000 persons capable of the full range of Petersberg tasks' (EU 1999: II, 28; Lachowski 2002).[42] The Headline Goal was thus very concrete and envisioned an active security role for the EU.[43]

The EU and NATO first began talking directly and regularly with each other towards the end of the 1990s. The NATO Washington summit in April 1999 set out the possibilities for close cooperation between the EU and NATO. NATO members agreed unanimously that they should 'define and adopt the necessary arrangements for ready access by the European Union to the collective assets and capabilities of the alliance, for operations in which the alliance as a whole is not engaged militarily' (EV 1999: 1). With this, the road was paved for a direct link between the EU and NATO.[44]; and after Washington and the EU Helsinki Headline Goal, the relations between the EU and NATO grew much more institutionalized. After a series of decisions in 2000, the EU started building military structures aimed at cooperation with NATO. First, four ad hoc working groups were created after a recommendation from the Feira European Council in June 2000 (EU 2000f: Article 9).[45] The groups were further specified at the Council meeting on July 5, 2000. The document set up an 'Ad hoc Working Group on Security Issues', an 'Ad hoc Group on Capability', an 'Ad hoc Group on the Provision of NATO Assets', and an 'Ad hoc Group on EU-NATO Permanent Arrangements' (EU 2000c). Furthermore, an 'Interim Military Body' was established by decision of the Council on February 14, 2000 (EU 2000a; EV 2000c), and an 'Interim Political and Security Committee' was established the same day (EU 2000b). A 'Capabilities Commitment Conference' constituted a first attempt to meet the capabilities goals set in Helsinki in 1999. The declaration issued after the conference shows that the EU had drawn on NATO expertise in preparing for the Conference and would continue to do so (EU 2000e).

After an interim period a permanent military staff was formed and weekly meetings with NATO were held. The EU Military Staff (EUMS) was established on June 11, 2001, which provided in-house military expertise for the Secretary General/High Representative. Javier Solana, who had previously been Secretary General of NATO, held this position.[46] The EU thus built structures designed to assume a greater role in European security from 1999 and onwards. In the process, stronger formal institutional ties with NATO were created. Many of the representatives in the EU structures were often also representatives in NATO. In NATO language, they were 'double-hatted': they held a seat in both the EU and NATO. This contributed to the strengthening of ties between the two organizations. Efforts were coordinated to a much greater degree than during the 1990s. Whereas competition had primarily characterized the 'conversation' between the two organizations in the 1990s, the formalization of relations meant instead that competition gave way to (a higher degree of) cooperation (Lachowski 2002: 157).

Informal contacts were one of the important aspects in moving the relationship forward:

> What has ... helped to overcome such rivalries was the fact that the former Secretary General of NATO, Javier Solana, had moved over to become both the EU's High Representative and Secretary General of the Council, and Secretary General of the WEU, and was intimately involved in the discussions.
>
> (Cornish and Edwards 2001: 591)

Weekly informal breakfasts between Solana and the new Secretary General Lord George Robertson provided an invaluable link and facilitated the cooperation between NATO and the EU (EV 2000c).[47] The informal links were thus growing stronger, and the formal links were developing rapidly after a decade of negligence – and then rivalry – between the two organizations.[48] The institutional distance between NATO and the EU thus came closer to the actual physical distance between the two organizations in Brussels to the extent where the editor of NATO Review argued that 'NATO's most important relationship in the coming years will likely be that with the European Union, as that organisation seeks to enhance its security – including military – capabilities' (Bennett 2003: 4). In support of this, the EU took over NATO's 'Allied Harmony' operation in Macedonia (under the name Concordia) on March 31, 2003. This was the first joint EU-NATO crisis management operation under the Berlin-plus framework (Missiroli 2003: 5).[49]

NATO's relations with European (security) organizations thus changed over the course of the 1990s. The WEU was important in the beginning of the 1990s, but dropped out of the game towards the end of the decade. The OSCE continued to live in the shadow of NATO and never seriously challenged the position of the alliance. A division of labour between the OSCE and NATO defined their relations. The greatest change took place between the EU and NATO: from having no formal contact at all, the two organizations ended the decade with formal institutional arrangements. The relations between the EU and NATO thus stand out as the most important relations when it comes to European organizations in the field of European security. Chapter 6 on doxic battles will pick up on this point and analyse how both the EU and NATO participated in the doxic battles that came to restructure the field.

## Think tanks and research centres

As argued in Chapter 4, knowledge-producing activities between theory and practice seemed to play an important role in European security in the 1990s. I shall therefore turn to the links NATO created with this type of agency in the 1990s and show that contacts between NATO and think tanks increased towards the end of the 1990s and became an everyday practice in the new millennium. NATO actively targeted this group through formal science programmes and informal links to research centres and think tanks were also initiated.

### *Science for Peace and Security*

NATO had created links to think tanks and research environments through a series of programmes for several decades. The NATO Science for Peace and Security Programme was established in 2006 on the basis of a merger of two former NATO science programmes: 'The NATO Security through Science Programme' from 1956 and 'The Committee on the Challenges to Modern Society' from 1969. The initial aim of the latter was to address problems affecting the environment of the nations and the quality of life of their peoples. The former programme was established after the report submitted by the 'three wise men' (NATO 1967) had concluded that developments in the fields of science and technology could be decisive for the development of the security situation for the allies (see also Nierenberg 2001; Carvalho-Rodrigues 2001). The NATO Science Programme was established to promote scientific collaboration, and such collaboration between scientists in NATO countries was supported for the next 40 years through various measures. The focus was on the technical and natural sciences (see Garfield 1987 for a description; see Nierenberg 2001 for discussion).[50]

Through various programmes, NATO was nurturing a scientific network of 'civil science', which could help create security and stability.[51] The Science for Peace and Security Programme can thus be seen as the latest institutional face of a process that has been ongoing in NATO.[52] Throughout the 1990s, the budget for science programmes in NATO has, however, stagnated or been cut. 'Civil science has proved to be a highly effective vehicle for international dialogue, due to its universality and dependence upon international networks. The talent garnered in these scientific networks can be applied to emerging threats faced by the Alliance' (NATO 2007f).[53]

The science programmes constitute part of NATO's strategy to remain central in European security through building formalized relations with a variety of actors. The cooperation between research institutes under the Science for Peace and Security Programme (and former programmes) primarily addressed technical problems and ways of identifying concrete threats. It did not challenge the status of NATO as a central organization, as such. Instead, the programme helped identify new threats to the alliance in a situation in which its defining counterpart had withered away and where arguments about NATO's lack of a future flourished. The technical research networks were therefore an important part of NATO's strategy to remain central in European security after the fall of the Cold War enemy.

### The PfP Consortium

One of the other platforms for promoting formalized relations with research centres and think tanks is the PfP Consortium (PfPC). The Partnership for Peace initiative not only worked to enhance cooperation between *states*; it also targeted a range of actors on the European security scene who had not previously been addressed directly. In 1998, *The PfP Consortium of Defence Academies and Security Studies Institutes* was established after decision by the US and German governments. Since then, it has grown into 'a massive forum for education in the liberal-democratic 'spirit of PfP'' (Gheciu 2007: 187; see also NATO 2007d).[54] The NAC and EAPC summits in April 1999 officially tasked the PfP Consortium to act 'as a vehicle to extend participation in PfP to include universities and non-governmental institutes' (NATO 2007c).[55] One of the main objectives of the Consortium was thus to create relations between security institutes, universities, and NATO, and to formalize these ties under the PfP umbrella. The text describing the tasks of the PfP Consortium supports this: the Consortium 'aims at enhancing multinational education through collaborative approaches *linking defence practitioners, scholars, and experts* into activity-based networks that facilitate information sharing. It may also extend participation in PfP to *include universities and non-governmental institutes*' (NATO 2007d: Article 12, my emphasis). An increase and strengthening of the number of links to NATO was thus actively targeted by the PfP Consortium: networks with both actors from universities, think tank experts and other researchers were the aim of the programme; they helped consolidate NATO's position in the European field of security.[56] The main type of actor in the programme was a social science-oriented research institute or think tank with expertise in security – often with a militarily influenced perspective. The technical science support for NATO under the Science for Peace and Security Programme was thereby complemented by a social science-oriented programme.

The *Science for Peace and Security* (and former programmes) and the *PfP Consortium* represent formalized NATO attempts to create links to think tanks broadly defined. As such, the two programmes constituted attempts by NATO to bolster its position in the field of European security, but NATO was also linked to other think tanks through more informal contacts. I review some of these contacts in the next section on public relations and outreach. I return to links with this type of agency from the perspective of the Secretaries General later. Both analyses show that towards the end of the 1990s and into the new millennium, the contacts were strengthening and becoming more frequent.

## Informal links: website and NATO Review

In a speech given to the Atlantic Council in the UK in 1997, then-NATO Secretary General Javier Solana expressed the need for good public relations: 'The need for public support of the alliance remains crucial. As an alliance of democratic nations, NATO draws its legitimacy from a broad public appreciation of its policies' (Solana 1997: 8). During the Cold War, the purpose of the alliance was much clearer to people and governments in member countries, and the audience of the alliance's press releases was largely limited to formal member states; however, that situation changed in the 1990s. NATO used different public relations strategies to an increasing degree from 1990 onwards. Its audience widened and the tools with which to reach out to other actors diversified. The NATO website and the *NATO Review* were both central in the creation of informal links with think tanks and contributed to the growing enmeshment of NATO in a wider field of European security.

### *Website*

Technological developments in the 1990s made the creation of a NATO website possible. The NATO website soon developed into a sharp tool for researchers and a public face for the alliance. Originally, the page contained archives with all of the major political texts agreed to in the history of NATO, and a user-friendly set-up that allowed everyone to search for topical issues. Press releases, photographs and taped recordings of press meetings were just a few of the resources available on the site. During the Kosovo Campaign (Operation Allied Force), the website was updated on a daily basis, and information was shared with the public. Every morning, NATO spokesman

Jamie Shea gave a briefing to the press at nine o'clock. This was a great change from earlier, where the public was not invited in to the same extent. The alliance issued brief press statements, and the national publics were largely informed about NATO initiatives through Heads of State and Government, Foreign and Defence Ministers, who returned from meetings in Brussels and reported on the progress made (Hansen 2002: 1). Today, the website has changed substantially. It no longer resembles a library database but rather a social media platform.

The creation of the NATO website enabled NATO to provide up-to-date versions of the alliance's policies as well as providing a platform for others to understand NATO. This even included live footage from operations. Hansen (ibid.: 7) describes how 111 videotaped bombings from Operation Allied Forces were made available on the NATO website (ibid.). With one mouse click, the internet user could follow the bombings of jeeps, bridges and even the Serbian Ministry of the Interior in Belgrade.

### NATO Review

The strategy of creating informal links with a variety of actors was also pursued through the publication of *NATO Review*. *NATO Review* is a publication that focuses on alliance policies and priorities. It provides analyses from a variety of perspectives and includes articles written by persons such as the Secretaries General, international staff, military staff, ambassadors to NATO and researchers. The use of *NATO Review* further confirms that NATO was increasingly creating links to think tanks and research centres.

All issues of *NATO Review* published since 1991 have been made available online on the NATO website.[57] Several prominent researchers/members of think tanks have published there. Among them are Francois Heisbourg, who has published extensively on European security, has been the director of the *Geneva Center for Security Policy*, chairman of the International *Institute for Strategic Studies* (IISS) and Director at the *Fondation pour la Recherche Stratégique* in Paris (Heisbourg and Wijk 2001), and Joseph S. Nye, who has also published extensively on security and was Dean of the *Kennedy School of Government* and a former US Assistant Secretary of Defense (Nye 1999).

An interesting article pitted Ronald D. Asmus (senior fellow for European studies at the *Council on Foreign Relations* (CFR)[58] and former Deputy Assistant Secretary of State for European affairs at the US State Department between 1997 and 2000, where he was responsible for NATO and European security issues) against Charles Grant (who was the director of the London-Based *Centre for European Reform*). The title of the debate was: 'Can NATO remain an effective military and political alliance if it keeps growing?' (Asmus and Grant 2002). Grant's answer was a 'no' – Asmus's answer a 'yes'. Charles Grant and the Centre for European Reform (CER) were central figures in the field of European security towards the end of the 1990s. My research shows that the CER was very successful in creating links with other think tanks, the

EU and with NATO through both *NATO Review* and with Secretaries General Solana and Robertson. Choosing Charles Grant to debate the future of NATO in NATO's flagship publication indicates that NATO considered him a player in the field and therefore also relevant to NATO. Grant argues against Asmus that 'When you talk of NATO being strong, you mean militarily strong. I think the Alliance will remain politically significant, but I think its military importance has diminished and will diminish further' (ibid.: 14). The importance of including Grant in an exchange in NATO Review – and even letting him argue that NATO's military role had played itself out – indicates that NATO has found it important to address this type of argument and this type of actor (a think tank representative). Pitting him against Ronald D. Asmus, one of the driving forces behind the enlargement of the alliance in the 1990s. Asmus, testifies to the importance ascribed to the CER and its director (Asmus 2002a, 2002b). NATO was using *NATO Review* as part of the battlefield in the fight for recognition after the Cold War.

Looking through the volumes of *NATO Review*, several other actors from think tanks and universities appear as invited discussants – and thus as informal links to NATO. Yves Boyer and Burkard Schmitt (respectively, deputy-director of the Paris-based *Fondation pour la Recherche Stratégique* and senior research fellow at the *European Union Institute for Security Studies, EUISS*) were invited to discuss under the title 'Can and should Europe bridge the capabilities gap?' (Boyer and Schmitt 2002). Steven Everts (senior researcher at the *Centre for European Reform*) was asked to debate whether 'Military Power was still the key to international security' with Gary Schmitt (executive director of the *Project for a New American Century*[59]) (Everts and Schmitt 2002). Francois Heisbourg of the *Fondation pour la Recherche Stratégique* discussed with Steve Larrabee of *RAND* (Larrabee and Heisbourg 2003) and Fraser Cameron (Director of studies at the *European Policy Centre* in Brussels) discussed with Andrew Moravcsik (Professor of Government and Director of the European Union Programme at Harvard's *Centre for European Studies*) (Cameron and Moravscik 2003). Among the other research centres and think tanks involved in debates in *NATO Review* were *Stiftung Wissenschaft und Politik* (Berlin), *Center for Defence Information* (Brussels), *Royal Institute for International Affairs at Chatham House, European Stability Initiative* (Berlin), *International Crisis Group* (Brussels), *Danish Institute for International Studies* (DIIS), *NATO Defense College* (Rome) and the *Clingendael Institute* (The Hague). In fact, in the late 1990s it became a standard feature to have think tank employees or researchers discuss the future of NATO under the heading 'debate', and also as contributors of articles and background pieces.

In sum, as seen from the perspective of NATO as a whole, the Alliance created both formal and informal links to think tanks and research centres over the 1990s. Some formalized programmes attached great numbers of this type of actor to NATO, such as the *Science for Peace and Security* and the *PfP Consortium* . SPS consisted mainly of technical think tanks and research centres that helped NATO define and analyse new threats, whereas the PfPC consisted of social science think tanks and research centres which could potentially challenge NATO's role in European security. The latter especially made attempts to influence the battle for recognition in the emerging field of European security towards the end of the 1990s. In addition to the formal programmes, NATO created informal links to think tanks and research centres through both the NATO website and *NATO Review*. A rising number of think tank members and experts were invited to analyse the future of the alliance and contributed side by side with  ambassadors and international staff. NATO was truly becoming enmeshed in a web of relations in European security that had not seemed as important to the alliance prior to the end of the Cold War. Think tanks and research centres constituted an increasingly important part of this web.

## The changing practices of the Secretaries General 1990–2003

The Secretaries General are important agents in the Atlantic Alliance – and increasingly so since the end of the Cold War.[60] In this section, I address the strategies of four NATO Secretaries General (SGs) during the 1990s: Manfred Wörner (1988–1994), Willy Claes (1994–1995), Javier Solana (1995–1999), and Lord George Robertson (1999–2003)[61] by focusing on the number and location of speeches from 1990–2003 (NATO 1990–2003) and the number of press releases recorded for the period 1991–2003 (NATO 1991–2003). The number of speeches and press releases say something about the importance attached to activities outside of the alliance. The changing locations of spee-ches given tell us something about the changing practices of the SGs: from being focused on relations within NATO, the SGs attached great value to travelling to research centres and universities towards the end of the 1990s.

The first striking aspect of Manfred Wörner's period as NATO Secretary General  is the limited number of speeches made by the SG himself and other NATO spokespeople in comparison with Javier Solana and Lord George Roberson. Manfred Wörner was clearly a Secretary General of the Cold War variety, whereas Solana marked the advent of a new post-Cold War type of Secretary General who strove to remain relevant in European Security:[62] the number of speeches given quadrupled when Solana took office.

Manfred Wörner made only a few speeches to think tanks. In 1990 he spoke at the *Institut Francais des Relations Internationales* in Paris and to the *National Defence Institute* in Lisbon. In 1993 he gave speeches at the *IISS* in Brussels and at the *Centro Alti Studi Difesa* in Rome (in addition to a few other places). The overviews of press releases support this finding. In 1991, there is only one (single) press statement on record, whereas 34 press releases are recorded for 1993. In comparison, a total of 170 press releases are on record from 1996, when Javier Solana had taken up the post as Secretary General. This underscores not only that Javier Solana was much more active in creating contacts outside of the alliance, but also that the alliance as such had assumed a more active public relations strategy.

Manfred Wörner worked for creating better relations between former enemies and has been mentioned as one of the early advocates for the creation of the NACC (Hendrickson 2004: 1). Manfred Wörner thus focused on institutional links with states and within the alliance itself.

Willy Claes became NATO Secretary General at a time when the wars in the Balkans were at their peak (1994–1995), but he only held the post for a limited period.[63] In 1994 he spoke at the CSCE Summit in Budapest in December; apart from that, mostly NAC and NACC speeches are on record. In 1995, he spoke at the *Grandes Conferences Catholiques* in January and at the *Munich Conference on Security Policy* in February. In October 1995, acting Secretary General Sergio Balanzino gave speeches to the *National Press Club* in Washington DC, to the *Atlantic Treaty Organization* in Toronto, and spoke at a *RAND* seminar in Brussels. But apart from that, Willy Claes' period as Secretary General did not involve extensive involvement with actors outside of the alliance or its formal programmes (NACC, PfP etc.) He gained some measure of renown, however, for stating that Islamic fundamentalism could be the threat to replace the former Communist threat and provide NATO with a new *raison d'être*.

Javier Solana was a real player in the emerging field of European security; he valued the dialogue with other players in the field to a much greater extent than had been the case with previous Secretaries General. For a long time, he was at the centre of things crucial to shaping the European field. Javier Solana was Secretary General to NATO from December 2, 1995, until Lord George Robertson took over on October 14, 1999. This was immediately after the Dayton Peace Accords and the NATO bombings in Bosnia (the first major military operation of NATO), and included the Madrid Declaration (Declaration, Madrid 1997), where the enlargement of the alliance was decided upon; the historic agreement with Russia on the creation of a joint NATO-Russia Partnership Council (NATO 1997a) and the Kosovo Air Campaign (1999). After having served as NATO Secretary General, Solana became the *High representative for Foreign and Security Policy* in the European Union and the first Secretary General of its Council of Ministers in 1999. He was also appointed as Secretary General to the WEU on November 25, 1999. These circumstances make Javier Solana highly important when plotting the shifting institutional practices in the Alliance. Solana personified the relations between important political actors in the field (NATO–WEU–EU) towards the end of the 1990s. The *European Voice* reported that Solana 'has acted as an invaluable bridgehead between the two organisations [EU and NATO]' (EV 2000c: 1).

The secretaries general before him had generally focused on the internal politics of the alliance, with only few public appearances in universities and think tanks (Hendrickson 2006). When Solana assumed the post as NATO Secretary General, the number of public speeches and press releases increased dramatically. For example, he talked at Georgetown University and the University of Warsaw in 1996; at the American and Columbia Universities in July

1997; and Stanford University and Universitat Pompeu Fabra in Barcelona in October 1997. Furthermore, he gave a speech at the Oxford University Union Society in May 1998. He opened the academic year at the Université Libre de Bruxelles (ULB) in October 1998 and gave speeches at l'Institut des Hautes Etudes de Défense Nationale (IHEDN) in Paris, at the Royal United Services Institute (RUSI) in London, and at the Instituto Da Defesa Nacional in Portugal in March 1999. In September 1999, he spoke at the National Defense University in Washington.

Furthermore, he gave several speeches to different think tanks. For example, he spoke at the *International Institute for Strategic Studies* (IISS) in London in September 1996; the Instituto de Estudos Estratégicos e Internacionais (IEEI) conference in Lisbon in November 1996; and the *Friedrich Ebert Stiftung* in Bonn and *Institut Royale des Relations Internationales* in Paris in January 1997. He also gave speeches at the *Royal Institute for International Affairs* (RIIA) at Chatham House, London, in March 1997; the *UK Atlantic Council* in November 1997 and at the *RAND* and the *Konrad Adenauer Stiftung* in Berlin in November 1997. In addition, he visited the *Aspen Institute* in Berlin in February 1999 and the *Council on Foreign Relations* in Washington in March 1999.

Solana also spoke at the *Munich Conference on Security Policy* in 1996 and 1998. Being a prominent participant in the Munich Conference placed the Secretary General at one of the important sites for exchanging views on security and meeting a great number of other actors in the field. The Munich Conference is an annual event that brings together agents spanning the theory/practice continuum in the security field.[64]

Solana was thus present in the European field of security to a much higher degree than previous Secretaries General had been.[65] A series of joint press conferences held after Solana became High Representative to the EU with the participation of Javier Solana and Lord Robertson (and later Jaap de Hoop Scheffer) testify to the fact that Solana remained at the heart of the field and that close relationships between top figures in the three organizations (the EU, WEU and NATO) continued to be important. Alyson J.K. Bailes, then political director to the WEU, has argued that Solana's role was central for EU success:

> at Köln, the EU leaders chose the new High Representative for Common Foreign and Security Policy ('Mr. CFSP') who is meant to give greater coherence to their external policy and action, and will no doubt have a key role also in the EU/NATO interface: *a task made easier by the fact that his name is Javier Solana.*
>
> (Bailes 1999: 316, my emphasis)

George Robertson (1999–2003) continued the trend started by Javier Solana, thereby consolidating the position of NATO in the field of European security. He spoke at the French Institute for International Relations (IFRI) in November 1999; at a conference organized jointly by the *Aspen Institute* in

Berlin and the *Philip Morris Institute* in Rome in January 2000; and at the *IISS* in London in March 2000. In May the same year, he gave a speech at a conference organized by *Centro Studi di Politica Internazionale/Instituto Affari Internazionali*, Rome, spoke at the *Slovak Foreign Policy Association*, and at the *Institut de Relations Internationales et Stratégiques* (IRIS) in Paris. He continued his visits to think tanks and research centres in September 2000 with a speech to the *Marshall Center* in Garmisch Partenkirchen and at the *NATO Defense College* in Rome. In October 2000 he spoke at the *Atlantic Club* of Bulgaria, and twice at the *Centre for European Policy Studies* in Brussels in November 2000. The Centre for European Policy Studies was a very influential think tank in the EU quarter in Brussels at the time, and it is important and interesting that the NATO Secretary General was invited to speak there.

In 2001, Lord Robertson continued to create informal links to a range of different actors. He gave speeches to the *Konrad Adenauer Stiftung* and the *Federal Security Academy* in Berlin, and he spoke about the 'ESDI and Transatlantic Defence Cooperation' at *Chatham House* in London. In February, he gave a speech to the *Nobel Institute* in Oslo, and to the *University of Edinburgh* and *University of Dundee* in Scotland (title: 'NATO in the New Millennium'). He continued to give speeches at the *Royal United Services Institute* (RUSI) in London, the *American Enterprise Institute*[66] in Washington DC, at the *Warsaw University* in March, and at the *Erasmus University* in Rotterdam in April 2001. In May, he gave a speech at a conference organized by the *Centre for European Security Studies*, in June he spoke about 'European Defence: Challenges and prospects' at the *Royal Institute for International Affairs* (RIIA) at Chatham House in London as well as at the *Chicago Council on Foreign Relations*. After several speeches at various think tanks and universities over the course of the following months, the Secretary General spoke at a *Konrad Adenauer Stiftung/Friend of Europe* roundtable in Brussels in December.

In 2002, Lord Robertson continued to create and strengthen relations with think tanks and research centres. He visited *Chatham House* in London, the *NATO Defense College* in Rome, the *Potsdam Center* in Potsdam, the *Aspen Institute* in Berlin, and the *Hanns Seidel Stiftung* in Brussels. Moreover, he gave speeches at the *Charles University* in Prague, the *Istituto Affari Internazionali* in Rome, the *Royal United Services Institute* (RUSI) in London and the *Forum Europe* in Brussels. In June, he returned to the *American Enterprise Institute* and gave a speech entitled 'Tackling Terror: NATO's New Missions'. In September he spoke at *IFRI* in Paris about 'Euro-Atlantic Security One Year after 11 September'. Furthermore, he spoke at a *European Policy Centre* breakfast briefing in Brussels in November and, once again, at the *Konrad Adenauer Stiftung* in December. In 2003, the trend was maintained. His speaking engagements that year included the *Geneva Centre for Security Policy*, the *World Economic Forum* in Davos, Switzerland and at *Leeds University*.

Overall, Lord Robertson continued the work started by Javier Solana by giving speeches to think tanks and universities while attending to his more formal obligations at the NAC and various NATO summits and meetings.[67]

In sum, the practices of the NATO Secretaries General changed during the 1990s. At the beginning of the decade, the SGs were predominantly occupied with the internal workings of the alliance and creating ties to former enemy states. Few press releases were published, and the number of speeches to think tanks and research centres was limited. In 1995, when Javier Solana assumed the post as NATO SG, this changed dramatically. The number of press releases and speeches increased and the character of the actors addressed changed: think tanks, universities and research centres became part of the audience that NATO addressed and engaged with. Lord Robertson continued this trend.

## Conclusion: changing institutional practices in NATO

An important difference between the tightly knit fields which Bourdieu primarily studied and the transnational field under reconstruction in Europe exists: no equivalent to the boundary around a nation state can work as an a priori delimitation in international relations in general and with regards to the field under study here. An empirical confirmation of the existence of a field was therefore required. This was the task of the present chapter.

In general, a trend towards increasing and intensifying the number of links surrounding the alliance was present: NATO initiated links with a growing number of states through the adoption of, for example, the Partnership for Peace initiative and other dialogue programmes. Furthermore, the alliance created stronger institutional links to other European organizations – especially the WEU in the beginning of the decade and the EU towards the turn of the millennium. In addition, various think tanks and research centres were invited to comment in. *NATO Review* and participated in a number of different activities surrounding NATO. The practices of Javier Solana and Lord Robertson supported this trend.

Through these practices, NATO became increasingly entangled with other actors on the European security scene. This makes it possible to argue that there was indeed a field in the making in which NATO has struggled to remain relevant and recognized. 'Today, barely a week goes by without either the NATO Secretary General meeting with the head of another international organisation or the leader of a Partner country, or a visit to alliance Headquarters by an individual of similar standing' (Bennett 2003: 1). To that, I can add that NATO's Secretary General was also regularly in contact with think tanks and research centres, which constituted an increasingly powerful type of agency in the field of European security.

## Notes

1 This point shares similarities with Onuf's division between studies that define their subject matter in terms of *attributes* and studies that define their subject matter in terms of *relations*. The practical patterns of interaction which I intend to study will define the relevant agency through relations (Onuf 1995: 50–51).

2 Mannfred Wörner (1988–1994), Willy Claes (1994–1995), Javier Solana (1995–1999) and Lord George Robertson (1999–2003).

3 West Germany joined NATO in 1955 as a sovereign state with the right to arm. It agreed not to create a general staff. This effectively subordinated its armed forces to SACEUR (Wallander 2000: 716).

4 The possibility of inviting new members was inscribed in the Washington Treaty of April 4, 1949, Article 10: 'The Parties may, by unanimous agreement, invite any other European State in a position to further the principles of this Treaty and to contribute to the security of the North Atlantic area to accede to this Treaty'.

5 The enlargement of NATO was far from everyday business for at least two reasons: first, the very stable configuration of NATO standing opposed to the Soviet Union to the East during the Cold War made enlargement across that very border difficult. Hence the formulation: 'NATO's enlargement must be understood as only one important element of a broad European security architecture that transcends and renders obsolete the idea of *"dividing lines"* in Europe' (NATO 1995: Chapter 2, para A9). Second, the strong predictions regarding NATO's demise made enlargement a counter-intuitive strategy. In fact, the central question for NATO in the beginning of the 1990s was not enlargement, but institutional survival (Fierke and Wiener 1999) in the face of the strong doxic practice in the field as discussed earlier. In addition to the difficulties with crossing the former East-West divide and the strong doxic practice that foresaw NATO's demise, the security guarantee of the Washington Treaty prevented NATO from accepting members who did not fully live up to the criteria in the Study of Enlargement (Solana 1997: 2).

6 The *Study on Enlargement* was accepted by the NATO Council in September 1995. It concluded that enlargement should 'complement the enlargement of the EU, a parallel process which also ... contributes significantly to extending security and stability to the new democracies in the East' (cited in Forster and Wallace 2001: 114).

7 NATO was not alone in using enlargement as a strategy to 'pile up' social capital. The EU's parallel drive towards enlargement was much more specific and changed the internal structure of states to a much greater degree than the prerequisites for NATO membership did. By using the *Acquis Communautaire* to establish standards for the coming members of the EU, the EU's move in the field to accumulate social capital was potentially much stronger and ran deeper (Fierke and Wiener 1999: 722; Michalski and Wallace 1992). The EU had also been open to enlargement from the outset. Enlargement was already a 'political obligation' in the 1957 Treaty, which founded the European Community (Cecchini *et al.* 2001: 155) and had become 'normal business' since then. Fierke and Wiener demonstrate that the EU's stand on enlargement after the end of the Cold War changed from a reluctant position to a commitment to enlargement. At the beginning of the 1990s, deepening integration (closer cooperation between member states) was more popular than widening integration (inclusion of more member states) (Fierke and Wiener 1999).

8 NATO underwent major changes in its command structure during 2002–2003. Allied Command Transformation (ACT) took the place of the former SACLANT (Allied Command Atlantic) and Allied Command Operations (ACO) took the place of ACE (Allied Command Europe). They officially opened in June 2003. ACO's headquarters are placed in Mons, Belgium and is often referred to as SHAPE: Supreme Headquarters Allied Powers Europe. Further transformation took place in 2011–2012 and will be fully implemented in 2015.

9 On a concrete, day-to-day basis, there are many institutional contacts with states. Over 300 committees covering everything from political issues to improving capabilities and technical issues related to the alliance's military 'interoperability' meet regularly at every level of the committee structure – i.e. from diplomats to

ministers to heads of state and government. All committees are led by international NATO staff, thereby connecting the officials from the NATO member states with the organization staff. The principal NATO committees are the North Atlantic Council (NAC), the Defence Planning Committee (DPC), the Nuclear Planning Group (NPG) and the Military Committee. The formal contacts between member states are thus dense and varied. The meeting schedule is tight, and a long list of issues are worked with in various settings simultaneously.

10  This magnetic pull is also described and analysed by Adler and Barnett (1998a).

11  The creation of the NACC followed a decision at the London Summit in 1990 to intensify visits and diplomatic contacts with the former Warsaw Pact countries.

12  The Soviet Union actually disintegrated during the NACC's inaugural meeting. Consequently, the Soviet ambassador present was only able to speak on behalf of the Russian Federation by the end of the meeting (Bennett 2003: 1).

13  The North Atlantic Council (NAC) is the only body in NATO that derives its legitimacy directly from the Washington Treaty and is formally the most important forum in the alliance. In practice, however, most of the actual work is carried out in other committees (NATO 2001: Chapter 7).

14  The security guarantee of the Washington Treaty of 1949 (Article V) states that: 'The Parties agree that an armed attack against one or more of them in Europe or North America shall be considered an attack against them all and consequently they agree that, if such an armed attack occurs, each of them, in exercise of the right of individual or collective self-defence recognised by Article 51 of the Charter of the United Nations, will assist the Party or Parties so attacked by taking forthwith, individually and in concert with the other Parties, such action as it deems necessary, including the use of armed force, to restore and maintain the security of the North Atlantic area'.

15  Partners in Peace were not allowed to move as freely around the NATO HQ as full members. Different pass colours indicated whether a corridor/meeting room was off limits or not. But establishing offices in the NATO HQ was an important step in the direction of fostering new contacts – formal and informal alike.

16  Not only did the relationship give NATO power; the Partnership for Peace also entitled the 'active participants' in the programme to consultations if they felt threatened. Partnership for Peace members were thus de facto covered by Article Four in the Washington Treaty, which provides for consultation regarding out-of-area threats (see Brzezinski 1995: 41; Hunter 1995: 4).

17  Another programme was adopted in 1999: the Membership Action Plan (MAP). The programme prepared selected states for membership of NATO.

18  Central and Eastern European countries were targeted by a range of institutional arrangements, including 'the effort to organize hundreds of workshops and seminars, as well as formal and informal consultations targeting Central and Eastern Europeans' (Gheciu 2007: 184). The role of NATO as teacher and the CEECs as students was translated into a great number of interactions.

19  The establishment of the *Euro Atlantic Partnership Council* (EAPC) at the NATO Meeting of Foreign Ministers in Sintra, Portugal in May 1997 (EAPC 1997) constitutes another step in the process of linking non-members to NATO. It was designed to expand both the political and practical cooperation under PfP (ibid.: para. 2; see also Pouliot 2007) and replaced the NACC (NATO 2001: Chapter 2). The EAPC was tasked to provide the overarching framework for consultations 'as part of a process that will develop through practice' (EAPC 1997: para. 3). It would meet at the ambassadorial level in Brussels on a monthly basis (ibid.: para. 6) and semi-annually at both the foreign and defence minister levels (ibid.: para. 7). Additional meetings would be held as required, and meetings at the level of heads of state and government could be arranged if appropriate. All NACC members and PfP participating countries automatically became EAPC members if they so

desired, and the Partnership Council was also 'open to other OSCE participating states able and willing to accept its basic principles and to contribute to its goals' (ibid.: para. 12). The idea was for the EAPC to develop the kind of relationship with NAC that Partnership for Peace had with SHAPE (Wallander 2000: 722). The EAPC also worked as a link to other European security organizations: 'It will take full account of and complement the respective activities of the OSCE and other relevant institutions such as the European Union, the Western European Union and the Council of Europe' (EAPC 1997: Article 2). The EAPC was thus both a forum for contacts at the state and organizational levels in Europe.

20　The organization had no founding charter determining its membership, purpose and rules (OSCE 2007: 1). It began as an unofficial gathering of representatives from 35 countries across the East-West Divide towards the end of 1972 and in 1973. The representatives worked together as the Conference on Security and Co-operation in Europe (CSCE) for almost two years. In that period of time, the participants agreed on a number of military confidence- and security-building measures, and also decided to cooperate in other areas: economy, science, technology, environment, culture and humanitarian issues. The official CSCE started on July 3, 1973, and lasted for four days.

21　The question of the status of Berlin had been settled in 1971 (in the Quadripartite Agreement), and the Anti-Ballistic Missile Treaty had been signed by US President Nixon and Soviet President Brezhnev in 1972 (OSCE 2007: 2).

22　Finland offered to host the event, which led to the adoption of the *Final Recommendations of the Helsinki Consultations* (also known as the 'Blue Book') in 1973.

23　The second stage in the CSCE process started in September 1973 and lasted until July 1975. It took place in Geneva. The third stage included the first summit, which took place in Helsinki from July 30 to August 1, 1975. At the summit, 35 countries adopted the *Final Act of the Conference on Security and Co-operation in Europe* (also known as the *Helsinki Final Act*). After the Helsinki Final Act of 1975, the CSCE work was structured in four so-called 'baskets': a set of confidence- and security-building measures; cooperation on, amongst other things, trade, science, the environment, transport and technology; increased cultural and educational exchanges, dissemination of information and solution of humanitarian problems; and finally, follow up on the conference.

24　A series of meetings following up on the Helsinki Final Act sought to further implement the decisions made and to keep the momentum of the conference going. The meetings took place in Belgrade (October 4, 1977–March 8, 1978), Madrid (November 11, 1980–September 9, 1983), Vienna (November 4, 1986–January 19, 1989).

25　Towards the end of the 1980s, however, negotiations between NATO and the Warsaw Pact countries led to the conclusion of the OSCE-related *Treaty on Conventional Armed Forces in Europe (CFE)* in 1990. This testifies to the existence of informal links capable of leading to formal agreements.

26　Participating States drew up the *Charter of Paris for a New Europe*, a comprehensive compendium of common values that went beyond the Helsinki Final Act, affirming the direct relevance to security not only of the respect for human rights but also of democratic governance and a free market economy. The *Charter of Paris* and the *Treaty on Conventional Forces in Europe* were seen as formally ending the Cold War (Wallander 2000: 717).

27　Also at the 1992 Summit, participating States declared that fact-finding and *rapporteur* missions could be used as 'an instrument of conflict prevention and crisis management' and that the Committee of Senior Officials or the Consultative Committee of the Conflict Prevention Centre could decide by consensus to establish such missions. Long-term missions became one of the OSCE's most important tasks in the 1990s and remain a cornerstone of the work of the organization (OSCE 2007).

28  An international secretariat had been decided on in 1991 and was set up in Copenhagen the following year.

29  The Dayton Accords refer to the peace agreement reached at Wright-Patterson Air Force Base near Dayton, Ohio in November 1995, and formally signed in Paris on December 14, 1995. These accords brought an end to the three and a half-year-long war in Bosnia, one of the armed conflicts in the former Socialist Federative Republic of Yugoslavia.

30  A NATO 'activation order' of October 30, 1998, officially launched a verification mission (Operation Eagle Eye) in Kosovo to observe compliance with UN resolutions. The mission was coordinated with the OSCE. In addition to the aerial surveillance under Operation Eagle Eye, the NATO support for OSCE also included a special military task force (led by France) to be deployed in the former Republic of Macedonia. This task force was designed to rescue members of the verification mission if renewed conflict should put them at risk (Sloan 2005: 103).

31  The mission ceased after the OSCE monitors withdrew as a result of non-compliance by the Yugoslav government, who continued to build up their forces. In March 1999, NATO commenced its precision bombing to reach a solution to the Kosovo situation. In the words of the OSCE official handbook, the withdrawal of the Kosovo Verification Mission signalled an end to the wishes for a strong, unitary role for the OSCE in European security: 'its abortion, however, clearly demonstrated that the Organization was not to play the role of exclusive guarantor of European security that some may have envisaged at the Paris Summit in 1990' (OSCE 2007: 9). The sense of urgency that fired participating states at the Paris Summit in 1990 had dissipated by the time the decade drew to a close.

32  The WEU was created by the Treaty on Economic, Social and Cultural Collaboration and Collective Self-Defence signed at Brussels on March 17, 1948 (Treaty of Brussels 1948). A Protocol signed in Paris on October 23, 1954, modified and completed the Treaty, known as 'The Modified Brussels Treaty' (WEU 1954). The original treaty was signed by Belgium, France, Luxembourg, the Netherlands, and the United Kingdom, and its main feature was a commitment to mutual defence. In December 1950, the Brussels Treaty powers decided to merge their military organization into NATO, which had become the central element in the West European and North Atlantic security system after the signing of the Washington Treaty in 1949.

33  CJTF is 'a flexible, deployable, multinational, multiservice HQ using a building block approach. The build-up of the CJTF HQ would take place by selecting a nucleus (a permanent core staff element) from the parent HQ and augmenting it with modules (resources provided by other NATO or national sources) and individuals (personnel). Modular and individual augmentation would take place initially from within the Alliance's military structure before seeking additional augmentation from nations' (da Silva 1998). It was developed because NATO saw a need to respond to 'out-of-area' conflicts (Wallander 2000), but the CJFT concept would also later become a central feature in the debates about European autonomy in the Alliance (Terriff 2003).

34  In 2000 the publication *WEU today* divided the 28 WEU countries into four groups of membership: member states, associate members, observers and associate partners. The ten member states of the WEU were Belgium, France, Germany, Greece, Italy, Luxembourg, Netherlands, Portugal, Spain and the United Kingdom. The six associate members, who were also members of NATO, included the Czech Republic, Hungary, Iceland, Norway, Poland and Turkey. The five observers, who were also EU members, were Austria, Finland, Ireland and Sweden. In addition, Denmark had observer status, even though the country was member of

both NATO and the EU (because of a Danish opt-out in the EU on defence issues). The seven WEU associate partners, all of whom had signed a *Europe Agreement* with the EU, were Bulgaria, Estonia, Latvia, Lithuania, Romania, Slovakia and Slovenia. They received associate membership in 1994.

35 In 1997, the newly elected Blair government vetoed a merger of the EU and the WEU. The veto was motivated by the feeling that such a merger would weaken NATO (Howorth and Keeler 2003: 9). This effectively sidetracked the WEU, and the institutional battles became a matter of direct moves between the EU and NATO. The buffer role which the WEU had played during the first half of the 1990s, attempting to reconcile French Europeanism and British Atlanticism, was over. 'By 1997, WEU was perceived by many key analysts as part of (if not the) problem rather than as part of (if not the) solution' (Howorth and Keeler 2003: 10). More than three years passed before the organization was closed down, but the WEU was effectively stripped of its political clout after the Blair veto.

36 The EU decided at the Cologne European Council in 1999 to absorb the WEU. A number of options were considered, such as placing the WEU in a newly created Fourth Pillar or placing the WEU under the aegis of the EU Council, coordinated with the Common Foreign and Security Policy (CFSP) of the EU. The outcome was a decision to insert (not integrate) the WEU into the EU by joining it with the CFSP (Cornish and Edwards 2001). Hence, the parallel appointments of Javier Solana as High Representative for the CFSP, Secretary General of the EU Council,and Secretary General of the WEU. Hereafter, the direct contacts between the EU and NATO took over the contacts that had existed between the WEU and NATO in the 1990s.

37 In 1990, the EU members were Belgium, Germany, France, Italy, Luxembourg, the Netherlands, Denmark, United Kingdom, Ireland, Greece, Portugal and Spain. Austria, Finland and Sweden became members in 1995. In June 1993, the EU promised membership to the so-called Visegrad states (Poland, Hungary, Slovakia and the Czech Republic), but no date was set; they were already associate members of the WEU (MccGwire 1998: 24, footnote 4). In 2004, the Czech Republic, Estonia, Cyprus, Latvia, Lithuania, Hungary, Malta, Poland, Slovenia and Slovakia became members. Bulgaria and Romania joined the European Union in 2007.

38 Of course, the EU cannot be said to have spoken with a single voice on security issues throughout the 1990s. The documents included below, however, represent a consensus among the EU members. As such, a dialogue between a EU consensus and NATO documents can be found.

39 The process following the Berlin ministerial meeting is often referred to as Berlin+. See also Chapter 6.

40 The Americans were not slow to point out that the Europeans had significantly failed in the Balkans (White 2001: 2).

41 Even though the idea had been discussed on the fringes of the informal European summit in Pörtschach (Cornish and Edwards 2001: 588).

42 The Petersberg Tasks had recently been incorporated into the 1997 Amsterdam Treaty amending the Treaty of the European Union (Article 17).

43 At roughly the same time that the EU member states committed themselves to the Headline Goal, NATO members signed the Defence Capabilities Initiative (DCI), the alliance's programme to raise its military capabilities in order to meet the challenges of the 21st century. The two organizations thus appeared to dialogue through initiatives and declarations throughout the 1990s.

44 Important issues remained unsolved, however. Most importantly, NATO wanted to ensure the fullest possible involvement of non-EU European Allies (among these, most notably Turkey) in EU-led crisis management operations (building on existing consultation arrangements with the WEU) (EV 1999; see also Cornish and Edwards 2001: 592).

45 The Feira European Council Meeting in June 2000 agreed to establish inclusive structures that allowed for routine regular dialogue between NATO and the EU, which would 'intensify during a pre-operational phase, developing into an ad hoc committee for contributors when operations began' (Cornish and Edwards 2001: 590).

46 The EUMS received its tasks from the EU Military Committee (EUMC), which is the highest military body within the Council. It was composed of the Chiefs of Defence of the Member States, who were regularly represented by their permanent military representatives to NATO. The EUMC provided the permanent Political and Security Committee (PSC) with advice and recommendations on all military matters within the EU. Its main functions are to keep track of the international situation and help define policies within the Common Foreign and Security Policy (CFSP), including the ESDP. It works to prepare a coherent EU response to a crisis and exercises its political control and strategic direction. The Political and Security Committee is often called COPSI, which is the French acronym for the committee (Lachowski 2002).

47 This finding is supported by Forster and Wallace's analysis of the EU–NATO relationship after the September 11, 2001 attacks on New York and Washington:

> The symbolism of the special meeting of the NATO council on 12 September 2001 was striking. It was attended by the EU 'High Representative' for common foreign and security policy, Javier Solana, the EU Commissioner for External Relations, Chris Patten, and the President of the European Commission, Romano Prodi, sitting alongside ministers from the member states as they expressed their solidarity with the United States in the wake of the terrorist attack organised from outside the NATO area.
>
> (Forster and Wallace 2001: 119)

48 Especially after the change in the French position towards the inclusion of the alliance in EU security matters in April 2000 boosted cooperation: Lionel Jospin's government suggested holding meetings between EU and NATO officials to discuss key issues for the establishment of the crisis management capability (EV 2000b). In a joint British-French paper, four joint committees were proposed: joint security agreement, military capabilities, EU access to NATO equipment, and permanent arrangements for the two bodies (EV 2000a).

49 The operation was completed in December 2003.

50 The list of publications indicates this (NATO 2007g). It is not until 2004 that one of the publications is listed as 'Human and Societal Dynamics'.

51 As of the early 1990s, the Programme gradually became opened up to participation from non-NATO countries, thus providing a platform for cooperation between research institutes in the partnership countries and NATO. In 1999 it was almost completely converted to provide support for collaboration between scientists in NATO countries and those in the Partner countries or countries participating in the Mediterranean Dialogue.

52 A number of fellowships were also granted through the Partnership for Peace programme. This practice was changed from 2004 when reintegration grants substituted for the fellowships. The idea was to persuade researchers from partnership countries to return to their home countries and assist in strengthening ties with the Alliance (Pedrazzini 2004).

53 Concretely, the SPS programme has included activities funded directly by NATO, as well as nationally funded SPS activities. The research is divided into four sub-categories or panels: the chemistry/physics/biology (CPB) panel, the environmental security (ES) panel, the human and societal dynamics (HSD) panel, and the information and communications security (ICS) panel. The perspective of the

NATO science programme thus includes more than technical and natural sciences: NATO is also interested in the social dynamics of a society. However, it was not until after 2004 that the programme began publishing under a social science heading 'Human and Societal Dynamics' (NATO 2007g). The programme arranges Advanced Training Courses (ATC) (designed to enable specialists in NATO countries to share their knowledge with trainees from Partner and Mediterranean Dialogue countries), Advanced Research Workshops (ARW) (working meetings of up to four days where scientists informally discuss frontline issues), Advanced Study Institutes (ASI) (high-level tutorial courses of two weeks' duration where a subject is treated in depth by lecturers of international standing), and Advanced Networking Workshops (ANW). The Advanced Networking Workshops are either policy workshops or training courses. Their aim is to promote coordination during development of research networks (NATO 2007e) for a description of all of the types of activities and an activities calendar. The programme thus actively supports the creation of networks between think tanks and research centres in support of the NATO project and has done so for a number of years.

54　Former United States Secretary of Defense William Cohen and his German counterpart, former Minister of Defence Volker Ruehe, proposed the formation of the Consortium as jointly sponsored during the June 12, 1998 meeting of the Defence Ministers of the Euro-Atlantic Partnership Council (EAPC 1998).

55　The formal military point of contact for the Consortium was the NATO Defense College, which was actively involved in six out of ten working groups. The NATO Defense College was founded in 1951 in order to train individuals who were going to serve in key capacities in the Alliance (NDC 2011). The College has actively served as an informal meeting ground for new partners and countries with which NATO does not have any formal relations.

56　The programme appears to have been quite successful: Gheciu holds that in 2007 more than 260 defence academies, institutes, think tanks, universities and research centres located in allied countries and partner states forming part of the PfP consortium took part. Most of the institutions that are part of the Consortium offer a variety of courses targeting military personnel and civilian defence experts at various levels of seniority (Gheciu 2007: 187) and thus help substantiate the networks created under the PfP consortium.

57　*NATO Review*has existed in a print version since 1953 but has also been available on the internet since the 1990s.

58　The CFR HQ is in New York, but the think tank also has a Washington office.

59　The Project for a New American Century was a neoconservative, American think tank established in the spring of 1997. Robert Kagan was one of its directors. The think tank was closed in 2006.

60　Hendrickson argues that the Secretaries General in the 1990s and in the new millennium have had more room for manoeuvre in comparison to Cold War Secretaries General, who were often not seen as important as the SACEUR (Supreme Allied Commander Europe) (Hendrickson 2006).

61　Sergio Balanzino became acting Secretary General of NATO twice in the 1990s. First, when Manfred Wörner resigned in 1994 whilst in the last stages of cancer , and second in 1995, when Willy Claes had to step down after facing corruption charges. Because of the very short time Sergio Balanzino served as Secretary General, I have chosen not to include him in this chapter.

62　It is possible that the very few speeches Wörner made in 1994 (a total of four speeches) was a result of his health problems, which ultimately resulted in his resignation in September 1994. The picture is clear, however: in the beginning of the 1990s, the strategy had not yet turned towards the multitude of actors NATO addressed by the end of the 1990s.

63  He was charged with corruption in Belgium (dating back to the time when he was member of the Belgian government) and chose to resign.

64  Especially after its revival in the beginning of the 1990s, the Munich Conference was central in European security. As many will recall, the Iraq crisis in 2003 spurred very dramatic reactions at the conference in 2003: 'Excuse me, I am not convinced', German Foreign Minister Joschka Fischer began his talk at the conference concerning the 'evidence' of weapons of mass destruction in Iraq (Spoerle-Strohmenger 2003: 2).

65  Solana also directly addressed the European Parliament and the WEU assembly (once in 1996, twice in 1997). In 1998, he embarked on an Eastern European tour that included speeches to the Czech, Hungarian and Polish Parliaments (these countries were the first to enter NATO in the 1999 enlargements). The tour testifies to a wish to entangle the Eastern European countries in the web surrounding NATO through social practices: meetings, speeches and appearances in the capitals of former enemy countries. Trips to Slovenia and the Former Republic of Macedonia in the mid-1990s add to the same picture.

66  The American Enterprise Institute (AEI) became more widely known when George W. Bush was elected President of the United States. More than 20 AEI alumni and visiting scholars and fellows served in a Bush Administration policy post or on one of the many government panels and commissions (Bush 2003). The AEI supported the neoconservative trend in American foreign policy under Bush.

67  In addition to using his public appearances to create informal links with think tanks and research centres, Lord Robertson also addressed the OSCE Summit in November 1999 and the OSCE Permanent Council in November 2000 and November 2003. He spoke at the European Parliament Conference in Brussels in February 2002 under the heading 'A Global Dimension for a Renewed Transatlantic Partnership', and spoke at the important locus for European security: the Munich Conference on Security Policy in February 2001, 2002 and 2003.

# 6  Doxic battles in European security

## The mobilization and redefinition of capital

Doxic battles are basic struggles determining what is valued in the field and what is considered worthless. They are *world-making* battles in the sense that the agents participating in the battles strive to gain the power to impose the legitimate version of the social world and its divisions (Swartz 1997: 89). They concern the unspoken, common knowledge constituting social reality and exercise a misrecognized structural power on the practices in a field (Bourdieu 1977; Ashley 1989: 259). Doxic battles thus concern the mobilization of different types of capital in the quest for influence on doxic understandings and potentially a prominent position in the hierarchy in the field.

This chapter is organized around the three main types of capital defined and discussed in Chapter 4: scientific capital, military capital and social capital. NATO made several moves that included – and helped redefine – these types of capital over the 1990s.

The analysis reveals how the balance between and the value of the types of capital shifted over the course of the 1990s. Scientific capital was explicitly ridiculed towards the end of the 1990s – though only in a certain form – and remained in a central position for backing up strategies and moves in the field. Economic capital entered the game – but as a new kind of military capital. It was not a profit-maximising and money-accumulating type of capital, as in Bourdieu's initial definition of the term: economic integration became a process-oriented type of security strategy, cast as military capital primarily through moves of the EU. This changed the way security could be approached. The London-based think tank *Centre for European Reform* (CER) supported this shift in the meaning of security and military capital, arguing that 'Europe will run the 21st century' (Leonard 2005), where 'Europe' means the EU. This left NATO in an awkward position as the agent in the field with the highest amount of classical, military capital at its disposal – a type of capital that no longer carried the value it held during the Cold War. In addition to these moves and changes in the field, the question of 'who represents whom' also became an important power struggle in the field – a struggle tied to the amount of social capital an agent had accumulated and could mobilize. The struggle for the definition of European autonomy (what I refer to as the ESDI/CFSP/ESDP letter game), the activation of

Article V of the Washington Treaty following 9/11, and the presentation of the European Security Strategy were all major moves in the field tied to the accumulation of social capital.

The most important change in the value of capital was the decreasing value of military capital coupled with a devaluation of the strong scientific explanation of the balance of power that had guided the period preceding the demise of the Soviet Union and bipolarity. NATO struggled to keep the definitions of security tied to the traditional military instrument but failed to do so: the military instrument became a tool in crisis management and humanitarian conflicts to which NATO had to adjust.

## Scientific capital

Bourdieu defined scientific capital as 'cultural or informational capital, accumulated in the form of statistics, for example, and also in the form of instruments of knowledge endowed with universal validity' (Bourdieu 2005: 12). As argued in Chapter 4, scientific capital is a particular kind of symbolic capital based on knowledge and recognition. It is a power which functions as a form of credit tied to a specific kind of training and to belonging to a field (Bourdieu 2004: 34). Scientific capital thus concerns scientific knowledge and the recognition vested in actors capable of speaking on behalf of scientific knowledge.

In the context of doxic battles, scientific capital takes on a special meaning. Scientific statements, developed in Security Studies but imported into the field of European security by a variety of actors, can be mobilized by actors who themselves are actually outside or on the fringes of the scientific field. Because the relevant agency in the field shares common ground and because the social sciences are only semi-autonomous (see Chapter 4), scientific statements can be mobilized in the quest for recognition in the field by a variety of actors: NATO, the EU, think tanks and other agents can play the 'scientific card' in the doxic battles in the field of European security. Scientific capital was, hence, mobilized by diverse actors in the field in search of a place in the hierarchy.

The traditional concept of security, the broad concept of security, and the Democratic Peace thesis (to which I turn below) were all established in the scientific field through practices of objectivation before being imported into NATO practice and the emerging field of European security. Scientific capital was therefore not *produced* by the variety of actors that *mobilzsed* it (Büger and Villumsen 2007; Berling 2011). Nevertheless, the scientific capital mobilized still had to have a backing in the scientific field in order to have value in the European field of security. The potential power of scientific capital rested on the impartial and objective status of knowledge production in the scientific field of IR/Security Studies and on a resonance with the common ground shared by the relevant agency. Solana's insistence that NATO 'had proven theory wrong' seemed to challenge this trend, but his argument actually also rested on a scientific (anti)fact in the scientific field: Social Constructivism.

Nonetheless, the research environments in the field made few explicit moves. The special status of science as ideally 'objective' and disconnected from practice/reality possibly offer one explanation as to why the scientific environments did not make explicit moves in the field. If they engaged in the struggles openly, they would encounter problems upholding their integrity. In Bourdieu's terms, they would lose the veil of 'disinterestedness', which is a pivotal value in the scientific field.

In the following, I shall outline six examples of how the 'instruments of knowledge' which guided the understanding of security in Europe were put into play by relevant agency and how this constituted doxic battles in the field. First, I address the widening of the concept of security in NATO documents early in the 1990s and how this development was mirrored in security research by the reissuing of Barry Buzan's seminal work *People, States and Fear* (Buzan 1991 [1983]). Second, I analyse NATO's call for 'prudence' in the form of sticking to conventional wisdom about the meaning of security and how the strategic environment worked, as well as how this was turned down by security research in the field. Third, I address the 'causal law in policy' between security and peace – the Democratic Peace thesis – and how NATO used this item of scientific knowledge in its quest for institutional and political change. Fourth, I turn to the identification of NATO as a specific culture-as-civilization, opposed to Islamic fundamentalism, which drew inspiration from Huntington's clash of civilizations (Huntington 1993). Fifth, I turn to a different variant of civilization understood as a civilizing process, which flourished in the European security field, especially in discussion about the deteriorating situation in the Balkans in the mid- and late 1990s, and sixth, I address the battle over defining how practice could change the premises for theoretical explanations through an analysis of the quote that started this investigation in the first place: Solana's claim that practice had proven theory wrong by upholding a good relationship with Russia while at the same time proceeding with the Eastern enlargement of the alliance.

## Widening the concept of security, 1990

The debate and struggles for recognition in the field in the beginning of the 1990s can best be described as taking place 'on a conceptual building site' (Cornish 1996: 752). The questions following the demise of the Soviet Union were 'either impossibly abstract or only barely concrete: What did 'defence' and 'security' mean without the antagonism of the Cold War? (ibid.: 751). NATO struggled to respond to these questions. The predictions regarding the demise of NATO were strong and sustained in the aftermath of the Cold War due to a strong and recognized type of common sense that guided the doxic practice in the field. One of the first attempts to 'prove theory wrong' centred on a reformulation of the concept of security and thus on an attempt to redefine the recognized scientific capital.

As early as 1990, NATO's concept of security started to change. In Turnberry in June 1990, a broadening of the concept of security can be found in the conclusions of the Council: 'Although the prevention of war will always remain our fundamental task, the changing European environment now requires of us a *broader approach to security* based as much on constructive peacebuilding as on peace-keeping' (NAC 1990a: para. 20, my emphasis). In the Council meeting that followed, this was made more explicit; the broad concept of security became a central feature in NATO's vision of the world. Security came to mean much more than military security. The new concept of security was meant to uphold stability through 'not only traditional security aspects, but also economic, social, environmental and other factors' (NAC 1990a: para. 8).

In the ears of a security analyst, this list sounds rather familiar. Barry Buzan  listed the same dimensions of security in *People, States and Fear*, which soon became a Security Studies classic (Buzan 1991 [1983]: 116–134; Buzan and Hansen 2009; Huysmans 2006). Research on security in Europe had long argued for a new, widened concept of security, as well as emphasizing the political process tied to security to an extent where this understanding had moved centre stage. The largely American military version of the concept of security was therefore losing centrality in Europe. Envisioning security as a political process along the axes of understanding/misunderstanding was borrowed from the peace research agenda and soon translated into a strong Constructivist trend in European Security Studies (Guzzini 2004: 43). Huysmans (2006: 19) argues that Buzan's *People, States and Fear* became a classic because of institutional politics in an environment of security research that had taken a blow after the end of the Cold War:[1]

> The hierarchy of threats in the security field broke down thereby opening the field for a redefinition of core security concerns. With it the narrative through which the field of security experts reproduced its identity broke down. The bipolar setting offered the field a background history and implicit understanding of its expertise and what it contributed to this history. After the dramatic transformation in the main empirical references of this narrative – e.g. the Soviet Union as a superpower – it could not be reproduced in an unproblematic, quasi-ritualistic way.
>
> (Huysmans 2006: 17)

This development was reflected in NATO practice. The alliance drew heavily on the scientific capital of the broad concept of security in its attempt to redefine and adjust the valued type of scientific capital in the field. One might be tempted to say that NATO was doing what Buzan had previously attempted to build on the realist tradition but include more aspects of importance to security in order to make the framework fit reality.

It is interesting to note that NATO actually turned the broad concept of security on its head by making a move involving the broad concept of security. Because of its roots in peace research, the concept was formulated as a critique of the narrow, military concept, and as an attempt to demilitarize (or 'desecuritize' as it later came to be termed in the Copenhagen school) security issues. By including all of the dimensions of the broad concept of security in its documents, NATO instead securitized everything from the economy to the environment. The move was meant to manoeuvre NATO into a position of relevance on all aspects: if the alliance had stuck to a purely military argumentation and understanding of security, its role in European security would have been negligible and, as a consequence, it would have been confined to the margins of the field. According to Huysmans, actors in the field of security knowledge and security institutions faced the problematique that 'widening their interests was a necessity if they wanted to survive as security experts or institutions in the new political climate' (Huysmans 2006: 19).

NATO's adoption of the list of security threats from the new classic in the field of European security thus signified an important shift in the field of European security. NATO was not merely designating new threats to be countered; it was actually fighting for its position as an important actor in the definition game of security. Without this move, NATO would indeed have become the anachronism realists would have it be. A key to countering this development lay in scientific capital: 'When established knowledge patterns are challenged by means of shifting the meaning of one of its defining concepts both an identity and status problem occur' (ibid.: 21). NATO's position and status as the holder of authority over defining European security was at stake.

The move towards widening the concept of security was supported by Security Studies – especially in Europe (Guzzini and Jung 2004). Consequently, NATO also influenced what would count as legitimate knowledge and on what grounds expert status could be attributed to other actors in the field in the years to come. In that sense, NATO was also contributing to changing the rules of the game for other types of agency in the field. This move would later leave NATO in a weaker position, as it became clear that the instruments to achieve security under the broad concept of security were not exclusively (if at all) at NATO's disposal. For example, the EU seemed stronger when security was broadly defined. I return to this later.

### Prudence in the Strategic Concept, 1991

The broadening of the security concept was not the only trend prevalent in the early 1990s NATO documents and in the moves made by the alliance to retain a central position in the field of European security. For some time, there was a tendency to retain the well-known and well-established conventional knowledge from Strategic Studies. This tendency also thrived in academic circles (Buzan and Hansen 2009: Chapter 7). The debate was heated, and the defenders of the traditional, military concept of security held strongly that '[i]ndeed, given the cost of military forces and the risks of modern war, it would be irresponsible for the scholarly community to ignore the central questions that form the heart of the security studies field' (Walt 1991: 213; see also Huysmans 2006).

In NATO's Strategic Concept from 1991, scientific capital was at play in a version reflecting Walt's call for responsibility. Old wisdom was one of the anchoring points for NATO and was defined by the strategic studies version of the world from before the fall of the Berlin Wall (Walt 1987; Waltz 1979). Three important factors from that perspective had influenced NATO in its practices during the Cold War: first, the aggressive intentions of the opponent; second, the relative accumulation of military capabilities; and third, strategic balancing as a strategy for handling the combination of aggressive intentions and military capability. The first factor had fallen out of the equation when the Soviet Union and Warsaw Pact dissolved. This led NATO to an increased focus on military capability and strategic balancing. The strategic balance remained an important factor in NAC declarations until the middle of the 1990s: 'Even in a non-adversarial relationship, prudence requires NATO to counterbalance the Soviet Union's military capabilities' (NAC 1990a: para. 4). In support of this, an analyst held that NATO "preserves the strategic balance in Europe by neutralising the residual threat posed by Russian military power' (Duffield 1994: 767–768). In other words, the military capabilities of the former enemy needed to be balanced, even in a situation in which the aggressive intentions were no longer dominant. The narrow, realist, military concept of security therefore tied the 'residual threat' of military capabilities to the strategy of strategic balancing. It had worked for decades, and NATO used it by default (almost ritualistically, in the words of Huysmans)  for some years following the end of bipolarity (Huysmans 2006). The conclusions from Copenhagen in 1991 and the Strategic Concept from 1991 state that the guiding strategy of the alliance would be to 'preserve the strategic balance within Europe' (NAC 1991; NATO 1991: para. 20, IV) and work for 'balanced reductions' of arms. NATO actively denied having an enemy (NAC 1990a: para. 2 and 4; for discussion, see Behnke 2013: 76–81) but acted as though the enemy still existed.[2] The spatial demarcation line from the past created a sense of continuity and purpose for the alliance. And because the link between military capital and scientific capital had previously placed NATO at the top of the hierarchy in the field, NATO felt a habitual interest in keeping security narrowly defined and within the boundaries of what a military alliance could (traditionally) deal with. This corresponds to Huysmans' point about the utterance of security language:

> The speech act of security draws upon a historically constituted and socially institutionalized set of meanings. Like the grammar of language, it evolves over time but it cannot be changed at random. To retain the capacity to generate meaningful speech, the constellation has to retain some continuity in how it renders security meanings.
>
> (Huysmans 2006: 25)[3]

In the case of NATO after the Cold War, historically acquired knowledge structured the practices, even in a situation of fundamental change. In this case, NATO had an entire social science tradition – strategic studies – to back it up. The mobilization of a doxic practice in the form of a specific, strategic studies version of scientific capital, was thus to be expected.[4] The stable geography of the Cold War was dissolving, but the military dimension of security and the plot of strategic balancing remained as attempts to maintain the authority over the definition of what security was in Europe. But could the story hold? It would later become important that NATO stopped conceiving of the enemy in geographical terms and started seeing only a material capability as its enemy. This paved the way for successive NATO enlargements which crossed the geographical borders of the former division between 'East" and "West'. At this point in time, however, it was premature to talk about enlargement, as it was still believed that a new enemy could rise and fill the empty space left by the Warsaw Pact and Soviet Union.

These two moves – widening and retaining the Cold War concept of security – ran parallel to one another and testify to an alliance in crisis. As argued, the doxic practice that tied the scientific capital of Strategic Studies together with military capital – and which seemed to spell the doom of NATO – was Janus-faced. On the one hand, the technological and institutional history of NATO spurred interest in keeping security confined to the definition prevailing in the Cold War. On the other hand, however, NATO was hit just as hard as security research by the inadequacy of the narrow definition of security (see above and Huysmans 2006): in order to stay in the game after the Cold War, NATO needed a new narrative – a new definition of what constitutes alliances, and a new story of what the military instrument could be used for. This became evident as early as the Turnberry meeting in 1990 (NAC 1990a). NATO was caught between a rock and a hard place.

Both types of scientific capital could be backed by research in Security Studies. Which type was to become most valued was not clear at the time. The other relevant agency in the field of European security had not yet risen to challenge the pivotal role of NATO; however, this would soon change. The WEU and EU made important moves in the field early in the 1990s, thereby challenging the position of NATO. The WEU formulated the 'Petersberg Tasks', and the EU adopted several new documents designating a more active security role for the organisation. Both organizations built on a broad concept of security and a different reading of the strategic environment: strategic balancing was not the only way to practice security. This helped tip the balance in the direction of the broad concept of security and towards a more constructivist understanding of practices in the emerging field of European security.

For NATO, the solution became a focus on the link between democracy and security that gained ground in the wider field of Western security from the end of the 1980s and became the basis of US foreign policy and military strategy under the Clinton Administration (see Büger and Villumsen 2007). According to Williams:

> the power and persistence of NATO in the post-Cold War period derived in considerable part from the ability to maintain is military dimension

while at the same time combining that dimension with a powerful cultural and political narrative that overcame the challenges faced by a purely military representation of the alliance.

(Williams 2007: 91)

The Democratic Peace Thesis and Constructivist thinking helped spur that development, because 'the democratic peace is not just a theory: it was and is also part of the articulation of a field of security where culture and identity are key dimensions of power' (Williams 2007: 5).

### Democracy, peace and security, 1994

According to Williams:

the democratic peace can be viewed as one element within a broad strategy of cultural power during the period of its ascendance, as part of a process whereby the West appropriated the claim to represent democratic values, and asserted its own inherent peacefulness. In short, the idea of the democratic peace allowed the military conflict of the Cold War to be transformed into a cultural struggle, thus contributing to the exercise of specific strategies and forms of cultural power.

(Williams 2007: 40–41)

I agree. The Democratic Peace Thesis was not merely a theory; it became mobilized in a power struggle in the field, thus forming part of the important changes in the hierarchy in the field.[5]

The introduction of democracy as the most viable means for creating security and stability for NATO came gradually during the 1990s (Büger and Villumsen 2007).[6] The link between *peace* and democracy had been established as something close to a 'scientific law' (Levy 1988: 622) and what might 'well be a law of nature' (Bueno de Mesquita 2002: 5), especially in the debate in the American social sciences.[7] It was considered to be possibly the first causal law in the social sciences.[8] In the 1990s, the link was translated into a link between *security* and democracy in both the Clinton administration and NATO alike. The Democratic Peace thesis was thereby securitized (Büger and Villumsen 2007; see also Geis *et al.* 2006). The thesis became so well-known in the wider public that many hail it as being the first successful knowledge transfer from science to policy (Lepgold and Nincic 2002; Siverson 2000; Kruzel 1994; for discussion, see Williams 2001; Grayson 2003). Instead of accepting this version of how the democratic peace 'travelled' to the field of practice, however, another – Bourdieusian – reading is possible. Pouliot contends that a Bourdieusian analysis 'paves the way for an innovative understanding of international peace as a socially misrecognised form of domination, a welcome alternative to prevalent liberal views' (Pouliot 2004: 16). The DP [democratic peace] thesis was mobilized as a power strategy:

'Peace is not procedural; it is political. As unpleasant as it may seem, there exists power politics of peace just like there is for war; the only real difference being that in the former case, it is misrecognisable' (ibid.: 17).[9]

One of NATO's most well-known initiatives in the 1990s – the Eastern Enlargement – was built on the link between security and democracy. Assistant Secretary General Admiral Norman Ray held that 'NATO enlargement should ... be seen in the context of a strategy that has as its objective the building of a *peaceful*, undivided and *democratic* Europe' (Ray 1997: 2, my emphasis). The plans to enlarge the alliance exercised a subtle kind of power on the surrounding states and led them in the direction of becoming more democratic; of solving ethnic problems within the states: 'There appears to be a broad consensus that the basic criteria for membership include a stable democratic system' (Brzezinski 1995: 32). NATO thus used enlargement to shape the new democracies in the East in NATO's image. 'NATO's doors will remain open .... The incentive, therefore, remains for aspiring members to continue down the road of democracy and economic reform' (Solana 1997: 3). Nowhere in the criteria, set up primarily in the *Study on Enlargement* (1995), was there any detailed discussion of military or strategic criteria as a premise for NATO membership. 'NATO membership criteria would ... be a fundamentally political, and institutional function' (Kay 1998: 487). The premise for enlargement was therefore not formulated on traditional, military power terms. This constituted a new type of power practice in the field:

> The ability to present actions as arising not from the pursuit of the interests of power or victorious, but as obligations derived from imperatives, *or from social scientific knowledge of the links between peace and democracy*, provided important forms of power and strategy in the transformation of European security.
>
> (Williams 2007: 43, my emphasis)

NATO used the strong standing of the Democratic Peace Thesis as a means to seek to uphold a powerful position in the field.[10]

The link between peace and democracy was stated as a *fundamental value* in NATO from the beginning of the 1990s: '*peace through democracy* [is a] shared value  fundamental to the Partnership' (NATO 1994a: 1, my emphasis). But as early as the Turnberry Communiqué (1990), the link between democracy, peace and security was present. 'Europe is entering a new era. The countries of Central and Eastern Europe are taking decisive steps to establish *democratic institutions*' (NAC 1990a: para. 1, my emphasis). This process of 'becoming democratic' was seen as an important element in the future security and stability in Europe (ibid.: para. 9). In the London declaration from July that year, the alliance vowed to 'support ... security and stability with the strength of our shared *faith in democracy*' (NAC 1990b: para. 2, my emphasis). Promoting democracy in NATO's neighbouring states thus came to be discursively tied to security, stability and peace (Behnke 2013: 76–77).

With the introduction of a link between democracy and security, NATO gained new momentum in the struggle to define security in Europe. Successfully placing the alliance in a central position in support of this 'scientifically supported' link would enable NATO to move into an authoritative position for speaking legitimately about security in Europe after bipolarity. The fundamental value – and later fact – of linking peace, security and democracy was further translated into practical cooperation in the military alliance; first, through the creation of the North Atlantic Cooperation Council in 1991, and later through 'the quantum leap' (NATO 2002b: 3), which the creation of the Partnership for Peace (PfP) constituted for the alliance. This cooperation was outlined in practice: the NAC planned 'to offer permanent facilities at NATO Headquarters for personnel from NACC countries and other Partnership for Peace participants in order to improve our working relationships and facilitate closer cooperation' and to 'propose, within the Partnership framework, peacekeeping field exercises beginning in 1994' (NATO 1994b: 2).[11] The Partnership for Peace programme was thus a strategy designed to retain a central position in the field by mobilizing 'causal laws' in the social sciences. The decisions to intervene in the Bosnian war in 1994/1995 and later the Kosovo Crisis in early 1999 made this clear. NATO was ready to apply what the Copenhagen School of Security Studies would call *emergency measures* (Buzan *et al.* 1998) in the quest for civilized behaviour in the periphery of the cooperative security landscape of democracies (see Zizek 2004). This underlines the importance of the Democratic Peace scientific capital for the future purpose and role of NATO. The link between democracy and security/peace provided what the narrow military concept of security had not been able to: a future role in European security for NATO.

Towards the end of the 1990s, the link was no longer formulated as a value, instead it assumed a more solid character as a fact of the nature of democracy: 'Military forces which are accountable to a democratic civilian government are *much less likely* to be used for purposes that run counter to peace and stability' (NATO 1998: 2, my emphasis). The formulation 'much less likely' has the sound of the statistical conclusions drawn by democratic peace theorists (see for example Ray and Russett 1996).

NATO's narrative underwent profound changes. Not only had NATO securitized democracy, the alliance also reshaped its understanding of space on this basis: NATO was not fighting Serbia *per se,* but rather, the lack of democracy in the country. Williams and Neumann argue that: 'it is the absence of specific, democratic cultural and political institutions that comes to define the perception of security' (Williams and Neumann 2000: 369–70; see also Rasmussen 2003).

### Islamic fundamentalism as the new threat, 1995

In the mid-1990s, NATO was still struggling to find a new purpose in the European security landscape. One of the more controversial attempts to find new purpose came through the attempt to fill the void left by the Soviet Union with a new enemy: that of Islamic fundamentalism. During the Cold War, NATO had become accustomed to a world split between it and a massive, material and political counterpart. This world had been understood through the tight fit between scientific and military capital, but with the disappearance of the Soviet Union, NATO still held on to balancing the military capabilities of the former enemy for some time.

When then Secretary General Willy Claes voiced his views in 1995 about the greatest threat in the future, he was still thinking in terms of a world split in two, organized by the presence of military capabilities and working according to strategic balancing; NATO was defined by its counterpart. As mentioned in Chapter 3, Claes is quoted for having stated: 'Muslim fundamentalism is at least as dangerous as Communism once was ... It represents terrorism, religious fanaticism' (Fisk 1999: 2; see also Droziak 1995; Behnke 2000: 3; Bilski 1995). With a new threat of the same magnitude as the Communist threat during the Cold War, NATO had a clear and legitimate purpose for remaining relevant in the post-Cold War European field of security. However, this statement created more problems than solutions for the Secretary General. It was not *comme il faut* in the emerging European field of security to place religiously demarcated groups as a new counterpart to NATO. It was bad taste and did not fare well in the European field of security. The statement was repeatedly demented, but the move had been made. According to Claes, NATO was a certain type of community easily distinguishable from its enemy along cultural and religious lines. To remain central in the emerging field, however, this type of argument was not acceptable. It constituted a mobilization of the wrong concept of civilization and thus diminished the scientific capital base of the alliance.[12]

Just as Huntington's thesis in the 'The Clash of Civilizations?' (Huntington 1993) met with strong opposition (Buzan and Hansen 2009: 166), the Willy Claes statement was furiously shunned. For example, it is interesting to note that a search of the official NATO website finds no records of this statement ever having been said – or in the vocabulary of this thesis, of the move ever having been made. The opposition was so strong against this type of civilization argument that any proof of its association with the alliance was deleted. Daniel Pipes commented that 'his statements met with outrage from all over the Muslim world, and he was quickly forced to retract and to withdraw' (Pipes 2002: 2). Willy Claes' withdrawal included stating that '[r]eligious fundamentalism ... whether Islamic or other varieties, is not a concern for NATO' (Pipes 2002: 2; see also Behnke 2000: 3).

The Secretary General's move in the field was clumsy: 'A social performance may also be clumsy or maladroit, confusing its spheres of practice and its principles of conduct appropriate to them' (Ashley 1989: 262). Willy Claes overstepped the limits of what was considered to be appropriate and normal in the field of European security practice in the mid-1990s. It is therefore not surprising that NATO's website shows no sign of ever having advocated a view of civilizations, whose closest cousin was the pariah version of the clashes in the new security order: Samuel P. Huntington's 'The Clash of Civilizations?'. The mistake was grave, and NATO never again advocated such a version of 'civilization as culture'. Through different – and accepted – kinds of practices, NATO tried to situate itself at the centre of authority for defining European security.

However, the move made sense at the time from the perspective of NATO, because it mobilized a type of argument that fitted the doxic practice from the Cold War days. Replacing one threat with another, while upholding the image of a world divided into two, organized by military capabilities, and run by a logic of strategic balancing seemed straightforward. It drew in a new type of scientific capital – that of the clash of civilizations – but it was not accepted in the field nor in NATO itself. Profound changes at the doxic level had challenged the tight fit between Cold War scientific and military capital, and the rising value of new types of scientific capital – notably Social Constructivism and Democratic Peace Theory as discussed above – added to this development. Claes' statement therefore threatened to confine NATO to a corner of the field to which no authority over the definition of doxic practices of European security was tied.

### Civilization as process, 1999

The clumsy attempt to lock civilization in a concept of culture, which provided a clear enemy for NATO in 1995, was replaced by a concept of civilization understood as a process. In this understanding, civilization could be obtained through practice: a civilized state was achievable for all people, irrespective of cultural backgrounds. This fit nicely with the growing Constructivist and Democratic Peace trend in the field.[13]

When NATO started precision bombing Serbia after the ethnic unrest in the Kosovo area, NATO Secretary General Javier Solana justified the actions thus: 'Our actions are directed against the repressive policies of the Yugoslav government, which is refusing to respect civilized norms of behaviour in this Europe at the end of the 20th century' (Solana 1999c; see also Blair 1999; Huysmans 2002b; Donnelly 1998).[14] The civilized norms of behaviour were tied to democracy and the rule of law, and the mobilization of this concept of civilization as capital was therefore supported by the mobilization of the Democratic Peace thesis in the field. But where the mobilization of the Democratic Peace thesis had hitherto primarily spurred peaceful, practical cooperation with partners, its coupling with the concept of civilization meant that NATO was ready to apply what the Copenhagen School of Security Studies would term emergency measures in the quest for civilized behaviour in the periphery of the cooperative security landscape of democracies. The underlying logic was that civilization could be spread to the countries surrounding NATO by a variety of practices – including militarily supported practices.[15] But the 'continuation of politics with other means' (Clausewitz 1989) was only civilized behaviour if it was carried out by the post-modern, civilized world.[16] Only in relations between this post-modern, civilized world and the modern, barbaric periphery was the use of military means a legitimate continuation of politics. And only in one direction: from the post-modern core to the modern periphery. This could kick-start the civilizing process in the countries that remained locked in the past.

The mobilization of civilization-as-process was thus tied to the mobilization of the Democratic Peace thesis, but Solana also mobilized the civilization argument as scientific capital in a manner that made it compatible with a new trend in valued scientific capital at the time: Social Constructivism. Civilization-as-process was seen as carrying transformative potential along the lines of this new type of scientific capital in the field. Solana was familiar with the valued scientific vocabulary in the field and mobilized it in his attempts to place NATO centrally in European security: 'Security in the 21st century is what we make of it. The future can be shaped' (Solana 1999a: 3–4) (see also below). The power move of mobilizing civilization-as-process arguments as a justification for intervening in the Kosovo Crisis thus added further to the alliance's standing in the field[17].

Huysmans has argued that 'NATO ... increasingly positions itself in a civilisation game in which the construction of a pan-European community of values is at stake' (Huysmans 2002b: 600). I agree. But the concept of civilization had to be of a certain kind to count as valued capital in the emerging field of European security. The understanding of civilization as a cultural, immovable entity was shunned, and the adoption of a concept of civilization which emphasized the possibility of becoming civilized became prevalent. The statements made by Willy Claes could have been devastating for NATO had they not been removed entirely from the official records and actively dismissed through practices of democratization and civilization by the alliance. Towards the end of the 1990s, NATO and the field in general agreed on a concept of civilization that valued the option of change. This type of civilization argument could add to an agent's standing and fit well with the valued scientific capital towards the end of the 1990s. The combination of the 'causal link' between democracy and peace/security and the Constructivist paradigm which held that 'security is what we make of it' provided an increasingly powerful platform in the field, as we shall also see below.

### *'Proving theory wrong', 1999*

When Javier Solana stated that: 'Indeed, had we listened to theory, we would not have come half as far. Theory told us that NATO enlargement and a NATO-Russia relationship would be mutually exclusive goals. Practice proved otherwise' (Solana 1999b), he was making a new move in the domain of security in Europe involving scientific capital.[18] This time, however, the value of the scientific capital from the Cold War was not high. Admiral Norman Ray, Assistant Secretary General, stated in stronger terms that:

> The underlying idea seems to be that we can't have both: new members and a new relationship with Russia. This is nonsense. Those who believe that ... are stuck to a zero-sum mentality born at the time of the Cold War but increasingly obsolete in today's strategic environment.
>
> (Ray 1997: 3)

As early as 1996, Solana voiced a similar sentiment: '1996 could be the year in which *practice finally replaces theory* and the pieces of a new European security architecture can begin to come together' (Solana 1996: 1, my emphasis).

These statements must be read on the background and in the context of NATO's history and the dominant concept of security which had been gradually replaced from 1990 onwards – both in NATO documents and in the Security Studies literature. Even though NATO had actively sought to replace the old concept of security in its documents and through practices such as the Partnership for Peace Initiative and the Eastern Enlargement, the old concept of security remained out in the field and the alliance was still largely associated with this strategic studies type of argument.

The context in which the statements came about included a strong opposition towards NATO enlargement. John Lewis Gaddis asserted that:

> my normally contentious colleagues seem to be in uncharacteristic agreement ... that the NATO expansion initiative is ill-conceived, ill-timed, and above all ill-suited to the realities of the post-Cold War world ... Indeed I can recall no other moment, in my own experience as a practicing historian, at which there was within our community greater unanimity against, which is to say less support for, an official foreign policy position.
>
> (Gaddis quoted in Kay 1998: 489)

There were numerous reasons for opposing NATO expansion (see for example Kay 1998).[19]  In the article, 'NATO expansion: 'a policy error of historic importance'' (MccGwire 1998), the position of the counterpart in Solana's quote is well represented. First, Russia would oppose the enlargement plans and would again develop political and territorial aspirations spurring a new version of the strategic balance seen during the Cold War. Second, the expansion would draw a new line between 'ins' and 'outs' in Europe and foster instability. Third, the ability of the alliance to carry out its primary mission (collective defence) would be compromised. Fourth and finally, the US commitment to NATO would be called into question (MccGwire 1998: 23–24; see also Mandelbaum 1996; Brown 1995; Waltz 2001; for discussion, see Kay 1998). The results of a NATO expansion were thus seen as creating an extremely dangerous situation by some commentators.

The doomsday prophecies of commentators were built on neo(realist) versions of the nature of security and how to secure Europe – the doxic practice of the Cold War. But Solana did not accept this explanation and its predictions. Solana therefore directly stated that theory had been proven wrong by practice. In so doing, he argued that NATO and NATO's mission were no longer definable by Cold War concepts and that he no longer had faith in conventional wisdom (see Kay 1998). Consulting Bourdieu, Solana's move runs parallel to theoretical expectations: 'It is significant that breaks with the most orthodox works of the past, i.e. with the belief they impose on the newcomers, often take the form of *parody* … which presupposes and confirms emancipation' (Bourdieu 1993: 31). NATO had changed how an alliance could be understood and what strategies an alliance could use in order to *construct* peace and security. In support of this argument, a newcomer on the scene was drawn in to provide scientific backing for NATO's moves: Social Constructivism (Kay 1998). Williams argues with respect to Constructivism:

> If we treat scholarly analysis not as determined by political directives, but as taking place within a field of practice that contains academic expertise, policy analysis, and institutions, we might suggest that the rise and popularity of Constructivism, and particularly its analysis of culture and security, can in part be accounted for as a result of the fit between the policy dilemmas and the forms of (cultural) strategy that policy institutions adopted to resolve them.
>
> (Williams 2007: 122)

Solana's statement thus both shunned a knowledge instrument (the old wisdom of realism, balance of threats, and Strategic Studies) and hailed a different knowledge instrument (Social Constructivism, Practice Theory). He thereby mobilized a popular kind of scientific capital in the field. This could entail a powerful position in the field.

Social Constructivism had entered Security Studies and had preached that 'anarchy is what states make of it', to paraphrase Wendt (1992).[20] When Javier Solana wrote his last letter to *NATO Review* before leaving NATO in 1999, he stated that: 'Security in the 21st century is what we make of it. The future can be shaped' (Solana 1999b: 3–4) thereby making it absolutely clear that not only did he consider the strategic environment of the alliance to be shaped by intersubjective understandings and practices, but also that he was familiar with the vocabulary of the social Constructivist paradigm, which was becoming ever more influential in Security Studies in Europe.[21]

By paraphrasing Wendt's famous dictum, he made a move in the field that was powerful in the sense that it placed NATO amongst the actors that were in the loop when the definition of the common sense of security was fought over and determined. At the same time, however, the direct reference to security research was a move that testified to a NATO which was becoming increasingly entangled in the field of European security. Williams holds that:

> The theoretical possibility of a move away from a militarised, threat-based, balance-of-power understanding of security and security

institutions that was central to Constructivism's early (largely meta-theoretical) claims found a strong resonance in institutional strategies that advocated precisely the same point at a practical level.

(Williams 2007: 123)

This point fits the NATO case perfectly. And in this new role, NATO was not only listening to theory – it was engaging in actively creating it. It is in this light that we should read Mikkel Vedby Rasmussen's conclusion about NATO: 'NATO has not only reinvented itself; it has provided a Western forum for reinventing security' (Rasmussen 2001: 298).

When analysing the wider domain of security in Europe, it hardly seems surprising that NATO became Constructivist. The practical patterns of interaction were strengthening, and the doxic understanding of security was changing. NATO somehow had to become Constructivist in order to stay on top in the battle over the definitions of security in Europe. As the next section will show, however, this was not the only move NATO was forced to make in the field. On other dimensions – and by throwing other types of capital into the game – NATO changed its visions of the world in order to remain in the game.

## Military capital

Military capital – understood as 'a capital of physical force, in the form of the military and the police' (Bourdieu 2005: 12) – had traditionally been NATO's primary source of capital. Even though the NATO military capabilities had not been used in active operations[22], the value of the military capital during the Cold War was not diminished by this fact. This changed during the 1990s. Military capabilities had to be increasingly flexible and deployable – something the NATO military machine had not been used to. NATO remained the only organisation in possession of military capabilities in the traditional sense.

Even now that NATO identifies itself more explicitly as a project for constructing a community based on shared values, its possession of the most significant volume of military capital in contemporary Europe is one of the key factors which makes it different from other community building instruments like the OSCE and the EU.

(Huysmans 2002b: 611)

The moves that changed the value and meaning of military capital were therefore  primarily initiated by other actors. NATO thus found itself on the defensive in this struggle.

Over the 1990s, the meaning and value of military capital changed remarkably. Four different moves will highlight this process. First, the strong move by the WEU when the organization formulated the Petersberg Tasks in 1992 and redefined which missions military capability ought to be designed to deal with in order to secure Europe. Second, the EU's Helsinki Headline

Goal, which picked up the process started by the Petersberg Tasks but went a step further in outlining a European Rapid Reaction Force. Third, Jef Huysmans has argued that NATO – in an attempt to remain relevant – tried to convert its military capital into humanitarian capital in order to have a role to play in the Kosovo Crisis (Huysmans 2002b). Fourth, military capital was not only sought converted into other types of capital or into other areas of employment. Military capital *per se* was also shunned more directly by other relevant agency in the field of European security. The *Centre for European Reform* (CER) saw military capital in the traditional sense as detached from the positive value of security, and instead cast it as a source of insecurity and a sign of brutishness. In that same move, the CER advocated the European Union as the organization with the capacity to 'run the 21$^{st}$ century'.

### Petersberg Tasks – the WEU's strongest move, 1992.

The Western European Union played a pivotal role in the struggles in the field surrounding NATO in the beginning of the 1990s. The EU used the organization to challenge the central status of NATO, but the WEU also tried to gain ground for itself.[23] The most famous move in the field made by the WEU is the formulation of the so-called Petersberg Tasks. The Petersberg Declaration adopted at the WEU Council of Ministers in Bonn on June 19, 1992,[24] declared a strengthened operational role for the WEU and outlined a list of situations in which the WEU should be able to act. The member states declared that they were 'prepared to support, on a case-by-case basis and in accordance with our own procedures, the effective implementation of conflict-prevention and crisis-management measures, including peacekeeping activities' (WEU 1992: para. 2). In the future, the WEU should be able to carry out 'humanitarian and rescue tasks; peacekeeping tasks; tasks of combat forces in crisis management, including peacemaking' (ibid.: Chapter 4, para. 2).[25].

With the formulation of the Petersberg Tasks, the WEU made a strong move towards changing the meaning of military capital. The conventional defence role of the Cold War was no longer adequate: in order to meet the challenges of the new situation, humanitarian missions and peace-enforcement were necessary. Like the attempts of Leander's private military companies to lobby politicians to change their understanding of security in order to hire specific companies for security tasks , the WEU Petersberg Declaration represented an example of lobbyism (Leander 2005a). If the field accepted this understanding and definition of security and threats, the WEU could manoeuvre itself into a position in which security expertise – and perhaps even implementation – could become the 'natural' task of the organization.

The redefinition of security and threats along these lines created a problem for NATO. The military capabilities of NATO were static, not designed for rapid responses, nor deployable in any great measure to conflict areas outside of the NATO member states (Wallander 2000).[26] The Petersberg Tasks thus made the military machine of NATO seem antiquated.

So NATO had to make adjustments, even though WEU political director Alyson J.K. Bailes argued that the WEU was 'clearly no rival to NATO' and that by adopting the Petersberg Tasks, the WEU 'would limit itself henceforth to a range of crisis management missions from evacuation to peace-making' and leave collective defence to NATO (Bailes 1999: 311). The WEU was moving in to grasp a role in a domain that NATO had dominated since its creation in 1949: the military domain. WEU ministers 'declared that WEU, together with the European Union, was ready to play a full part in building up Europe's security architecture' (WEU 1992: para. 3). After decades of playing second fiddle to NATO, the WEU could now come into being as the security organization in Europe that could handle the new types of threats after the Cold War. Member states agreed to designate forces answerable to the WEU (FAWEU) and established a Planning Cell in the WEU Headquarters in Brussels. However, the ministers 'likewise reaffirmed their conviction that the Atlantic Alliance is one of the indispensable foundations of Europe's security' (ibid.: para. 3). Even though this reads like a call for cooperation, however, it did not mean that NATO could (or should) perform the Petersberg Tasks. Instead, NATO should only take care of collective defence – and leave crisis management to the WEU. 'The problem for NATO has been that its military capital has remained a key element in determining its political identity in the European security complex' (Huysmans 2002b: 617). This identity was tied to static collective defence and not to future threats and risks.

In the face of this development, NATO adjusted its military capital in the direction of the Petersberg Tasks over the 1990s. Lachowski argues that 'the post-cold war transatlantic 'division of labour' as regards security could no longer be predicated on the traditional division into military and non-military areas' (Lachowski 2002: 151). NATO understood that. Already in October 1992, NATO created its first headquarters for the rapid deployment of forces: the Allied Command Europe Rapid Reaction Corps (ARRC) in Moench-engladbach in Germany. The ARRC came to play a crucial role in the deployment of forces to Bosnia and Herzegovina and Kosovo.[27] It was no coincidence that NATO decided to move on the creation of rapid reaction capabilities so soon after the agenda was set by the WEU Petersberg meeting. Had NATO let the move go unnoticed or un-countered, the alliance would soon find itself in a marginalized position in the field. Instead, NATO began a restructuring of its forces. By 1999, NATO land, sea, and air units had been reduced by 30–40 per cent, with only 35–60 per cent kept at a thirty-day readiness level, as compared with 70–90 per cent kept at a minimum of two days' readiness in 1990. 'NATO shifted its military strategy from positional defense based upon its Main Defence Forces to ... Immediate and Rapid Reaction Forces and Augmentation Forces' (Wallander 2000: 718). The process included the 1999 Kosovo intervention and the 2002 Prague Summit, at which a NATO Reaction Force (NRF) with a global reach consolidated NATO's role as the 'globo-cop' of the new century (Kristiansen and Ringsmose 2006).[28]

The Petersberg Tasks redefined the type of mission military capital should be put into use for, thereby challenging NATO's position. At the same time, however, the Petersberg Declaration confirmed an interest in grounding the handling of European security in a strictly European organization. This presented a more direct challenge to NATO. WEU's cooperation with the EU supported this trend towards a European-led organization taking over responsibility for European security. The WEU encountered difficulties, however, because many of the EU members did not want the EU to have its own 'army' (Bailes 1999). The Petersberg Tasks were written into the Treaty of the European Union during the summit in Amsterdam in 1997. The wording of the EU glossary is an exact copy of the original text of the Petersberg Declaration (EU 2007). The move in the field was thus important in the redefinition of military capital, though it did not translate into a central role for the WEU in the long run.[29]. NATO countered the move by creating structures designed to address the very tasks mentioned in the Petersberg Declaration, and the EU moved to become a strong player by integrating the wording into Union documents.

One thing is worth pointing out: even though NATO's type of military capital was devalued during the 1990s, one part of it remained an asset. NATO's integrated command structure made it possible for the alliance to adapt to the new tasks. In an interview with Celeste Wallander, Phillip Gordon holds that this is one of the reasons why NATO prevailed and not the WEU:

> If, for example, NATO were just the Article 5 commitment without any of its assets, it would be the WEU. What made NATO possible in the 1990s was what was developed in the Cold War to deal with the Soviet threat and the alliance's internal tasks.
>
> (Gordon quoted by Wallander 2000: 725)

In other words, NATO's internal structures were already in place, and parts of its military capital could thus be reformed and put into practice more easily behind the Petersberg Tasks (this is supported by Williams 2007 and Huysmans 2002b).

### Helsinki Headline Goal, 1999

One of the defining moves in the field involving military capital was the 1999 EU adoption of the Helsinki Headline Goal. The Helsinki Headline Goal was formulated at the EU summit in Helsinki in 1999 following a shift in British policy towards the EU's role in security and the adoption of the joint Franco–British St Malo Declaration in 1998 (Franco–British Summit Declaration 1998).

The Helsinki Headline Goal drew on the WEU Petersberg Tasks. After the degradation of the WEU in the field, the EU took up the plans to be able to carry out missions across the full range of Petersberg Tasks by itself – involving neither the WEU nor NATO. And even though 'NATO's monopoly of collective defense would ... be no more challenged than it had been by WEU' (Bailes 1999: 314), this constituted a threat to NATO's recognition as the primary military organization in the field. If NATO was not fit to carry out crisis management the Petersberg way, the organization would move to the margins of the emerging field.

The Headline Goal called for EU member states to be able to deploy up to 50,000–60,000 personnel (corps level) within 60 days and sustainable for a year in support of the Petersberg Tasks. The forces pledged 'should be militarily self-sustaining with the necessary command, control and intelligence capabilities, logistics, other combat support services and additionally, as appropriate, air and naval elements' (EU 1999: II, Article 28 and Annex 4; for discussion, see Schuwirth 2002). The Helsinki Headline Goal was to be met by June 2003 if possible and by December Union 2003 at the latest.[30] In December 2001, the Laeken Presidency Conclusions noted that the ' Union is now capable of conducting some crisis-management operations' – signalling the operationalization of ESDP and advances in fulfilling parts of the Headline Goal. This position was confirmed and reinforced at the May 2003 General Affairs and External Relations Council: 'the EU now has operational capability across the full range of Petersberg tasks, limited and constrained by recognised shortfalls' (EU 2003).

The Helsinki Headline Goal represented 'a political commitment by the Member States' (EU 2000d: 2) but also went far towards describing the new concept of security in Europe and the new, crisis management-related capabilities needed to sustain security and peace. With the Helsinki Headline Goal, the EU signalled very strongly that it had decided on assuming a more important – and militarily more capable – role in the field. The EU was thus seeking a higher position in the field of European security by mobilizing the redefined type of military capital.

By adopting the Headline Goal, the EU contested the commonly held understanding in the field: that the EU could not live up to a military role. 'Europe's static conscript-dependent forces look increasingly like dinosaurs' (Economist 1999: 1).[31] This static type of military capability could have translated into recognized military capital during the Cold War. After the success of the concept of Petersberg Tasks, however, the static military capabilities of the EU countries were no longer recognized as valuable. The decreasing defence budgets throughout Europe had not made the EU role in security more credible, and the developments in the Balkans together with the European inability to act there had only strengthened the lack of confidence in European ambitions (Lachowski 2002: 152).[32] The decision to create a rapid reaction force capable of working on the whole range of Petersberg Tasks was thus important. With that, the EU suddenly found itself at the centre of the debates in the field. If the Headline Goal was met, the EU could gain a credible and central role in the field of European security – and challenge NATO.

### From military to humanitarian capital, 1999

As we have seen, military capital played a central role in many of the moves made in the 1990s. One of these moves was to enter a humanitarian field: NATO attempted to convert its traditional military capabilities into *humanitarian* capital, because the military instrument was no longer popular and did not ascribe a significant role to NATO in the developing crisis in Kosovo (Huysmans 2002b). By using the humanitarian card to redefine the chains of command in a humanitarian direction, NATO sought to stay on top. According to Huysmans, 'There is a structural link between the symbolic struggle in the humanitarian field and NATO's struggle in the contemporary European security complex' (ibid.: 600).

By trying to convert military capital into humanitarian capital, NATO not only challenged how military capability – and thus military capital – could be understood in the field; the alliance also supported the change in the rationality of the concept of security, which had formerly been tied to narrow military connotations. The widening of the concept, and the link between peace, security and democracy, which had been on the agenda early in the 1990s (see above), was now supported and stabilized in NATO by a change in the rationality towards establishing peace, stability and security through crisis management and disaster relief.[33] It changed the concrete practices on the ground (NATO undertook missions that were comparable to Petersberg Tasks), but also contributed to changing the position of NATO in the field. In this manner, the move towards reframing military capabilities as humanitarian capital in the service of an evolving process of civilization opened up space for NATO in the emerging field of European security. If military capital was accepted as being associated with the broad concept of security, democracy and a civilizing rationality, then NATO was once again in a position of authority in the field: 'By struggling to demonstrate the value of military capital for the assistance of refugees NATO struggled to credibly convert its military capital into political capital in the community of values game' (ibid.).

NATO took on the new role with relative ease, the logistical technologies and skills could quite smoothly be transferred from military to humanitarian tasks.[34] In the process, NATO's position in the field changed as it emerged as a military and diplomatic alliance as well as humanitarian agency (ibid.: 603). The strategy of casting the primary type of accumulated capital of the alliance in humanitarian terms was thus successful.

The homology between NATO's position and the related strategies in the Kosovo conflict on the one hand and its position and related strategies in the struggles for political authority in the European security complex made it structurally possible to directly capitalize in the post-Cold War European security game on the political and humanitarian capital acquired in the Kosovo conflict (ibid.: 617).

That NATO changed its conceptualization of military capital – and recast its capabilities in humanitarian terms – can be seen as a *field effect.*

According to Bigo (2006) field effects works invisibly to steer practices in a field. NATO worked to change the meaning and application of its military capital, because the field moved away from valuing how military capability had traditionally been perceived. This move was supported by the shifting understandings of scientific capital and the changing weights of social capital.

But NATO was countered in the field. According to Huysmans, 'The conversion of military capital into political authority is challenged by organisations that embody economic capital such as the European Union' (Huysmans 2002b: 600). I agree. And in support of the EU other types of relevant agency entered the struggles. Amongst them, a rising star on the sky of European security: the think tank entitled the *Centre for European Reform*.

### The underwhelming power of the EU, CER entering the scene

The Centre for European Reform (CER) made several moves to set the agenda and pull the field in a certain direction in the late 1990s and at the beginning of the 21st century. The think tank advocated the strength and role of the EU in security matters. If the CER had its way, NATO's military capital would no longer constitute a power base in the field, instead the alliance would have a position on the margins of the field. This largely followed the trend of redefining the meaning of scientific capital but also added to the struggles concerning military capital. The Centre for European Reform thus boldly entered the game in the field and challenged the limits of what security means and how security can be provided in Europe and its region. The process of redefining the meaning and role of military capital, which started with the formulation of the Petersberg Tasks and continued with the attempts by NATO to convert its military capital into humanitarian capital, was drawn by the CER in the direction of leaving the military instrument as largely a thing of the past.

The Centre for European Reform was one of the European think tanks that stood out as very well-connected in the field. The think tank was established in 1998 in Britain with the objective of improving the quality of debate of the EU in the UK. It played a special role in shaping the British debate and had relations with a long list of people, institutions and others with a central position in the European security landscape. In 2002, the CER stated in its annual report that it has 'become a truly European think tank, committed to reforming the European Union' (CER 2002). Its connections with especially former Secretary General of NATO and the High Representative for Foreign and Security Policy, Javier Solana, made the CER a centrally placed think tank in the practical patterns of interaction making up the field.

The CER worked for an 'outward-looking EU that is aware of its global responsibilities' (CER 2004: 2). Its publications stressed the importance of Eastern Enlargement and even took up the issue of embracing Turkey[35] and Georgia – issues still considered by most to be 'hot potatoes' in the EU enlargement debate. Furthermore, the CER published on the need for the EU to adopt its own security strategy and (not least) a more operative defence dimension. All of these publications represent moves in the field of European security and point in the direction of a reformulation of why military capital is no longer perceived as an asset. In a publication concerning the possible accession of Turkey to the EU, Steven Everts, senior research fellow and director of CER's transatlantic programme, spelt out the 'European way' as seen in opposition to a focus on the military instrument: 'The EU's approach is the opposite: indirect, underwhelming and economic-legal in nature' (Everts 2004: 1). According to Everts, the EU's approach created long-term results for the security and stability in the region. The *underwhelming* power of the EU consisted in the long-term transformation from instability and national selfishness to European, civilized space. This made it more powerful than brute, military power. In the words of Mark Leonard: 'To understand the shape of the twenty-first century, we need a revolution in the way we think about power ... The strength of the EU ... is broad and deep: once sucked into its sphere of influence, countries are changed forever' (Leonard 2005: 3–4).

The underwhelming soft power of the EU was pivotal in CER's understanding of how to provide security in Europe – and the world. Military capabilities were cast as a problem, whereas the process-oriented method of EU enlargement and the economic nature of relations were seen as the solution for the new century. According to the CER, a new kind of power needed to be understood and recognized, because it would take over the role of traditional, military power. It created peace and stability and was tied to the identity of Europe: peace-promoting, non-interventionist, culturally accepting. Mark Leonard confidently stated that this was what made the EU so powerful. 'We can see that a new kind of power has evolved that cannot be measured in terms of military budgets or smart missile technology. It works in the long term, and is about reshaping the world rather than winning short-term tussles' (Leonard 2005: 5). The underwhelming power of the EU thus clearly challenged the traditional type of military capital that NATO possessed so much of (and the EU so little of): according to the CER, NATO could only hope to win short-term tussles.

On the contrary:

> [f]or countries such as Turkey, Serbia, or Bosnia, the only thing worse than having the bureaucracy of Brussels descend on your political system, insisting on changes, implementing regulations, instigating state privatizations and generally seeping into every crack of everyday political life, is to have its doors closed to you.
>
> (Leonard 2005: 51)

As such, the underwhelming power of the EU not only consisted of the actual practices when the EU entered a region and slowly changed it by demanding structural and administrative changes in a country; it also worked before the EU entered a region: the economic power of the EU was so attractive to other countries that the risk of 'exclusion from the club' could make a country change in the direction that the EU wished for, even without being officially invited to join the EU. According to the CER, this was security politics. And it constituted a complete redefinition of the strength and value of military assets and capabilities.

The discussion of whether the EU could credibly take on a stronger role in European security was thus defined away by the CER: that the EU did not have operational capability (to an extent that equals NATO or the US) was not a problem; it was actually an *advantage*. The EU could credibly assume a strong role in the European security field *because* it was not burdened by the short-term successes of strong military power. The focus on the shrinking European defence budgets could thereby be brushed away as belonging to a discussion of the past.

The underwhelming power was modelled on Foucault's vision of power as surveillance. According to Leonard:

> Foucault's real insight is that efficient exercise of power depends *less on having military might* or the technology of deterrence than on *establishing legitimacy by making everyone complicit in the enforcement rules* ... This model of surveillance is what the European Union has achieved within its borders.
>
> (Leonard 2005: 40–41, my emphasis)[36]

The strongest trend in CER publications was generally an understanding of power almost void of military might. However, only some countries were on the path to democracy and would consequently be changeable through underwhelming power. Other countries were not yet on that path. These zones of turmoil (Cooper 1996) were different from the zones of peace and should be (and had to be) treated differently: 'Europeans have learned the hard way that to promote peace you sometimes need to go to war' (Leonard 2005: 68). So the military dimension was not completely forgotten (even though it was devalued). 'Europe's transformative power comes from its ability to reward reformers and withhold benefits from laggards. But passive aggression does not work on countries that do not want to join the club of law-abiding states. Dealing with them may involve using force' (ibid.: 56). The military instrument may thus be a necessity, but it would always be subordinated to the soft, Foucauldian, underwhelming power: "even with the development of European military capabilities, Europeans will rely less on the use of force to shape the world than any other major power' (ibid.: 68).

This type of argument had already been made by Robert Kagan, first in his famous article and later in his book *Of Paradise and Power* (2002, 2003). In the book, the European 'paradise' was juxtaposed with American power. Europeans, it was argued, needed to understand that the power-free 'paradise' could not easily be extended to areas outside of Europe. Through this juxtaposition, Europe's take on security was labelled naivety. Instead of merely accepting this reading of the 'European way', however, Leonard used the famous juxtaposition as a *power asset* for Europe – and not (as intended by Kagan) as a way to foreground European weakness and lack of sense of reality. In this manner, Leonard drew on distinctions already known to the field of security, but in a manner portraying military capability as brute force, a relic from the past. According to Leonard, the US was therefore not necessarily stronger because it was stronger militarily. Kagan's understanding of power was limited to military power and did not begin to understand the forms of power in play. Williams supports this, arguing that:

> Kagan's analysis ... demonstrates the perils of working with too restricted an account of power, because this tension is between the application and operation of different forms of strategy and power; it is not a tension between the principles of power and the principles of paradise. By generally reducing power to military power (occasionally mentioning, though failing to theorize, the importance of 'soft power'), his account fails to grasp the ways in which cultural power was essential in the reconstruction of security in post-Cold War Europe.
>
> (Williams 2007: 129)

It certainly failed to grasp the struggles within the European security field, which included the mobilization and redefinition of a various types of capital.

In sum, the meaning and value of military capital was challenged severely during the 1990s and into the new century. NATO's traditional, static, defensive forces were cast as a problem rather than an asset by diverse actors such as the WEU, the EU and think tanks in the field of European security. NATO moved to meet the demands of the new definitions of military capital. The alliance promptly created rapidly deployable forces and made attempts to convert its military capital into humanitarian capital when the tasks of a security organization moved to include humanitarian and rescue missions. By the end of the 1990s, however, the struggle over the value of military capital had yet to find a conclusion.[37] The tremendous adjustments the alliance had made ready to implement appeared futile in the face of the moves made by the Centre for European Reform.[38]

When airplanes hit the twin towers of the World Trade Center in New York in September 2001, NATO saw a chance to reclaim centre stage. The alliance mobilized its social capital and backed it up with military capital by activating the mutual defence clause of the Washington Treaty (Article V) for the first time in its history; however, the move was not successful.

## Social capital

The struggle in the field took place on other dimensions as well. It did not suffice to advocate the 'right kind' of scientific capital or to cast military capital in the right way to suit developments in the field. NATO also needed to lock itself into the social relations that were developing in the domain of security in Europe. These struggles concern social capital: 'Social capital is the capacity derived from being part of networks and from relations of acquaintance and mutual recognition' (Huysmans 2002b: 608). Social capital can add to the standing of an agent holding other types of valued capital in the field.

Chapter 5 on practical patterns of interaction constituted an analysis of social capital from the perspective of the *accumulation of contacts*. The chapter concluded that NATO actively sought to increase its social capital power base through initiatives such as the enlargement of NATO and the successful programme Partnership for Peace, as social capital became increasingly important over the 1990s. NATO also moved towards addressing the public in a much more open and inclusive way, testifying to the fact that in order to remain in the game of European security, social capital in the form of networks and being 'in the loop' institutionally and socially had become important for creating and sustaining a position in the field. The introvert stance of NATO and its Secretaries General from the Cold War was replaced by an active strategy of placing itself at the centre of debates and networks in Europe. In this chapter, I address what I call 'The ESDI/CFSP/ESDP letter game', the activation of Article V of the Washington Treaty on September 12, 2001, and the adoption of the European Security Strategy in 2003. These were moves in the field concerning social capital.

### The ESDI/CFSP/ESDP letter game

Who represents European security and its allies? Who gets to define where the lead in European security should be based institutionally? NATO, the WEU and the EU all sought the role as the primary entity in European security. It became a pastime for European organizations to fight over the social structuring of the European security landscape through the formulation of various new institutional arrangements – what I refer to as 'the ESDI/CFSP/ESDP letter game'. The ESDI (European Security and Defence Identity) was NATO's acronym for a European role in security in the 1990s. The ESDP (European Security and Defence Policy) was the EU's attempt to define the role to be played by the EU.[39] The WEU remained the compromise organization which was repeatedly chosen to bridge these two poles in the debate over who gets to represent European security – NATO or the EU.[40]

The ESDI was unofficially launched at the North Atlantic Council (NAC) meeting in Brussels in January 1994 and later agreed to in Berlin in 1996. It was initially conceived largely as a technical-military arrangement, allowing the Europeans to assume a greater share of the burden for security missions. The arrangement meant that the Europeans (through the WEU) would gain access to the capabilities that they did not possess themselves. The European capabilities could also be separated from the NATO force pool in missions that only the Europeans wanted to carry out (this idea was formulated as 'separable but not separate', see below). The formulation of the ESDI thus constituted a move in the field on the part of NATO. NATO sent a signal that it was ready to accept a more important role for the Europeans but that the alliance wanted to retain the European project for autonomy *within* NATO. Howorth and Keeler argue that '[t]he very fact that ESDI was about *identity* (within NATO) rather than about either *policy* or *capacity* indicated its limited ambition' (Howorth and Keeler 2003: 8). If NATO had talked about a European 'policy' or 'capacity', the European project for autonomy would be a step closer to completion and NATO's role in European security would subsequently diminish. NATO refrained from using such words (and thus making any promises), and stuck to the un-ambitious 'identity', thereby attempting to maintain the power to represent all of the alliance members (and European security in general).

However, '[u]ltimately ... the *political* message of ESDI – that a clearer, bigger European role was both acceptable and desirable – acquired more importance than the technical-military arrangements' (ibid.: 8). When NATO coined the ESDI in an attempt to lock European aspirations within the Alliance, it thereby also opened up the door to increased European influence. Sloan argues when concluding on the Berlin Accord from 1996 that '[i]t revealed transatlantic consensus on the need to accommodate development of greater European defence cohesion and military capabilities' (Sloan 2005: 102). I disagree. This reading underestimates and misjudges the game of '*prises de positions*', which the Berlin Accord was part of. While NATO wanted to keep European security centred on the alliance, the EU (especially France) wanted to invest its capital in a EU solution; and no consensus had been found on that point. The push towards European autonomy was strong, however, and NATO therefore had to come up with a counter-move. Without the formulation of the ESDI, NATO risked losing the right to represent the European Allies altogether – and thus risked losing important social capital in the field. But the formulation that the Europeans could only use the forces on a case-by-case basis – separable but not separate, as in the NATO language of the day – was pivotal. Establishing a separate capacity was not acceptable to NATO.[41]

## St Malo Declaration, 1998

The St Malo Declaration on European Defence was another important step in the ESDI/CFSP/ESDP letter game. 'St Malo represented a paradigm shift in European security thinking' because it created a strong platform for a European role in security. The declaration referred to a direct link between NATO and the EU (Howorth 2004: 222; see also Moens 2003). The WEU had been sidetracked by a British veto at the Amsterdam summit in 1997, and hopes for an autonomous European role in security appeared doomed. However, the new Labour government led by Tony Blair did not let the European role remain unfilled. Instead, he and French President Jacques Chirac formulated and adopted a joint French–British declaration at the Franco–British summit in St Malo on December 3–4, 1998 (Whitman 1999: 9). This left the British preference for using the WEU as a buffer between the EU and NATO behind (Moens 2003: 26).

The Declaration constituted the first time the two governments had agreed on such a bilateral statement on security and summed up a Franco–British common ground on five main points: first, the EU had to have the capacity to decide to act; to be able to act autonomously; and to be ready to do so in international crisis situations requiring military force. This point was spurred by European inaction in the crises in the Balkans throughout the 1990s. The UK, the former staunch defender of NATO's role, suddenly saw a role for the EU in security matters. The second point of common ground was that NATO was to remain the foundation of *collective defence* for Europe through Article 5 of the Washington Treaty. At the same time, the collective defence commitment related to Article V of the Brussels Treaty (WEU) should be maintained. This might appear to be a strengthening of the WEU, but it in fact constituted the opposite: the WEU had tried to go beyond the collective defence commitment in the Brussels Treaty by formulating the Petersberg Tasks in the early 1990s and had taken the lead in operationalizing a broader concept of security – and thereby a new role for military capital in the field of European security. France had supported this endeavour all along. By stating that the collective defence commitment of the WEU should remain was therefore tantamount to saying that none of the other tasks the WEU had attempted to take on should be maintained. This effectively constituted a weakening of the WEU and a simultaneous strengthening of the EU and possibly NATO. Third, the institutional arrangements for EU decision-making on defence matters were to remain intergovernmental. This point concerned the internal workings of the EU and underlined that defence was not to be 'communitarized'.[42] Nonetheless, the EU would have a clear security role. Fourth, in the future, the EU should develop capabilities to analyse, have access to sources of intelligence, and be able to plan to facilitate the decision-making and approval of circumstances under which military action was to be undertaken without the involvement of the entire Atlantic Alliance. This feature built on the role the WEU had gradually been taking on over the course of the 1990s: the EU was to take over the direct planning of military action without the participation of all NATO members. Fifth , the EU – i.e. its Member States – needed to give attention to creating armed forces capable of undertaking the military tasks that may be required without the involvement of the whole Atlantic Alliance. The St Malo Declaration thus foresaw a more important – and militarily underpinned – role for the EU in the future (Saint-Malo 1998).

The real surprise was that there was a document at all. The two countries had disagreed on each and every point about European security for years, and suddenly they were able to draft a document together. As late as the Intergovernmental Conference (IGC) in 1996, the British Conservative government had argued that no military role for the EU was acceptable and that no development beyond the Maastricht Treaty of 1991 could be envisioned. This meant that the WEU would remain the European organisation that would provide the framework for engaging in Petersberg Tasks (Whitman 1999: 9–10). The change in the British position at St Malo was therefore palpable.[43] One commentator explains it thus:

> When Blair was first properly briefed, in mid-1998, on Europe's seriously defective capacity to react to a hypothetical crisis in Kosovo, he was appalled. Europe, he concluded, simply had to turn its attention to defence. The rest followed: Pörtschach, St Malo, Cologne, Helsinki and Nice.
>
> (Howorth 2004: 221)

The St Malo declaration thus constituted a major move in the field over where to ground the legitimate right to represent European security. If Britain and France could agree to a text, an understanding in the field could be within reach. At first glance, the EU seemed immensely strengthened. However, the declaration actually split the social capital – and the answer to the question: who represents European security? Where Britain had formerly bet its money on NATO, and secondarily the WEU, the social capital was now divided between three organizations. The letter game 'ESDI/CFSP/ESDP' thus ended with no clear winner after St Malo.[44] The French hailed the St Malo Declaration as a clear EU/European response to NATO domination, while to Blair the declaration was more pragmatically understood as solving a problem within the Atlantic Alliance (Howorth 2004: 223). The North American allies could not be counted on to solve 'small European problems', such as Kosovo. For that reason, a European component had to be constructed. Moens supports this reading of the British position at St Malo:

> the British move was not so much an attempt to shift security and defense to Europe for the sake of creating a European rather than NATO defense capability as a move to pre-empt the loss of American interest in the alliance given the more pressing areas of military concern for the United States in Asia or the Middle East.
>
> (Moens 2003: 26)

The St Malo Declaration thus represented a compromise *par excellence.* 'The political Directors had struck a deal: 'European autonomy' would underpin the 'vitality of a modernised Atlantic Alliance'. The first element satisfied the French; the second satisfied the British' (Howorth 2004: 222).

But even though the UK emphasized the importance of NATO, the St Malo Declaration became an important step in the consolidation and construction of the European Security and Defence Policy (ESDP- or CESDP, as it was often referred to in order to distinguish it more clearly from ESDI) (Howorth and Keeler 2003: 10). The Franco–British agreement paved the way for a trilateral approach including Britain, France and Germany that brought London into both 'the Atlantic and European houses' (Moens 2003: 28). The

German presidency was crucial and instrumental in forwarding the rather vague St Malo Declaration and turning it into the embryo of an ESDP.[45]. This German process was supported in think tanks and policy circles (Howorth 2004: 224).

The language of the St Malo Declaration was carefully repeated in the NATO Washington Summit Communiqué in April 1999. It struck a balance between keeping the European efforts within the alliance and accepting the European wishes for some autonomy. However, the battle over European autonomy, and thus for the right to be the recognized and legitimate spokespersons, was not over. The ESDP project was launched at the June 1999 European Council Meeting in Cologne and further specified at the Helsinki European council meeting the same year. The new institutions of the ESDP were laid out and the 'Headline Goal' involving the creation of a European armed force capable of humanitarian, crisis management and peace enforcement operations was formulated. The Cologne summit went a step further than the St Malo Declaration. Where the St Malo Declaration said: 'In order for EU to take decisions and approve military action where the alliance as a whole is not engaged' (Saint-Malo 1998), the Cologne Council Declaration instead stated that 'The Union must have the capacity for autonomous action, backed up by credible military forces, the means to decide to use them, and a readiness to do so, in order to respond to international crises without prejudice to actions by NATO' (Cologne Council Declaration 1999: Annex III Article 1). In NATO and the Clinton administration, this was understood as leaving crisis management (the whole range of Petersberg Tasks, see above) to the EU, and only Article V collective defence to NATO. This was not acceptable to an alliance striving to remain atop the hierarchy in European security (Cornish and Edwards 2001). During the Helsinki European Council Summit – and after extensive critique from NATO and the United States – Blair convinced President Chirac to agree to go back to the wording from the St Malo Declaration (Moens 2003: 30). But the battle continued, testifying to the fact that the stakes were high. What may seem like small variations on the same theme spurred fierce reactions in the field, where the power hierarchy had not yet found its equilibrium after the end of the Cold War.

The Helsinki Conclusions implied that the EU was preparing for at least two types of capabilities and operations: its own operations without the use of NATO assets and capabilities, and EU-led operations with NATO assets and capabilities. The apparent dual purpose of the new EU capacity raised questions about the agreement the alliance had affirmed in Washington: 'our commitment to building the ESDI within the Alliance' (Moens 2003: 31). The formulation of the Headline Goal seemed to discount the role of NATO. The project was thought to have at least one serious shortcoming, however: 'The EU's military inadequacy, compounded by the unavailability of U.S. assets ... remains the Achilles heel of the ESDP project' (Howorth and Keeler 2003: 16). The lack of military capital therefore caused a problem of accumulating social capital for the EU. Even though the concept of military capital had changed over the 1990s in the direction of economic and crisis management capabilities, the EU still had to have some credible amount of hardware in order to be recognized as a legitimate spokesperson on security matters by the end of the 1990s (CER's move to claim EU's subtle *underwhelming* power was later). Many commentators thus concluded that 'only after NATO has declined to intervene could ESDP be activated' (Hulsman 2000: 44).

The letter game continued, re-emerging as late as 2002 when NATO Secretary General Lord Robertson held that 'The EU's European Security and Defence Identity conceived at St Malo was in part at least my brainchild' (Robertson 2002b: 5). At first glance this would seem to be an uncontroversial (yet perhaps slightly narcissistic) statement. However, what was agreed to in St Malo was the EU concept of ESDP (Franco–British Summit 1998) – not the NATO concept of ESDI. To state that the Franco–British summit had agreed on the ESDI was to argue that NATO's version had won.

Even though the developments in the Balkans made it difficult to keep Europeans tied into the alliance, one commentator pointed at NATO as the winner of the letter game: 'NATO has effectively won the 'war of the alphabet soup' ... emerging as the dominant security organization in competition with its institutional rivals' (Hyde-Price 2000: 141). I disagree: in the context of this book, the letter game (or the alphabet soup) should not be read in isolation from the multitude of actors and different types of capital that came to structure European security. And the battle continued.

## Activation of Article V of the NATO Treaty, 2001

The activation of Article V of the NATO Treaty on September 12, 2001, was a symbolic act and constituted a move in the emerging field of European security involving the mobilization of social capital.[46] NATO tried to mobilize the social capital it had accumulated during the 1990s by stating that the attacks on New York and Washington were to be considered an attack on all of the allies – and associated countries – of the North Atlantic Treaty Organization. The social capital of the PfP and the EAPC was thus mobilized in an attempt to take on an important position in the field: NATO was no longer merely an alliance of 19 members. Instead, it was argued: 'Today, the Atlantic Alliance is bigger than its 19 member nations. To all intents and purposes, it has become a coalition of 46' (Robertson 2001b: 5). And looking back in 2002, Lord Robertson argued that, 'In the wake of the terrorist attacks on the United States, the 46 countries of the Euro-Atlantic Partnership Council proved to be the world's largest permanent coalition' (Robertson 2002b: 2).

By invoking the common defence clause, the alliance not only signalled that it was behind the US and against the terrorists, who had carried out the attacks on New York and Washington; the alliance was also signalling that it still wanted to be the common reference point for security. The Europeans wanted America to consult more after 9/11 (*Economist* 2003a: 1–2), and NATO offered itself up as the locus for future negotiations.

Contrary to what could be expected, the invocation of the collective defence guarantee of the Washington Treaty was therefore not primarily a military move (even though it obviously could have developed in that direction).[47] Lord Robertson stressed this repeatedly during a press conference on September 12, 2001 (Robertson 2001d).[48] The alliance cast itself as the symbolic expression of a large community of states standing behind the United States after the attacks.

> Article 5 is not just a statement of solidarity. It is also a commitment by Allies to offer practical support. And the response by America's Allies reveals a basic truth about the transatlantic relationship: that as we enter the 21st century, NATO remains the pre-eminent and unrivalled forum for preserving the security of all its members.
>
> (Robertson 2002a, 2001a)

Through a combination of social and military capital, NATO thus offered itself as a natural centre for providing security. The activation of NATO's collective defence clause was meant to bring the alliance back in the game.

By backing up the bid for centrality with military capital, NATO's statement of support seemed stronger than the similar statements given in the days following the terrorist attacks by for example, the EU and the OSCE. On September 14, 2001, the EU 'condemned the perpetrators" and announced that it would make every possible effort to ensure that those responsible for these acts of savagery [were] brought to justice and punished' (EU 2001b: 1). September 14, 2001, was declared a 'day of mourning' and was used to express solidarity with the American people. However, a statement on the role of international organizations did not mention NATO. Instead, it held that 'the United Nations in particular, must make this an absolute priority" (ibid.). It was stressed that the CFSP and CESDP should be strengthened, making it 'operational as soon as possible" (ibid.: 3). That the EU joint declaration did not mention NATO is a statement in itself. The North Atlantic Treaty Organization had invoked Article V of the Washington Treaty for the first time in its history just two days earlier, thereby mobilizing both military and social capital in the field of European security. The High Representative of the CFSP had even been present in the NATO HQ for the meeting on September 12, 2001 (Forster and Wallace 2001). To neglect such an important move by the oldest security organization in Europe seems odd at best. Seen from the perspective of this book, the explanation is that the battle to be the legitimate and recognized spokesperson was carried on in these statements of solidarity with the US after 9/11. The EU was attempting to undermine the standing of NATO by devaluing its symbolic act.

Some argued that the terrorist attacks on the United States rendered the ESDI/CFSP/ESDP letter game obsolete: 'European Security is no longer seen as a potential threat to the integrity of NATO. In the age of global terrorism, any capacity is welcome' (Moens 2003: 35). This does not seem to be the most prevalent conclusion drawn by observers and practitioners, however.[49] To most, the NATO move to activate Article V constituted a failure: 'Paradoxically, NATO's invocation of Article V, high in political symbolism, could prove to be the historical swan song of the alliance *as a military instrument*' (Howorth and Keeler 2003: 13–14, italics in original).[50] Even the NATO Secretary General seemed reluctant in the months following 9/11. 'NATO may not be the lead organization combating global terrorism' (Robertson 2001c: 3; see also NAC 2001: para. 9; for discussion, see Coker 2002, 2003).

## The European security strategy, 2003

The process leading up to the presentation of the European Security Strategy by EU High Representative Javier Solana in December 2003 included the activation of Article V and an internal NATO situation in February 2003, which has been described as 'one of the worst crises the alliance has faced' (CESD 2003: 1). The United States had been arguing – and preparing – for an intervention in Iraq for several months, but the interest in intervention was not shared by many of the European allies.[51] The situation started with a US request to provide assistance to Turkey, the only NATO member to share a border with Iraq. Giving the go-ahead for NATO to plan for providing assistance to Turkey was seen as 'entering the logic of war' by especially France, Belgium and Germany. They consequently refused to accept the decision (Economist 2003a: 1).[52] As a consequence of this refusal, Turkey invoked Article IV of the Washington Treaty, which states that members will 'consult together whenever, in the opinion of any of them, the territorial integrity, political independence or security of any is threatened' (NATO 1949: Article IV). This was the first time a country had invoked Article IV. The ensuing deadlock in NATO was broken by the transfer of the decision to assist Turkey to the Defence Planning Committee (DPC), NATO's highest body for decisions regarding military matters at the time,[53] on which France was not represented.[54] Consensus was reached between the eighteen participating members, but only after six emergency NAC meetings over eleven days.

The 'situation' that arose over the US request for assistance to Turkey testifies to the fact that the fight for being the primary, legitimately recognized security organization in Europe was not over for NATO. As one NATO insider speculated after the bumpy February days in 2003, 'this row might exert negative spill-over effects onto the other issues, such as the NATO-EU cooperation' (CESD 2003: 2). Indeed, the three countries that had refused to capitulate to the 'logic of war' were European allies and EU member states. The ensuing disappointment with NATO on this point together with the strong anti-war sentiments in many European countries formed an important background on which the European security strategy was laid forward later that same year.[55]

The European Union had moved boldly following the Franco–British St Malo Declaration in 1998 by adopting the 'Headline Goal' in Helsinki in 1999. In 2003, the EU went a step further in the consolidation process of the

European Union as a security organization. The High Representative for Foreign and Security Policy, Javier Solana, formulated a 'European Security Strategy', which was adopted at the European Council in Brussels in December of 2003 (European Security Strategy 2003; for discussion, see Duke 2004; Toje 2005). The EU wanted to be seen not just as a European player but as a *global* player with global responsibilities:

> As a union of 25 states with over 450 million people producing a quarter of the world's Gross National Product (GNP), and with a wide range of instruments at its disposal, the European Union is inevitably a global player ... Europe should be ready to share in the responsibility for global security and in building a better world.
>
> (European Security Strategy 2003: 1)

At the same time, however, the EU stressed that in the new situation, where threats were no longer 'massive, visible' (ibid.: 8) and 'none of these threats is purely military' (ibid.: 7), the European Union was 'particularly well equipped to respond' (ibid.: 7) This vision of the EU as being superior to NATO and other organizations for dealing with security is very similar to the vision forwarded by the *Centre for European Reform* (see above). The European Security Strategy thus constituted a strong move towards gaining central ground in the field of European security on the part of the EU. Backed up by the process beginning with the formulation of the Headline Goal and the reformulation of military capital and the concept of security in the field of European security since the beginning of the 1990s, the European Union High Representative, Javier Solana, was able to (more) credibly – and perhaps even legitimately – talk as if the EU was a recognized spokesperson in European security. 'A more capable Europe is within our grasp' (ibid.: 12).

The relationship with NATO was downplayed in the security strategy. NATO was mentioned in the introduction in relation to the role played by the US during the Cold War and as a collective defence mechanism in the 1990s. However, the document then talks about the UN, the WTO, the OSCE and the Council of Europe before it returns (on p. 12) to the role of NATO in European security:

> The EU-NATO permanent arrangements, in particular Berlin Plus, enhance the operational capability of the EU and provide the framework for the strategic partnership between the two organisations in crisis management. This reflects our common determination to tackle the challenges of the new century.
>
> (European Security Strategy 2003: 12)

The role of NATO was limited (in the document) to enhancing the operational capability of the EU – a role, NATO was probably not content to play. Instead of talking about the EU–NATO relationship, the document proceeded to talk about a direct EU–US relationship: 'The transatlantic relationship is irreplaceable. Acting together, the European Union and the United States can be a formidable force for good in the world' (European Security Strategy 2003: 13). This direct reference to a EU-US relationship instead of an EU–NATO relationship constitutes a move to sidetrack NATO. The underlying logic seems to be that if the EU was negotiating directly with the US about European – and even global – security, then the EU must be the most important security organization in Europe. If this were the case, then NATO had a serious problem when attempting to remain at the centre of European security.[56]

## Conclusion: the new structure of the European security field

The field emerged on the background of a game involving three types of capital from the beginning of the 1990s. A number of *prises de positions* were important for the construction of the valued types of capital in the emerging field. The biggest change in the field was tied to breaking the tight fit between military and scientific capital, which had guided the alliance until the end of the Cold War. New types of scientific capital were mobilized, and a profound redefinition of the military instrument meant that the former positions of power could no longer hold. In the process, 'theory' entered the struggles in the field as a *factor* – a valued type of capital – in the doxic battles. Not only agency tied to the scientific field of Security Studies could mobilize this type of capital: the EU and NATO also actively pursued strategies in which scientific capital was mobilized.

Scientific capital was explicitly ridiculed towards the end of the 1990s – but only in a certain form – and remained in a central position for backing up strategies and moves in the field. Old wisdom from strategic studies was countered by the mobilization of redefined scientific capital: the broad concept of security, the scientific link between democracy and peace, civilization-as-process, and Social Constructivism were drawn from Security Studies and International Relations more broadly and used in the doxic battles in the field. Economic capital entered the game – but as a new kind of military capital, not as a profit-maximising and money-accumulating type of capital, as was Bourdieu's initial definition of the term: economic integration became a process-oriented type of security strategy cast as military capital, primarily through moves of the EU, but supported by the London-based think tank the *Centre for European Reform* . Military capital was also redefined by the formulation of the Petersberg Tasks, which set the agenda for what military capability should be used for. The static, defensive type of military capital from the Cold War no longer held its previous value. This left NATO, the agent in the field with the highest amount of classical military capital at its disposal in an awkward position, and the EU in a potentially powerful position.

In addition to these moves and changes in the field, the question of 'who represents whom' also became an important struggle in the definition of the field – a struggle tied to the amount of social capital an agent had accumulated. The Franco–British St Malo Declaration and the struggle for the definition of European autonomy (the ESDI/CFSP/ESDP letter game), the activation of Article V of the Washington Treaty, and the presentation of the European Security Strategy were taken as examples of moves in the field tied to the accumulation and mobilization of social capital. No clear winner was found in the battle over the right to be the legitimate spokesperson for European security based on social capital. NATO had accumulated social capital through various programmes and strategies. Ultimately, however, its strongest mobilization of its newly accumulated social capital was a failure: the activation of Article V of the Washington Treaty after 9/11/2001 showed that social capital alone did not make for a central position in the field.

The combination of different types of capital became a prerequisite for success in the field. Combining the valued type of scientific capital with a high amount of recognized social capital could lead to a strong position in the field. But the possession of the wrong kind of military capital could detract from this strong position. Only when mobilized in the manner that was becoming recognized in the field would the different types of capital be of value to the agents fighting for recognition in the field.

This chapter constituted the final part of the three-step analysis developed in Chapter 3. It added a dynamic dimension to the study of field-specific capital (Chapter 4) and practical patterns of interaction (Chapter 5). Taken together, these three types of analysis make it possible to answer the empirical question of this book: how NATO was related to theory in the 1990s. At the same time, however, the framework for analysis can be applied to IR more generally. It reformulates philosophically based claims about the existence of fields and discourses in sociological, empirical terms and points to how analyses of the international after the linguistic turn can be carried forward.

## Notes

1  Guzzini and Jung argue that the widened debate on security has roots in peace research, which had a considerable impact on the restructuring of security agendas in e.g. Germany in the 1980s. The peace research trend was carried forward by a group of researchers at The Copenhagen Conflict and Peace Research Institute (COPRI) amongst them Barry Buzan and Ole Wæver, who later coined the term 'securitization' and founded the Copenhagen School of Security Studies (Wæver 1995a, 1995b; Buzan *et al.* 1998).

2  Analysts were uncertain of whether the aggressive intentions would re-emerge: 'Nor can anyone be certain that this military power will never again be used for hostile purposes … it has not yet been possible to rule out the prospect of a return to a more confrontational, even expansionist posture' (Duffield 1994: 768).

3  Bourdieu calls this tendency to focus on the past 'the primacy of yesterday's man' (Bourdieu 1977: 81). 'Yesterday's man'is meant to signify the constraints and limits of possibility that personal history and social history have on the actions (practice) of human beings.

4  David Gress calls this constellation the 'Cold War West' story (Gress 1998: 422–423). Gress argues that NATO has largely focused on the strategic and military elements and has forgotten the two other norms about open markets and the right

to self-determination, which Churchill and Roosevelt introduced in the transatlantic relationship during World War II in the Atlantic Charter from 1941.

5 Risse even argues that the democratic peace can be considered a 'common lifeworld' in international relations (Risse 2000: 15).

6 The idea that NATO was always a security community was revived in the 1990s in the security communities-literature on NATO. The Harmel Report (NATO 1967) played a central role in this re-telling of NATO's story (Risse-Kappen 1994, 1995, 1996; Adler 1997a; Solana 1997; Adler and Barnett 1998b). See Gress (1998) for a more provocative and entertaining version of this story. Wallander and Keohane have also contributed to retelling the story of NATO (Wallander and Keohane 1999; see also Keohane and Wallander 1996). To them, NATO is a 'security management organization' which has always sought to deal with more than external threats (for discussion of this argument, see Gheciu 2007). Deutsch laid the groundwork for talking about security communities (Deutsch 1954, 1957).

7 Williams holds that 'numerous analyses declared that Kant had basically been right all along, and that the link between democracy and peace – and particularly the claim that liberal-democracies do not go to war with one another – constitutes one of the most important discoveries concerning the nature of security, and the one of the most important insights for its construction.

8 The Democratic Peace Thesis in the contemporary American version was built on statistical evidence from the Correlates of War Project and the Polity Dataset (see e.g. Singer 1972).

9 Williams supports this: 'The power of this strategy lies precisely in its apparently uncoerced nature – in its specifically 'disinterested' forms – and it is all the more effective as a result. The status of the 'Kantian' democratic peace as objective knowledge, or as universal principles of right and obligation disconnected (and sometimes even at odds with) from the interests of those who promote it, are important elements of the cultural and symbolic capital and power at work in the restructuring of security practices' (Williams 2007: 60).

10 Also, the PfP constituted a move in the field that attempted to cast NATO as the guarantor of democracy (and following from this security) and as the natural centre for democratic reform in the former enemy states. The EU also used this type of argument in the later pushes for enlargement. In fact, both the EU and NATO developed a specific Western identity that was embedded in the construction of shared democratic norms (Fierke and Wiener 1999: 723).

11 In 1997, the PfP Programme was extended to include Russia in a Euro Atlantic Partnership Council (EAPC). NATO declared: 'No European democratic country whose admission would fulfil the objectives of the Treaty will be excluded from consideration' (NATO 1997b: para. 8). The alliance wanted to build a cooperative security landscape (NAC 1996a: para. 4), inhabited by a certain type of actor – as the title of the Partnership for Peace-programme had already foretold. The 'objectives to be fulfilled' included democratization as a central – and non-negotiable – condition. In the Membership Action Plan from 1999, which created a forum for discussion with applicant countries, democracy was declared to be one of the basic principles of the alliance and a prerequisite for membership (NATO 1999: 2).

12 It is interesting to compare this point with Hansen's analysis of a 'Balkan' and a 'Genocide' discourse surrounding the Bosnian war in the mid-1990s. 'The Balkan discourse draws upon and reproduces the Balkanization discourse's construction of 'the Balkans' as violent, passionate, and backward' (Hansen 2006: 108). The Genocide discourse, on the other hand, constructed Bosnia as a victim by '[l]ifting 'Bosnia' out of the Balkanized spatial and temporal construction of the Other' (ibid.: 112). Hansen finds that the Balkan discourse was common in the US in the beginning of the 1990s but later shifted towards the genocide discourse. The UK was especially reluctant to surrender the Balkan discourse.

13 Compare with Hansen's discussion of a standard of civilization as an Enlightenment discourse (Hansen 2006: 101–102).

14 The civilizing process is often associated with Norbert Elias (2000); for discussion, see Linklater (2004). Fukuyama's end-of-history argument is a related discussion (Fukuyama 1989, 1992).

15 Hansen finds a similar trait in her analysis of the Bosnian War: sometimes the West had to force other civilisations onto the path of the civilised world, as this was believed to be 'in their own best interest' (Hansen 2006: 102).

16 NATO does not call itself a post-modern world but stresses the civilized nature of the Alliance and the democratic peace which it claims to institutionalize. It is my reading that this is similar to arguments about a post-modern core and a modern periphery (Singer and Wildavsky 1993; van Ham 2001).

17 The trend to downplay culture and ethnicity was strong in the moves leading up to the Kosovo air campaign in March 1999 and they constitute a perfect opposite to Claes' earlier move. Tony Blair's speeches are probably the most telling in their symbolism. Blair spoke many times about the justification for NATO's intervention in Kosovo, thereby mobilizing a certain type of scientific capital as the background for the alliance's willingness to act. In April 1999, he spoke to the *Economic Club of Chicago*: 'Awful crimes that we never thought we would see again have reappeared – ethnic cleansing, systematic rape, mass murder' (Blair 1999: 1). The lines of conflict which Willy Claes had used in an attempt at reviving NATO and bringing it a new purpose were shamed and placed as a thing of the past, confined to areas which had not yet moved from barbaric to civilized. The British Foreign Minister Robin Cook made this argument very clearly when defining two types of space fighting for the future: 'There are now two Europes competing for the soul of our continent. One still follows the race ideology that blighted our continent under the fascists. The other emerged fifty years ago out from behind the shadow of the Second World War. The struggle between the international community and Yugoslavia is the struggle between these two Europes' (Cook 1999: 1).

18 Solana had previously made similar statements concerning the role of 'theory' or 'commentators', e.g.: 'Some commentators have predicted problems for NATO' (Solana 1997: 5). Admiral Norman Ray, Solana's Assistant Secretary General, also held that, 'Among some analysts, there is the view that somehow NATO has to 'choose' between NATO enlargement and good relations with Russia' (Ray 1997).

19 The term 'expansion' was later replaced by the euphemism 'enlargement', which was not as directly associated with military vocabulary from the age of territorial warfare. Being part of a strategy that tied security with peace and democracy, 'expansion' was not an appropriate word for the initiative. Interestingly, Russia stuck to the concept of NATO expansion.

20 This does not mean that Social Constructivist researchers were walking the halls of power and giving strategic advice in any direct manner. But in Oren's words: 'the scholar's personal independence ... does not necessarily guarantee that her scholarship ... [is] "uncontaminated" by the politics of ... security' (Oren 2000: 546). Williams argues similarly, that 'the relationship between Constructivist Security Studies and institutional strategies is not one of direct, personal links, but one of affinity with this field, and of a (largely misrecognized) participation in its production and reproduction' (Williams 2007: 123–24).

21 The quote is almost a direct paraphrasing of the most commonly known Constructivist mantra from the 1990s by Alexander Wendt (1992; see also NAC 1996b: paras. 1 and 10).

22 The first time in its history NATO used force was on February 28, 1994, when four Bosnian Serb war planes breached the UN-imposed no-fly zone over Bosnia and Herzegovina (Hendrickson 2004: 2).

23 The WEU Council and Secretariat-General completed relocation from London to Brussels in January 1993, thereby joining the 'capital of European security', which already housed the NATO headquarters and the EU. This enabled the organization to be close to the policy process that was restructuring the European security architecture while at the same time being able to draw on the military expertise of the member state delegations to NATO.

24 The declaration got its name from the hotel in which the meeting was held near Bonn: The Hotel Petersberg.

25 The WEU also held on to the common defence contributions in accordance with Article 5 of the Washington Treaty (NATO) and Article V of the modified Brussels Treaty (WEU 1954).

26 In connection with the deteriorating situation in the Balkans in the early 1990s, Wallander holds that 'NATO still had a collective defense mindset and structure, and it had not exercised, and practiced for anything other than its Cold War mission under Article 5' (Wallander 2000: 719). This was about to change.

27 The ARRC Headquarters assumed, for the first time, command of the land component of the NATO-led Peace Implementation Forces (IFOR) in Bosnia and Herzegovina on December 20, 1995 (NATO 2001: Chapter 12).

28 The Prague summit created 'a NATO Response Force (NRF) consisting of a technologically advanced, flexible, deployable, interoperable and sustainable force including land, sea, and air elements ready to move quickly to wherever needed, as decided by the Council' (NATO 2002c: para. 4a).

29 The WEU continued to exist as an organization. In practice, however, it was no longer a player in European security after the NATO Washington summit in 1999, the EU Cologne Council the same year, the WEU Marseille Declaration of November 2000, and the 1352nd meeting of the Council of Western European Union in June 2001. Before that, however, the organization made several attempts to regain a central position in European security. Examples include the 2000 CRISEX , which was a desk exercise about the designation of NATO assets and capabilities to a WEU-led mission based on a Petersberg scenario (NATO 2000). In practice, the results of the cooperation between WEU and NATO were transferred to the EU–NATO relationship after 2001.

30 Given this deadline, it is sometimes referred to as the Headline Goal 2003.

31 Especially the lacking European capabilities relating to 'lift' were held up as evidence that Europe would be unable to play a credible military role for the foreseeable future. 'Lift' concerns the ability to transport a fighting force: 'unglamorous, logistical lift is probably the key component in fighting a war in the post-Cold War era' (Hulsman 2000: 48).

32 The EU felt the need to be able to carry out missions similar to IFOR, SFOR and KFOR – what Bailes calls Europe's 'Kosovo motivation' (Bailes 1999: 316). This motivation unavoidably carried hints of competition and differentiation between the EU and NATO. There would be little point in pushing for a European alternative in crisis management if it did not "imply flying a European flag more often' (ibid.).

33 An official reported to Wallander that 'since 1994 NATO has been an Article 4 institution', meaning that the alliance had shifted its focus from collective defence to consultations on issues that effect common security (Wallander 2000: 739). 'The Parties will consult together whenever, in the opinion of any of them, the territorial integrity, political independence or security of any of the Parties is threatened' (NATO 1949: Article 4).

34 Huysmans mentions two exceptions to this easy transference of capabilities: that NATO organized training seminars with humanitarian organizations to improve co-operation; and that the humanitarian and military command structures did not work according to the same principles (Huysmans 2002b: 607).

35  In 2004 alone, CER published three essays and ran five seminars on Turkish accession to the EU (CER 2004).

36  It is interesting that Mark Leonard uses this understanding of power to describe the EU in a positive way. Foucault wrote his analysis in an attempt to uncover the hidden power in society and has usually been used as a critique of power holders.

37  The Afghanistan mission has shown that military capability in deployable versions has become the top priority for NATO. The recent developments in Ukraine may tip this balance.

38  The CER was not the only think tank or agent to advocate the view that soft, normative power was the superior type of power in the post-Cold War field. For more, see Everts *et al.* (2004); Manners (2002); Diez (2005); Matlary (2006).

39  The CFSP was the EU programme that preceded the ESDP. It was introduced with the Maastrich Treaty.

40  Hyde-Price refers to this as 'alphabet soup' and includes the WEU, the UN and the OSCE in the game. I have chosen to focus on the institutional battles between the EU and NATO, as they were heated and very defining at the time (Hyde-Price 2000: 141).

41  After the Berlin Accord – the process known as Berlin+ – French President Chirac played a strong card: he suggested to President Clinton that the position of Supreme Allied Commander over the Allied Forces South be transferred from the US to a European country (Sloan 2005: 102; Howorth and Keeler 2003). This suggestion was doomed to failure (France being the primary motor behind the European bids for autonomy) and to leave the American ally with no option other than to decline. The French President wanted to show that NATO was never going to be the right organization for handling European security by demonstrating that the Europeans would even not be given the lead in their own backyard. The French preferred the EU to take over security matters – first through the WEU and later through the EU. The French and American versions of the Berlin Accords paint a rather clear picture of what was at stake in the ESDI/ESDP letter game: the legitimate position as spokesperson and representative of European security.

42  In the EU language at the time, this meant that security would remain in the 'second pillar' of the European Union and not be moved to the first, which included decision procedures whereby a majority vote would be enough to pass a decision. Security would remain an issue on which unanimity was required and decisions were made by the Council of Ministers.

43  The change did not only surprise people outside Britain. Howorth argues that "It is no exaggeration to say that fewer then two dozen individuals were involved in constructing the co-ordinated discourse that generated the UK side of the St Malo paradigm shift' (Howorth 2004: 221). According to Howorth, there was no discourse surrounding the decision to sign St Malo (ibid.: 222–223).

44  Reactions in the US were, however, quite strong: 'When Madeleine Albright and the Washington community woke up on the morning of 5 December, they were shocked by the St Malo text. Albright responded with her famous "Three D's" (Howorth 2004: 222). The three D's were: no duplication of NATO assets in the EU, no discrimination of non-EU NATO members, and no decoupling of Europe from North America (Albright 1998; for discussion, see Bailes 1999 and Bozo 2003).

45  The Franco–British consensus did not concern all aspects of security, to say the least. The Franco–British summit at Le Touquet in February 2003 on closer policy co-operation in the Balkans 'had the paradoxical effect, in the spring of 2003, of seeing Britain and France screaming at one another over Iraq, while simultaneously embracing one another over many ongoing dimensions of ESDP' (Howorth 2004: 230).

46 Article Five of the North Atlantic Treaty states: 'The Parties agree that an armed attack against one or more of them in Europe or North America shall be considered an attack against them all and consequently they agree that, if such an armed attack occurs, each of them, in exercise of the right of individual or collective self-defence recognised by Article 51 of the Charter of the United Nations, will assist the Party or Parties so attacked by taking forthwith, individually and in concert with the other Parties, such action as it deems necessary, including the use of armed force, to restore and maintain the security of the North Atlantic area' (NATO 1949).

47 The United States would provide most of the military hardware in the search for the perpetrators of the attacks themselves – NATO Article V or not (US and UK began action on October 7, 2001, without the NATO apparatus). NATO did, however, send seven NATO AWACS radar aircraft to help patrol the skies over the United States from mid-October 2001 to mid-May 2002 and assisted with elements of the Standing Naval Forces to patrol the eastern Mediterranean from October 26, 2001 and, in March 2003, the Strait of Gibraltar (NATO 2007a: 1–2)

48 The military dimension of the decision was regulated by the Washington Treaty (Article V), which states that in the case of an American demand, the member states should take 'such actions as it deems necessary, including the use of armed forces' (NATO 1949). The article would only come into effect if it could be confirmed that the attack came from *abroad*.

49 The comment of Moens was probably written with the terrorist attacks as a recent background for evaluating the relationship between the EU and NATO – and before the presentation of the European Security Strategy, which constituted a new bold move in the field by the EU.

50 That the alliance was not included in the American plans to intervene in Afghanistan and that the NATO ISAF (International Security Assistance Force) was only created in December 2001 *after* the Americans had removed the Taliban regime themselves support this reading. Many perceived this as a devaluation of NATO as a central security organization, and prophecies about the end of NATO re-emerged. Recent history including the Libya intervention in 2011 seems to have proven this wrong.

51 This was the situation when US Defense Secretary Donald Rumsfeld drew the distinction between 'old Europe' and 'new Europe'. 'New Europe' included the European countries that supported the American plans to intervene in Iraq. In a newspaper add printed in several European newspapers, the leaders of Britain, Spain, Portugal, Italy, Denmark, Hungary, Poland and the Czech Republic expressed solidarity with the American position (*Economist* 2003b: 3).

52 Technically France, Germany and Belgium broke the 'silence procedure' on the decision to provide assistance to Turkey. The silence procedure gives the member countries a set amount of time in which to 'break silence' if they disagree with the text laid forward for decision in e.g. NAC. If no one breaks the silence before the deadline, the decision stands. This technique is used especially in heated discussions. It takes the debate out of the face-to-face interaction and gives the states time to consider their position and negotiate informally with other member states. Wallander reports from interviews with senior US officials to NATO that the culture in the alliance has developed so that 'countries do not want to break silence' (Wallander 2000: 724).

53 The DPC was dissolved following a review of committees in 2010. Its responsibilities were absorbed by the North Atlantic Council (NAC).

54 France withdrew from the integrated military structure of NATO in 1966.

55 It can also be read as a response to the adoption of the new National Security Strategy of the United States of America from September 2002 and the NATO Prague Summit Conclusions of November 2002. In Prague, NATO cast away its

'European straightjacket' and put its capabilities behind the quest for global security. In the European Security Strategy, the EU also envisions a global role for itself.

56 As early as 2001–02, Forster and Wallace foresaw a development in this direction: 'The parallel enlargement of the EU [and NATO] and the expansion of EU capabilities – from economic integration and diplomatic consultation towards limited defence integration – suggests that the relationship between EU and the US may progressively displace NATO as the forum for negotiating the terms of transatlantic partnership"' (Forster and Wallace 2001: 117).

# 7 Conclusion

Looking back at the years after the end of the Cold War from today's perspective not only provides an interesting historical insight. This book also suggests that security is not a stable concept or phenomenon and that it is continuously negotiated with the means of different types of power (capital) and with different strategies. It may seem anachronistic to put such emphasis on a security situation, which seems so long ago and so far away from how we have conceptualized security in NATO for more than two decades. But events in Ukraine in the spring of 2014, when Russia annexed the Crimea region despite international pressure and NATO cut all contacts with Russia as a result, show us that this is far from a dull exercise. Security remains contested, and with the Ukraine situation, Russia might have finally wrestled itself into a position in which it gets to define the shape of what security means for the foreseeable future. Only future analyses will be able to determine in what way this affects the balance of power – in terms of valued types of capital – in the European security field. Has everything changed? Probably not. For as Bourdieu would have it, the field perspective captures change within the logic of reproduction. It is my contention that there will continue to be more than military power in the equation. A Bourdieusian analysis helps us keep an open mind towards this fact.

NATO came out of the 1990s with a dramatically changed understanding of its strategic environment, of military capabilities, and of the possibility to change the future in a more peaceful direction. Over a decade later – after the long Afghanistan mission and other central military operations including Libya and anti-piracy actions – NATO still held this view of the world in many respects. It was possible to change the strategic environment by the spread of democracy (sometimes backed up with military forces). Social networks and scientific capital backed up this doxa.

Ukraine might carry the potential to change that conception (even if the similar situation in Georgia in 2008 did not). But as I argue in this book, the changes after the Cold War were gradual and did not happen overnight. Russia may have pushed conventional deterrence to the top of the agenda for 2014 and beyond, and NATO may have to rethink how the military instrument should function in the future. Is a rapid reaction force (NATO Response

Force, NRF) adequate in the face of a massive Russian army? Will NATO direct its missile shield against Russia? Or turned on its head: is Russia even interested in competing with NATO? Will it  what Russia does matter at all for the conceptualization of security in the European region? I will contend that only time will tell. In times of change, there is a tendency to fall back to common sense conceptualizations of how security mechanisms play out. And there is a real risk that analyses for the foreseeable future will overemphasize the crude, military hardware and balance of power understanding of European security. But this would be a serious mistake.

Theoretically speaking, this book has insisted that there is more to change than discourse, and more to security than military power. Bids for domination need to be meticulously analysed, taking into account a range of actors not normally present in security analyses and  sources of power not typically considered powerful as such for security. Who could have foreseen that theoretical statements would become so powerful in the restructuring of European security after the end of the Cold War with the conventional Security Studies toolbox as guidelines? Not many. And who could afford to dismiss military hardware as a thing of the past entirely? Many tried (none mentioned, none forgotten) but this book has argued that the military instrument – which in some phases during the 1990s seemed a burden rather than an asset – remained relevant. Relevant in new ways, and sometimes depending, not on actual military strength, but on the conceptualization of military capital in a specific field. At the same time – and this will also remain true for the future – social networks (capital) remained a cornerstone of European security. Questions to be followed in this regard are how NATO will develop its partnership policy and how the relations with other international organizations – notably still, the EU – will play out. Does NATO still get to speak for European security in the future? Or will the EU take over this role? How will the science programmes be followed up and in what way can science assist in the new situation?

NATO transformations were at the heart of discussions in this book. But in order to grasp these, I zoomed in on two pivotal theoretical challenges with relevance for IR and Security Studies more broadly. First, I argued that fundamental assumptions underpinning the orthodox understanding of the theory/practice relationship in IR and Security Studies had created a blind spot towards practice. A discussion and reformulation of how the science/policy nexus had been understood was therefore called for. The second theoretical challenge lay in the construction of an approach which went beyond epistemology and philosophy and added sociological patterns of practice to the methodological toolbox. I set out to construct an approach which translated the epistemologically formulated claims about the impossibility of detached knowledge production into concrete analyses of *how* theory and practice hung together.

These endeavours were necessary for understanding the specific constellation and changes underpinning European security in the 1990s. The empirical challenge thus became to show how theory and practice in Europe 'hung together': what relation (if any) was there between theory and NATO practice in Europe in the 1990s, and how did this influence the constitution of important issues? The answers to these questions followed from my turn to reflexive sociology. The 'link' or 'hanging together' was thus conceptualized as being part of a wider power struggle in which 'theory' was both a specific type of *practice* connected to expertise and a specific type of *resource* (capital) which can be mobilized dynamically in struggles. The link between NATO and 'theory' thus became a question of changing relations with 'theory-type agency' *and* a question of how theory is mobilized as a weapon or resource in social struggles.

A key term or impulse in this book has been to focus on 'the struggle'. By insisting on never to take statements at face value or letting theoretical or philosophical standpoints take the place of empirical research the question 'struggle over what?' has performed as the leitmotif through theoretical and empirical discussions. By posing this very basic question, the book has tried to turn studies of NATO in particular, and studies of International Relations/ Security Studies in general, meticulously empirical and critical. There is no external vantage point from where the researcher can observe without influencing the object of study, the philosophy of knowledge debates would have it. Instead, the researcher and knowledge need to be integrated into accounts of social phenomena – including security issues – the sociology of knowledge argument would reply. This book has tried to set an agenda for doing exactly that.

# Bibliography

Abelson, Donald E. (2002) *Do Think Tanks Matter? Assessing the Impact of Public Policy Institutes*, London, Montreal and Kingston: McGill-Queen's University Press.

Abelson, Donald E. (2004) The business of ideas: the think tank industry in the USA. In: Stone, D. and Denham, A. (eds) *Think tank traditions. Policy research and the politics of ideas*, Manchester and New York: Manchester University Press, 215–231.

Adler, Emanuel. (1992) The emergence of cooperation: national epistemic communities and the international evolution of the idea of nuclear arms control. *International Organization* 46: 101–145.

Adler, Emanuel. (1997a) Imagined (Security) Communities: Cognitive Regions in International Relations. *Millennium. Journal of International Studies* 26: 249–278.

Adler, Emanuel. (1997b) Seizing the Middle Ground: Constructivism in World Politics. *European Journal of International Relations* 3: 319–363.

Adler, Emanuel. (2002) Constructivism and International Relations. In: Carlsnaes, W., Risse, T. and Simmons, B.A. (eds) *Handbook of International Relations*, London: Sage, 95–118.

Adler, Emanuel and Barnett, Michael. (1998a) A framework for the study of security communities. In: Adler, E. and Barnett, M. (eds) *Security Communities*, Cambridge: Cambridge University Press, 29–65.

Adler, Emanuel and Barnett Michael. (1998b) *Security Communities*, Cambridge: Cambridge University Press.

Adler, Emanuel and Pouliot Vincent. (2011) *International Practices*, Cambridge: Cambridge University Press.

Adler-Nissen, R. (2009) The Diplomacy of Opting Out: A Bourdieudian Approach to National Integration Strategies. *Journal of Common Market Studies* 46: 663–684.

Adler-Nissen, Rebecca. (2011) Opting Out of an Ever Closer Union: The Integration Doxa and the Management of Sovereignty. *West European Politics* 34: 1092–1113.

Adler-Nissen, Rebecca. (ed.). (2012) *Bourdieu in International Relations. Rethinking key concepts in IR*, London: Routledge.

Adler-Nissen, Rebecca. (2014) *Opting Out of the European Union. Diplomacy, Sovereignty and European Integration*, Cambridge: Cambridge University Press.

Albright, Madeleine. (1998) The Right Balance will Secure NATO's Future. *Financial Times* December 7.

Art, Robert J. (1996) American Foreign Policy and the Fungibility of Force. *Security Studies* 5: 7–42.

Art, Robert J. (1999) Force and Fungibility Reconsidered. *Security Studies* 8: 183–189.

Ashley, Richard K. (1984) The Poverty of Neo-realism. *International Organization* 38: 225–286.

Ashley, Richard K. (1987) The Geopolitics of Geopolitical Space: Toward a Critical Social Theory of International Relations. *Alternatives* 12: 403–434.

Ashley, Richard K. (1988) Untying the Sovereign State: A Double Reading of the Anarchy Problematique. *Millennium: Journal of International Studies* 17: 227–262.

Ashley, Richard K. (1989) Imposing International Purpose: notes on a problematic of governance. In: Czempiel, E.O. and Rosenau, J.N. (eds) *Global Changes & Theoretical Challenges. Approaches to World Politics for the 1990s*, Lexington, MA: Lexington Books, 251–290.

Asmus, Ronald D. (2002a) Having an Impact: Think Tanks and the NATO Enlargement Debate. *U.S. Foreign Policy Agenda* November: 1–4.

Asmus, Ronald D. (2002b) *Opening NATO's Door. How the alliance remade itself for a new era*, New York: Columbia University Press.

Asmus, Ronald D. and Grant Charles. (2002) Can NATO remain an effective military and political alliance if it keeps growing? *NATO Review* 1: 13–17.

Bailes, Alyson J.K. (1999) NATO's European Pillar: The European Security and Defence Identity. *Defense Analysis* 15: 305–322.

Baldwin, David A. (1989) *Paradoxes of power*, New York, NY: Basil Blackwell.

Baldwin, David A. (1999) Force, Fungibility, and Influence. *Security Studies* 8: 173–183.

Baldwin, David A. (2002) Power and International Relations. In: Carlsnaes, W., Risse, T. and Simmons, B.A. (eds) *Handbook of International Relations*, London and Thousand Oaks, CA: Sage, 177–191.

Bartelson, Jens. (1995) *The Genealogy of Sovereignty*, Cambridge: Cambridge University Press.

Behnke, Andreas. (2000) Inscriptions of Imperial Order: NATO's Mediterranean Initiative. *The International Journal of Peace Studies* 5: available at http://www.gmu. edu/academic/ijps/vol5_1/behnke.htm (accessed 30 August 2007).

Behnke, Andreas. (2013) *NATO's Security Discourse after the Cold War. Representing the West*, London: Routledge.

Bennett, Christopher. (2003) Building Effective Partnerships. *NATO Review*: 1–4 (web edition).

Berling, Trine  Villumsen. (2011) Science and Securitization. Objectivation, the authority of the speaker, and mobilization of scientific facts. *Security Dialogue* 42: 385–397.

Berling, Trine  Villumsen. (2012a) Bourdieu, International Relations, and European Security. *Theory and Society* 41: 451–478.

Berling, Trine  Villumsen. (2012b) Knowledges. In: Adler-Nissen, R. (ed.) *Bourdieu in International Relations: Rethinking Key Concepts in IR*, London: Routledge, 59–77.

Berling, Trine  Villumsen. (forthcoming) *Exploring the social landscape of expertise: Think tank practices in European security.*

Berling, Trine  Villumsen and Bueger Christian. (2013) Practical Reflexivity and Political Science: Strategies for Relating Scholarship and Political Practice. *PS: Political Science and Politics* 46: 115–119.

Berling, Trine  Villumsen and Bueger Christian. (2015) *Security Expertise. Practice, Power, Responsibility*, London: Routledge.

Bigo, Didier. (2000) Liaison officers in Europe: New officers in the European security field. In: Sheptycki, J. (ed.) *Issues in Transnational Policing*, London: Routledge, 67–99.

Bigo, Didier. (2002a) Border Regimes and Security in an Enlarged European Community. Police Cooperation with CEECs: between trust and obligation. In: Zielonka, J. (ed.) *Europe Unbound: enlarging and reshaping the boundaries of the European Union*, London: Routledge, 213–239.

Bigo, Didier. (2002b) Security and Immigration: Toward a Critique of the Governmentality of Unease. *Alternatives: Global, Local, Political* 27: 63–92.

Bigo, Didier. (2005) Frontier Controls in the European Union: Who is in Control? In: Bigo, D. and Guild, E. (eds) *Controlling Frontiers: Free Movement into and Within Europe*, Aldershot: Ashgate, 49–99.

Bigo, Didier. (2006) Globalized-in-security: The Field and the Ban-opticon. In: Solomon, J. and Sakai, N. (eds) *Translation, Biopolitics and Colonial Difference*, Hong Kong: University of Hong Kong Press, 109–156.

Bigo, Didier. (2012) Security. Analysing transnational professionals of (in)security in Europe. In: Adler-Nissen, R. (ed.) *Bourdieu in International Relations. Rethinking Key Concepts in IR*, London and New York: Routledge, 114–130.

Bigo, Didier and Guild, Elspeth. (2005) *Controlling Frontiers: Free Movement into and Within Europe*, Aldershot: Ashgate.

Bigo, Didier and Walker, R.B.J. (2007) Political Sociology and the Problem of the International. *Millenium: Journal of International Studies* 35: 725–739.

Bilski, Andrew. (1995) Islamic Fundamentalism. *Maclean's*.

Blair, Tony. (1999) *Doctrine of International Community*, Economic Club of Chicago: Prime Minister's Office. Available at http://number-10.gov.uk/public/info/index.html.

Booth, Ken. (1991) Security and Emancipation. *Review of International Studies* 17: 313–327.

Booth, Ken. (1997) Discussion: a reply to Wallace. *Review of International Studies* 23: 371–377.

Bourdieu, Pierre. (1971) Intellectual field and creative project. In: Young, M.F.D. (ed.) *Knowledge and Control: New Directions for the Sociology of Education*, London: Collier-Macmillan, 166–188.

Bourdieu, Pierre. (1972) *Esquisse d'une théorie de la pratique, précedé de trois etudes d'ethnologie kabyle*, Geneve and Paris: Librairie Droz.

Bourdieu, Pierre. (1977) *Outline of a theory of practice*, Cambridge: Cambridge University Press.

Bourdieu, Pierre. (1986 [1979]) *Dinstinction. A Social Critique of the Judgement of Taste*, New York and London: Routledge.

Bourdieu, Pierre. (1988) *Homo Academicus*, Cambridge: Polity Press.

Bourdieu, Pierre. (1990) *The Logic of Practice*, Cambridge: Polity Press.

Bourdieu, Pierre. (1993) *The Field of Cultural Production. Essays on Art and Literature*, New York: Columbia University Press.

Bourdieu, Pierre. (1998a) *Practical Reason*, Cambridge: Polity Press.

Bourdieu, Pierre. (1998b) *The State Nobility*, Cambridge and Oxford: Polity Press.

Bourdieu, Pierre. (2000) *Pascalian Meditations*, London: Stanford University Press.

Bourdieu, Pierre. (2004) *Science of Science and Reflexivity*, Cambridge: Polity Press.

Bourdieu, Pierre. (2005) *The Social Structures of the Economy*, Cambridge: Polity Press.

Bourdieu, Pierre and Wacquant, Loic, J.D. (1992) *An invitation to reflexive sociology*, Cambridge: Polity Press.

Bourdieu, Pierre and Wacquant, Loic, J.D. (2004 [1996]) *Refleksiv sociologi – mål og midler*, Copenhagen: Hans Reitzels Publishers.

Boyer, Yves and Schmitt, Burkardt. (2002) Can and should Europe bridge the capabilities gap? *NATO Review* 3: 12–16.

Bozo, Frédéric. (2003) The Effects of Kosovo and the Danger of Decoupling. In: Howorth, J. and Keeler, J.T.S. (eds) *Defending Europe: The EU, NATO and the quest for European Autonomy*, New York and Houndsmills: Palgrave Macmillan, 61–77.

Breitenbauch, Henrik Ø. (2013) *International Relations in France. Writing between Discipline and State*, London and New York: Routledge.

Brown, Michael E. (1995) The flawed logic of NATO Expansion. *Survival* 37: 34–52.

Brzezinski, Zbigniew. (1995) A Plan for Europe. *Foreign Affairs* 74: 26–42.

Bueger, Christian and Bethke, Felix. (2011) *Boundary Concepts and the Interaction of Communities of Practice. Lessons from the Security-Development-Nexus*, London: Annual Conference of Millenium: Journal of International Studies.

Bueger, Christian and Bethke, Felix. (2013) Actor-Networking the 'failed state' – and enquiry into the life of concepts. *Journal of International Relations and Development* doi: 10.1057./jird. 2012. 30: 1–31.

Bueno de Mesquita, Bruce. (2002) Domestic Politics and International Relations. *International Studies Quarterly* 46: 1–10.

Bush, George W. (2003) President Discusses the Future of Iraq, [Speech to the American Enterprise Institute, Washington Hilton Hotel].

Buzan, Barry. (1991 [1983]) *People, States and Fear: An agenda for international security studies in the Post-Cold War Era*, London: Harvester Wheatsheaf.

Buzan, Barry, de Wilde, Jaap and Wæver, Ole. (1998) *Security: A New Framework for Analysis*, Boulder, CO: Lynne Rienner.

Buzan, Barry and Hansen Lene. (2009) *The evolution of international security studies*, Cambridge: Cambridge University Press.

Büger, Christian and Gadinger, Frank. (2007) Reassembling and Dissecting: International Relations Practice from a Science Studies Perspective. *International Studies Perspectives* 8: 90–110.

Büger, Christian and Villumsen, Trine. (2007) Beyond the Gap: Relevance, Fields of Practice and the Securitizing Consequences of (Democratic Peace) Research. *Journal of International Relations and Development* 10: 417–448.

C.A.S.E. (2006) Critical Approaches to Security in Europe: A networked Manifesto. *Security Dialogue* 37: 443–487.

C.A.S.E. (2007) Europe, knowledge, politics – Engaging with the limits: The C.A.S.E. collective responds. *Security Dialogue* 38: 559–576.

Calhoun, Craig, Gerteis, Joseph, Moody, James, *et al.* (2002) *Contemporary Sociological Theory*, Oxford: Blackwell.

Callon, Michel and Latour, Bruno. (1981) Unscrewing the big Leviathan: How actors macrostructure reality and how sociologists help them to do so. In: Knorr Cetina, K. and Cicourel, A.V. (eds) *Advances in Social Theory and Methodology. Toward an Integration of Micro- and Macro-Sociologies*, Boston, MA: Routledge and Kegan Paul, 277–303.

Cameron, Fraser and Moravscik, Andrew. (2003) Should the European Union be able to do everything that NATO can? *NATO Review* 3: 20–25.

Campbell, David. (1992) *Writing Security: United States Foreign Policy and the Policy of Identity*, Manchester: Manchester University Press.

Carvalho-Rodrigues, F. (2001) NATO's science programs: origins and influence. *Technology in Society* 23: 375–381.

Cecchini, Paolo, Jones Erik and Lorentzen Jochen. (2001) Europe and the Concept of Enlargement. *Survival* 43: 155–165.

CER. (2002) *Centre for European Reform Annual Report 2002*, London: Centre for European Reform.

CER. (2004) *Centre for European Reform Annual Report 2004*, London: Centre for European Reform.

CESD. (2003) 16-to-3: The Allies at loggerheads over Iraq. *NATO Notes, Centre for European Security and Disarmament* 5: 1–2.

Chalmers, Malcolm. (1990) Beyond the Alliance System. *World Policy Journal* 7: 215–250.

Chalmers, Malcolm. (2001) The Atlantic burden-sharing debate – widening or fragmenting? *International Affairs* 77: 569–585.

Chamberlin, Jeffrey. (2004) *Comparisons of U.S. and Foreign Military Spending: Data from Selected Public Sources*, Washington: Congressional Research Service. Library of Congress.

Chan, Steve. (1995) Grasping the Peace Dividend: Some Propositions on the Conversion of Swords into Plowshares. *Mershon International Studies Review* 39: 53–95.

Ciuta, Felix. (2002) The end(s) of NATO: Security, strategic option and narrative transformation. *Contemporary Security Policy* 23: 35–62.

Clausewitz, Carl von. (1989) *On War*, Princeton, NJ: Princeton University Press.

Cohn, Carol. (1987) Slick 'Ems, Glick Ems, Christmas Trees and Cookie Cutters: Nuclear language and How we Learned to Pat the Bomb. *Bulletin of Atomic Scientists*: June, 17–24.

Coker, Christopher. (2002) *Globalisation and Insecurity in the Twenty-first Century: NATO and the Management of Risk*, London: International Institute for Strategic Studies, Adelphi Paper 345.

Coker, Christopher. (2003) From MAD to Nomad: 9–11 and the Future of the Western Alliance. In: Heurlin, B.M.V.R. (ed.) *Challenges and Capabilities. NATO in the 21st Century*, Copenhagen: Institute for International Studies, Security and Defence Studies Programme, 11–23.

Cologne Council Declaration. (1999) *Presidency Conclusions.*, Cologne: European Council 3–4 June, 1999.

Cook, Robin. (1999) It is fascism that we are fighting. *The Guardian*.

Cooper, Robert. (1996) *The Post-Modern State and the World Order*, London: Demos.

Cornish, Paul. (1996) European security: the end of the architecture and the new NATO. *International Affairs* 72: 751–769.

Cornish, Paul and Edwards, Geoffrey. (2001) Beyond the EU/NATO dichotomy: the beginnings of a European strategic culture. *International Affairs* 77: 587–603.

Cox, Michael. (2005) Beyond the West: Terrors in Transatlantia. *European Journal of International Relations* 11: 203–233.

Cox, Michael. (2006) Let's Argue about the West: Reply to Vincent Pouliot. *European Journal of International Relations* 12: 129–134.

Cox, Robert W. (1981) Social Forces, States and World Orders: Beyond International Relations Theory. *Millennium* 10: 126–155.

Croft, Stuart. (2000) The EU, NATO and Europeanisation: The Return of the Architechtural Debate. *European Security* 9: 1–20.

Crossley, Nick. (2004) On Systematically Distorted Communication. Bourdieu and the Socioanalysis of Publics. *The Sociological Review* 52: 88–112.

CSCE. (1973) *Blue Book: Final Recommendations of the Helsinki Consultations*, Helsinki: Conference on Security and Co-Operation in Europe.

da Silva, Lt. General Mario. (1998) Implementing the Combined Joint Task Force Concept. *NATO Review* 46: 16–19.

Dahl Kelstrup, Jesper. (2007) Tænketanke i forandring – imellem national sikkerhed og globalt risikosamfund. *Militært Tidsskrift* 136: 131–142.

Daugbjerg, Carsten and Marsh, David. (1998) Explaining policy outcomes: integrating the policy network approach with macro-level and micro-level analysis. In: Marsh, D. (ed,) *Comparing Policy Networks*, Buckingham and Philadelphia, PA: Open University Press, 52–71.

De Santis, Hugh. (1991) The Graying of NATO. *Washington Quarterly* 14: 51–65.

Denham, Andrew and Garnett, Mark. (2004) A 'hollowed-out tradition? British Think tanks in the twenty-first century. In: Stone, D. and Denham, A. (eds) *Think tank traditions. Policy Research and the politics of ideas*, Manchester and New York: Manchester University Press, 232–246.

Der Derian, James. (1992) *Antidiplomacy. Spies, Terror, Speed, and War*, Cambridge and Oxford: Blackwell.

Deutsch, Karl W. (1954) *Political Community at the International Level: Problems of Definition and Measurement*, New York: Doubleday.

Deutsch, Karl W. (1957) *Political Community and the North Atlantic Area*, Princeton, NJ: Princeton University Press.

Dezalay, Yves and Garth, Bryan G. (2006) From the Cold War to Kosovo: The Rise and Renewal of the Field of International Human Rights. *Annual Review of Law and Social Science* 2: 231–255.

Dezalay, Yves and Garth, Bryant G. (2002) *The Internationalization of Palace Wars. Lawyers, Economists, and the Contest to Transform Latin American States*, Chicago, IL and London: The University of Chicago Press.

Diez, Thomas. (2005) Constructing the Self and Changing Others: Reconsidering 'Normative Power Europe'. *Millennium* 33: 613–636.

Donnelly, Jack. (1998) Human Rights: A New Standard of Civilization? *International Affairs* 74: 1–23.

Droziak, William. (1995) NATO turns attention to Islamic Extremists. *International Herald Tribune.*

Duffield, John S. (1994) NATO's Functions after the Cold War. *Political Science Quarterly* 109: 763–787.

Duke, Simon. (2004) The European Security Strategy in a Comparative Framework: Does it make for Secure Alliances in a Better World? *European Foreign Affairs Review* 9: 459–481.

Eagleton-Pierce, Matthew. (2013) *Symbolic Power in the World Trade Organization*, Oxford: Oxford University Press.

EAPC. (1997) *Basic Document of the Euro-Atlantic Partnership Council*, Sintra, Portugal: NATO Press Release M-NACC-EAPC-1(97)66 30 May 1997.

EAPC. (1998) *Chairman's Summary of the Meeting of the Euro-Atlantic Partnership Council in Defence Ministers Session*. Brussels: NATO Press Release M-EAPC-12 June 1998.

*Economist.* (1999) Armies and Arms. *The Economist* April 22: 1-4 (web edition).

*Economist.* (2003a) A Fractured Alliance. *The Economist* February 13: 1–2 (web edition).

*Economist*. (2003b) How deep is the rift? *The Economist* February 13: 1–3 (web edition).

Elias, Norbert. (2000) *The Civilizing Process*, Oxford: Blackwell Publishers.

Emirbayer, Mustafa. (1997) Manifesto for Relational Sociology. *American Journal of Sociology* 103: 281–317.

Emirbayer, Mustafa and Johnson, Victoria. (2008) Bourdieu and Organizational analysis. *Theory and Society* 37: 1–44.

Eriksson, Johan. (1999a) Debating the Politics of Security Studies: Response to Goldmann, Wæver and Williams. *Cooperation and Conflict* 34: 345–352.

Eriksson, Johan. (1999b) Observers or Advocates? On the Political Role of Security Analysts. *Cooperation and Conflict* 34: 311–330.

Eriksson, Johan and Sundelius, Bengt. (2005) Molding Minds that Form Policy: How to Make Research Useful. *International Studies Perspectives* 6: 51–72.

EU. (1999) *Helsinki Headline Goal: Presidency Conclusions*, Helsinki: European Council.

EU. (2000a) *Council Decision of 14 February 2000 setting up the Interim Military Body, Council of EU*, Brussels: The Council of the European Union, 2000/144/CFSP, 14 February.

EU. (2000b) *Council Decision of 14 February setting up the Interim Political and Security Committee, Council of EU*, Brussels: The Council of the European Union, 2000/143/CFSP, 14 February.

EU. (2000c) *EU-NATO ad hoc working groups, Council of EU*, Brussels: Council of the European Union, 10025/1/00 Rev 1, PESC 328, COSDP 26, 5 July.

EU. (2000d) *Food for Thought: Preparatory Document related to CESDP. Elaboration of the Headline Goal. 'Food for Thought'* , Brussels: European Council Press Release number 6765/00, 14 March.

EU. (2000e) *Military Capabilities Commitment Declaration*, Brussels: French Presidency on behalf of the European Union.

EU. (2000f) *Santa Maria da Feira European Council 19 and 20 June 2000* Feira: Portuguese Presidency of the EU.

EU. (2001a) *European Commission: Financing of Civilian Crisis Management Operations*, Brussels: European Union Commission. Communication from the Commission to the Council and the European Parliament, COM (2001) 647 final, 28 November.

EU. (2001b) *Joint Declaration by the Heads of State and Government of the European Union, The President of the European Parliament, The President of the European Commission, and The High Representative for the Common Foreign and Security Policy*, Brussels: EU.

EU. (2003) Declaration on EU Military Capabilities: EU External Relations Council 9379/03 (Presse 138), May.

EU. (2007) *Glossary EU*, http://europa.eu/scadplus/glossary/petersberg_tasks_en_htm: 17 September.

EU. (2008a) *The CFSP Budget*, www.diplomatie.gouv.fr/en/european-union_157/eu-in-the-world_1491/common-foreign-and-security-policy_5463/operation-of-the-cfsp_5467/cfsp-decision-making-processes-and-instruments_5473/the-cfsp-budget_8753.html.

EU. (2008b) *Fifth EU Framework Programme*, http://cordis.europa.eu/fp5/src/budget.htm: 7 May.

EU. (2008c) *Fourth EU Framework Programme*, http://cordis.europa.eu/guidance/fp4_en.html: 7 May.

EU. (2008d) *Overview of EU Framework Programmes*, http://www.eurosfaire.prd.fr/bibliotheque/pdf/FP7_Complete_presentation_April_2005.pdf: 13 May.

EU. (2008e) *Sixth EU Framework Programme*, http://cordis.europa.eu/fp6_glance.htm#: 7 May.

European Security Strategy. (2003) *A Secure Europe in a Better World*, Thessaloniki: European Council, 20 June 2003.

EV. (1999) Europe takes first steps on road to becoming a military superpower. *European Voice* 5: 1–2 (web edition).

EV. (2000a) Early EU-NATO talks likely on protecting military secrets. *European Voice* 6: 1 (web edition).

EV. (2000b) France softens stance on NATO's involvement in EU defence policy. *European Voice* 6: 1 (web edition).

EV. (2000c) A safe pair of hands at the heart of Union's foreign policy. *European Voice* 6: 1–2 (web edition).

Everts, Steven. (2004) *An Asset but not a Model: Turkey, the EU and the Wider Middle East*, London: Centre for European Reform Briefing Note.

Everts, Steven, Freedman, Lawrence, Grant, Charles, *et al.* (2004) *A European Way of War*, London: Centre for European Reform.

Everts, Steven and Schmitt, Gary. (2002) Is military power still the key to international security? *NATO Review* 4: 17–22.

Feldman, Jonathan. (1993) Broadening the Peace Dividend. *Society* 30: 32–40.

Fierke, KM and Wiener Antje. (1999) Constructing Institutional interests: EU and NATO enlargement. *Journal of European Public Policy* 6: 721–742.

Fieschi, Catherine and Gaffney, John. (2004) French think tanks in comparative perspective. In: Stone, D. and Denham, A. (eds) *Think tank traditions. Policy research and the politics of ideas*, Manchester and New York: Manchester University Press, 105–120.

Fisher, Donald. (1990) Homo Academicus. *Journal of Higher Education* 61: 581–591.

Fisk, Robert. (1999) The West's Fear of Islam is no Excuse for Racism. *The Independent* 3 November: 1–3.

Forster, Anthony and Wallace, William. (2001) What is NATO for? *Survival* 43: 107–122.

Franco–British Summit Declaration (1998). Joint Declaration on European Defense, Saint-Malo, The Heads of State and Government of France and the United Kingdom.

Friedrichs, Jörg and Kratochwil Friedrich. (2009) On Acting and Knowing: How Pragmatism Can Advance International Relations Research and Methodology. *International Organization* 63: 701–731.

Friis, Lykke. (1997) *When Europe Negotiates. From Europe Agreements to Eastern Enlargement*, Copenhagen: Institute for Political Science, University of Copenhagen. Ph.D. Series.

Fukuyama, Francis. (1989) The End of History. *The National Interest* 16: 3–35.

Fukuyama, Francis. (1992) *The End of History and the Last Man*, Harmondsworth: Penguin.

Gadea, M. Dolores, Pardos, Eva, Pérez-Forniés, Claudia, *et al.* (2004) A long-rund analysis of defence spending in the NATO countries (1960–1999). *Defence and Peace Economics* 15: 231–249.

Galvin, John C. (1994) Breaking Through and Being Heard. *Mershon International Studies Review* 38: 173–174.

Garfield, Eugene. (1987) NATO's Strategy for Science. *The Scientist* 1: 9.

Geis, Anna, Brock, Lothar and Müller, Harald. (2006) *Democratic Wars. Looking at the dark side of democratic peace*, Basingstoke: : Palgrave MacMillan.

George, Alexander L. (1993) *Bridging the Gap: Theory and Practice in Foreign Policy*, Washington, DC: U.S. Institute of Peace Press.

George, Alexander L. (1994) Some guides to Bridging the Gap. *Mershon International Studies Review* 39: 171–172.

George, Jim. (1993) Of Incarceration and Closure: Neo-realism and the New/Old World Order. *Millennium: Journal of International Studies* 22: 197–234.

George, Jim. (1994) *Discourses of Global Politics: A Critical (Re) Introduction to International Relations*, Boulder, CO: Lynne Rienner.

Gheciu, Alexandra. (2007) Security Institutions as Agents of Socialization? NATO and the 'New Europe'. In: Checkel, J.T. (ed.) *International Institutions and Socialization in Europe*, Cambridge: Cambridge University Press, 171–207.

Gibbons, Michael, Limoges, Camille, Nowotny ,Helga, *et al.* (1994) *The new production of knowledge. The dynamics of science and research in contemporary societies*, Los Angeles, CA and London: Sage Publications.

Giddens, Anthony. (1984) *The Constitution of Society*, Cambridge: Polity Press.

Glaser, Charles L. (1993) Why NATO is Still Best. Future Security Arrangements for Europe. *International Security* 18: 5–50.

Go, Julien. (2008) Global Fields and Imperial Forms: Field Theory and the British and American Empires. *Sociological Theory* 26: 201–229.

Goldmann, Kjell. (1999) Issues, Not Labels, Please! *Cooperation and Conflict* 34: 331–333.

Gray, Colin S. (1992) New Directions for Strategic Studies? How can Theory help Practice? *Security Studies* 1: 611–635.

Grayson, Kyle. (2003) *Democratic Peace Theory as Practice: (Re)Reading the Significance of Liberal Representations of War and Peace.* YCISS Working Power Series 22.

Gress, David. (1998) *From Plato to NATO – The Idea of the West and its Opponents*, New York: The Free Press.

Grieco, Joseph M. (1988) Anarchy and the limits of cooperation: A realist critique of the newest liberal institutionalism. *International Organization* 42: 485–508.

Guilhot, Nicolas. (2005) *The Democracy Makers: Human Rights and International Order*, New York: Columbia University Press.

Gusmao, R. (2001) Research networks as a means of European integration. *Technology in Society* 23: 383–393.

Guzzini, Stefano. (1994) Power Analysis as a Critique of Power Politics: Understanding Power and Governance in the Second Gulf War, European University Institute, Florence, unpublished Ph.D. thesis.

Guzzini, Stefano. (2000) A Reconstruction of Constructivism in International Relations. *European Journal of International Relations* 6: 147–182.

Guzzini, Stefano. (2001) The Significance and Roles of Teaching in International Relations. *Journal of International Relations and Development* 4: 98–117.

Guzzini, Stefano. (2003) 'Self-fulfilling geopolitics'? Or: the social production of foreign policy expertise in Europe. DIIS Working Paper 23: 1–22.

Guzzini, Stefano. (2004) 'The Cold War is what we make of it'. When peace research meets Constructivism in International Relations. In: Guzzini, S. and Jung, D. (eds) *Contemporary Security Analysis and Copenhagen Peace Research*, New York: Routledge, 40–53.

Guzzini, Stefano. (2005) The Concept of Power: a Constructivist Analysis. *Millennium: Journal of International Studies* 33: 495–521.

Guzzini, Stefano. (2006) Applying Bourdieu's framework of power analysis to IR: opportunities and limits, Paper prepared for the 47th Annual convention of the International Studies Association in Chicago 22–25 March.

Guzzini, Stefano and Jung, Dietrich. (2004) *Contemporary Security Analysis and Copenhagen Peace Research*, New York: Routledge.

Hacking, Ian. (1999) *The social construction of what?*, Cambridge, MA and London: Harvard University Press.

Hamati-Ataya, Inanna. (2012) IR Theory as International Practice/Agency: A Clinical-Cynical Bourdieusian Perspective. *Millenium* 40: 625–646.

Hamati-Ataya, Inanna. (2013) Reflectivity, reflexivity, Reflexivism: ir's "Reflexice Turn" and Beyond. *European Journal of International Relations*: 669–694.

Hansen, Lene. (1995) NATO's new discourse. In: Hansen, B. (ed.) *European Security – 2000*, Copenhagen: Copenhagen Political Studies Press, 117–135.

Hansen, Lene. (2002) Internettets Sikkerhedspolitik: Legitimitet og institutionel identitet i en virtuel tidsalder. *Politologiske Studier* 4: 1–9 (web edition).

Hansen, Lene. (2006) *Security as Practice. Discourse Analysis and the Bosnian War*, London: Routledge.

Haraway, Donna. (1992) The Promises of Monsters: A Regenerative Politics for Inappropriated Others. In: Grossberg, L., Nelson, C. and Treichler, P. (eds) *Cultural Studies*, London: Routledge, 295–337.

Hassner, Pierre. (1990) Europe Beyond Partition and Unity: Disintegration or Reconstitution? *International Affairs* 66: 461–475.

Hay, Colin. (1998) The tangled webs we weave: the discourse, strategy and practice of networking. In: Marsh, D. (ed.) *Comparing Policy Networks*, Buckingham and Philadelphia, PA: Open University Press, 33–51.

Heisbourg, Francois and de Wijk, Rob. (2001) Is the fundamental nature of the translatlantic security relationship changing? *NATO Review* 49: 15–19.

Hendrickson, Ryan C. (2004) Manfred Wörner: NATO visionary. *NATO Review* 3: 1–3 (web edition).

Hendrickson, Ryan. (2006) *Diplomacy and War at NATO. The Secretary General and Military Action after the Cold War*, Columbia: University of Missouri Press.

Holbrooke, Richard. (1995) America, A European Power. *Foreign Affairs* 74: 38–51.

Hollis, Martin. (1996) The Last Post? In: Smith, S., Booth, K. and Zalewski, M. (eds) *International Theory: Positivism and Beyond*, Cambridge: Cambridge University Press, 301–308.

Homan, Kees. (2006) *NATO, Common Funding and Peace Support Operations: A comparative perspective*, The Hague: Netherlands Institute of International Relations 'Clingendael'.

Hopf, Ted. (2002) *Social Construction of International Politics: Identities & Foreign Policies, Moscow, 1955 and 1999*, Ithaca, NY: Cornell University Press.

Howorth, Jolyon. (2004) Discourse, Ideas, and Epistemic Communities in European Security and Defence Policy. *West European Politics* 27: 211–234.

Howorth, Jolyon and Keeler John, T.S. (2003) The EU, NATO and the quest for European Autonomy. In: Howorth, J. and Keeler, J.T.S. (eds) *Defending Europe: The EU, NATO and the quest for European Autonomy*, New York and Houndsmills: Palgrave Macmillan, 3–21.

Hulsman, John C. (2000) The guns of Brussels: Burden sharing and power sharing with Europe. *Policy Review* 101: 35–49.

Hunter, Robert E. (1995) Enlargement: Part of a strategy for projecting stability to Central Europe. *NATO Review* 3: 3–8.

Huntington, Samuel P. (1993) The Clash of Civilizations? *Foreign Affairs* 72: 22–49.

Huntington, Samuel P. (1996) *The Clash of Civilizations and the Remaking of World Order*, New York: Simon and Schuster.

Huysmans, Jef. (2002a) Defining social Constructivism in security studies: The normative dilemma of writing security. *Alternatives* 27: 41–62.

Huysmans, Jef. (2002b) Shape-shifting NATO: Humanitarian Action and the Kosovo Refugee Crisis. *Review of International Studies* 28: 599–618.

Huysmans, Jef. (2006) *The Politics of Insecurity. Fear, migration and asylum in the EU*, London and New York: Routledge.

Hyde-Price, Adrian. (2000) The Antinomies of European Security: Dual Enlargement and the Reshaping of European Order. *Contemporary Security Policy* 21: 139–167.

Ibrügger, Lothar. (1998) *The Revolution in Military Affairs*, Brussels: NATO Parliamentary Assembly Special Report, Science and Technology Committee.

IISS. (2003) 2003–2004. *Military Balance* 103: 1–309.

Ish-Shalom, Piki. (2006) Theory as a Hermeneutical Mechanism: The Democratic Peace Thesis and the Politics of Democratization. *European Journal of International Relations* 12: 565–598.

Jackson, Patrick T. (2011) *The Conduct of Inquiry in International Relations. Philosophy of Science and its implications for the study of world politics*, London and New York: Routledge.

Jasanoff, Sheila. (2004a) The idiom of co-production. In: Jasanoff, S. (ed.) *States of Knowledge: The co-production of science and social order*, New York: Routledge, 1–12.

Jasanoff, Sheila. (2004b) *States of Knowledge: The Co-Production of Science and Social Order*, London and New York: Routledge.

Jentleson, Bruce W. (2002) The Need for Praxis. Bringing Policy Relevance Back In. *International Security* 26: 169–183.

Johnson, Randal. (1993) *The Field of Cultural Production. Essays on Art and Literature*, Cambridge: Polity.

Jørgensen, Knud Erik. (2000) Continental IR Theory: The Best Kept Secret. *European Journal of International Relations* 6: 9–42.

Kagan, Robert. (2002) Power and Weakness. *Policy Review*, 113 June/July.

Kagan, Robert. (2003) *Paradise and Power: America and Europe in the New World Order*, London: Atlantic Books.

Katzenstein, Peter J. (1996) *The Culture of National Security: Norms and Identity in World Politics*, New York: Columbia University Press.

Kauppi, Niilo. (2003) Bourdieu's political sociology and the politics of European integration. *Theory and Society* 32: 775–789.

Kay, Jean. (1998) Deconstructing an Alliance. *International Politics* 35: 485–503.

Keohane, Robert O. (1988) International Institutions: Two Approaches, ISA presidential address. *International Studies Quarterly* 32: 379–396.

Keohane, Robert O. and Wallander, Celeste A. (1996) Why does NATO persist? An Institutional Approach: Center of International Affairs, Harvard University.

King, Gary, Keohane Robert O. and Verba Sidney. (1994) *Designing Social Inquiry. Scientific Inference in Qualitative Research*, Princeton, NJ: Princeton University Press.

Klein, Bradley S. (1988) Hegemony and Strategic Culture: American Power Projection and Alliance Defence Politics. *Review of International Studies* 14: 133–148.

Klein, Bradley S. (1994) *Strategic Studies and World Order: The Global Politics of Deterrence*, Cambridge: Cambridge University Press.

Klein, Bradley S. (1998) Politics by Design: Remapping Security Landscapes. *European Journal of International Relations* 4: 327–345.

Krais, Beate. (1994) I mellemtiden har jeg lært alle den sociologiske forståelses sygdomme at kende (Interview with Pierre Bourdieu). In: Callewaert, S., Munk, M., Nørholm, M., *et al.* (eds) *Pierre Bourdieu. Centrale tekster inden for sociologi og kulturteori*, Copenhagen: Akademisk Forlag, 111–128.

Kratochwil, Friedrich. (2007) Of false promises and good bets: a plea for a pragmatic approach to theory building (the Tartu lecture). *Journal of International Relations and Development* 10: 1–15.

Krause, Keith and Latham Andrew. (1998) Constructing non-proliferation and arms control: the norms of Western practice. *Contemporary security policy* 19: 23–54.

Krause, Keith and Williams Michael C. (1997) *Critical Security Studies*. Minneapolis: University of Minnesota Press.

Krige, John. (2000) NATO and the strengthening of Western science in the Post-Sputnik era. *Minerva* 38: 81–108.

Kristensen, Kristian Søby. (2011) *More than an Alliance: Theorizing Security Community and the Practice of Strategic Discourse in NATO*, Copenhagen: University of Copenhagen.

Kristiansen, Kristian Søby and Ringsmose, Jens. (2006) NATO: Dette århundredes globo-cop? *Udenrigs* 2: 58–68.

Kruzel, Joseph. (1994) More a Chasm Than a Gap, But Do Scholars Want to Bridge it? *Mershon International Studies Review* 38: 179–181.

Kundera, Milan. (1984) The Tragedy of Central Europe. *New York Review of Books* 26 April: 33–38.

Lachowski, Zdzislaw. (2002) The military dimension of the European Union. In: SIPRI (ed) *SIPRI Yearbook 2002: Armaments, Disarmament and International Security*, Stockholm: SIPRI, 151–173.

Laffey, Mark and Weldes, Jutta. (1997) Beyond Belief: Ideas and Symbolic Technologies in the Study of International Relations. *European Journal of International Relations* 3: 193–237.

Larrabee, Steve and Heisbourg, Francois. (2003) How global a role can and should NATO play? *NATO Review* 1: 13–17.

Latour, Bruno. (1983) Give Me a Laboratory and I Will Raise the World. In: Knorr-Cetina, K. and Mulkay, M.J. (eds) *Science Observed: Perspectives on the Social Study of Science*, London: Sage, 141–170.

Latour, Bruno. (1988) *The Pasteurization of France*, Cambridge, MA: Harvard University Press.

Latour, Bruno. (1993) *We Have Never Been Modern*, Cambridge, MA: Harvard University Press.

Law, John. (1992) Notes on the theory of the actor-network: Ordering, strategy, and heterogeneity. *Systems practice* 5: 379–393.

Leander, Anna. (2002a) The Cunning of Imperialist Reason: Using a Bourdieu Inspired Constructivism in IPE. COPRI Working Paper 33: 4–32.

Leander, Anna. (2002b) Do we really need reflexivity in IPE? Bourdieu's two reasons for answering affirmatively. *Review of International Political Economy* 9: 601–609.

Leander, Anna. (2005a) The market for force and public security: destabilizing consequences of private military companies. *Journal of Peace Research* 42: 605–622.

Leander, Anna. (2005b) The power to construct international security: on the significance of private military companies. *Millenium* 33: 803–826.

Leander, Anna. (2006) The 'Realpolitik of Reason': Thinking International Relations through Fields, Habitus and Practice , Paper Presented at the International Studies Association Annual Convention, San Diego 22–25 March.

Leander, Anna. (2008) Thinking Tools. In: Klotz, A. and Prakash, D. (eds) *Qualitative Methods in International Relations*, New York: Palgrave Macmillian.

Leander, Anna. (2010) Staging International Relations Practicing Bourdieu's Sociology. Annual Conference of the International Studies Association (ISA), 17–20 February. New Orleans.

Leonard, Mark. (2005) *Why Europe will run the 21st century*, London and New York: Fourth Estate.

Lepgold, Joseph. (1998) Is Anyone Listening? International Relations Theory and the Problem of Policy Relevance. *Political Science Quarterly* 113: 43–62.

Lepgold, Joseph and Nincic Miroslav. (2001) *Beyond the Ivory Tower. International Relations Theory and the Issue of Policy Relevance*, New York: Columbia University Press.

Lepgold, Joseph and Nincic, Miroslav. (2002) *Being Useful. Policy Relevance and International Relations Theory*, Ann Arbor: University of Michigan Press.

Linklater, Andrew. (2004) Norbert Elias. 'The Civilising Process' and the Sociology of International Relations. *International Politics* 41: 3–35.

Luhmann, Niklas. (1998) *Observations on Modernity*, Stanford, CA: Stanford University Press.

Mandelbaum, Michael. (1996) *The Dawn of Peace in Europe*, New York: The Century Foundation.

Manners, Ian. (2002) Normative Power Europe: A contradiction in terms? *Journal of Common Market Studies* 40: 235–258.

Markusen, Ann. (1992) Dismantling the Cold War Economy. *World Policy Journal* 9: 389–399.

Maastricht Treaty. (1991) *Treaty of the European Union*, Maastricht: Members of the European Community, negotiated 1991, signed 1992 and entered into force 1 January 2003.

Matlary, Janne Haaland. (2006) When Soft Power Turns Hard: Is an EU Strategic Culture Possible? *Security Dialogue* 37: 105–121.

MccGwire, Michael. (1998) NATO expansion: 'a policy error of historic importance'. *Review of International Studies* 24: 23–42.

McCourt, David M. (2010) Rethinking Britain's Role in the World for a New Decade. The Limits of Discursive Therapy and the Promise of Field Theory. *The British Journal of Politics and International Relations* 13: 145–164.

Mearsheimer, John J. (1990) Back to the Future: Instability in Europe after the Cold War. *International Security* 15: 5–56.

Melescanu, Teodor. (1993) Security in Central Europe. a positive-sum game. *NATO Review* 41: 12–18.

Mérand, Frédéric. (2008) *European Defence Policy: Beyond the Nation State*, Oxford: Oxford University Press.

Michalski, Anna and Wallace, Helen. (1992) *The European Community: The Challenge of Enlargement*, London: The Royal Institute of International Affairs.

Milliken, Jennifer. (1999) The Study of Discourse in International Relations: A Critique of Research and Methods. *European Journal of International Relations* 5: 225–254.

Missiroli, Antonio. (2003) *Financing ESDP*, Paris: EU-ISS.

Moens, Alexander. (2003) ESDP, the United States and the Atlantic Alliance. In: Howorth, J. and Keeler, J.T.S. (eds) *Defending Europe: The EU, NATO and the quest for European Autonomy*, New York and Houndsmills: Palgrave Macmillan, 25–37.

Moravscik, Andrew. (1998) *The choice for Europe*, London: UCL Press.

Morgenthau, Hans J. (1986[1948]) *Politics Among Nations. The Struggle for Power and Peace*, New York: Knopf.

Myles, John F. (2004) From Doxa to Experience. Issues in Bourdieu's Adoption of Husserlian Phenomenology. *Theory, Culture & Society* 21: 91–107.

NAC. (1990a) *Final Communiqué*, Brussels, Belgium: North Atlantic Council Ministerial Communiqué, 17–18 December.

NAC. (1990b) *London Declaration on a Transformed North Atlantic Alliance*, London: Issued by the Heads of State and Government participating in the meeting of the North Atlantic Council, London 5–6 July.

NAC. (1991) *NATO's Core Security Functions in the New Europe*, Copenhagen, Denmark, Press Communiqué M-1(91)44: North Atlantic Council Meeting in Ministerial Session, Ministerial Communiqué 6–7 June.

NAC. (1992) *Final Communiqué*, Oslo, Norway: North Atlantic Council, 4 June.

NAC. (1994) *Declaration of Heads of State and Government*, Brussels, Belgium. Press Communiqué M-NAC-1(94)3: North Atlantic Council Ministerial Communiqué, 11 January.

NAC. (1996a) *Final Communique*, Brussels, Belgium: Press Communique M-NAC-2(96) 165: North Atlantic Council Ministerial Meeting Communique, 10 December.

NAC. (1996b) *Final Communiqué*, Berlin, Germany. Press Communiqué M-NAC-1 (96)63: North Atlantic Council Communiqué, 3 June.

NAC. (1999) *Washington Summit Communiqué*, Washington, DC: Issued by the Heads of State and Government participating in the North Atlantic Council in Washington D.C. on 24th April.

NAC. (2001) *NATO's Response to Terrorism*, Brussels, Belgium. Press Release M-NAC-2(2001)159: Statement issued at the Ministerial Meeting of the North Atlantic Council, 6 December.

NATO. (1949) *The North Atlantic Treaty*, Washington, DC: NATO.

NATO. (1967) *The Harmel Report. Text of the Report of the Committee of Three on Non-Military Cooperation in NATO. The Future Tasks of the Alliance*, Brussels: NATO, 13–14 December.

NATO. (1990–2003) *Overview of NATO Secretary General speeches*, at www.nato.int/docu/speech, accessed 13 May.

NATO. (1991) *The Alliance's Strategic Concept. Agreed by the Heads of State and Government*, Rome: North Atlantic Council, 8 November.

NATO. (1991–2003) *Overview of NATO press releases*, at www.nato.int/docu/pr: accessed 13 May 2008.

NATO. (1994a) *Partnership for Peace: Framework Document, Annex to M-1(94)2*, Brussels, NATO Headquarters: Issued by Heads of State and Government participating in the Meeting of the North Atlantic Council, 10–11 January.

NATO. (1994b) *Partnership for Peace: Invitation, Press Communiqué M-1(94)2*, Brussels, NATO Headquarters: Issued by the Heads of State and Government Participating in the Meeting of the North Atlantic Council, 10–11 January.

NATO. (1995) *Study on NATO Enlargement*, www.nato.int/docu/basictxt/enl-9501. htm: NATO.

NATO. (1997a) *Founding Act of Mutual Relations, Cooperation and Security between NATO and the Russian Federation*, Paris: NATO and Russia.

NATO. (1997b) *Madrid Declaration on Euro-Atlantic Security and Cooperation*, Madrid, Spain: North Atlantic Council. Issued by Heads of State and Government. Press Release M-1(97)81, 8 July.

NATO. (1998) *Partnership for Peace. A political view: Secretary General's Remarks*, Oberammergau: PfP Defense Planning Symposium, 15 January.

NATO. (1999) *Membership Action Plan, NATO Press Release NAC-S(99)66*, Washington: NATO Washington Summit.

NATO. (2000) *First joint WEU/NATO crisis management exercise – CMX/CRISEX 2000 – to be held from 17 to 23 February 2000*, Brussels: NATO Press Release (2000), 31 January.

NATO. (2001) *NATO Handbook*, Brussels: NATO Office of Information and Press.

NATO. (2002a) *Financial and Economic Data Relating to NATO Defence. Defence Expenditures of NATO Countries 1980–2002*, Brussels: NATO Press Release M-DPC-2 (2002): 139.

NATO. (2002b) *Partnership in Action*, Brussels: NATO Office of Information and Press.

NATO. (2002c) *Prague Summit Declaration*, Prague, Czech Republic: Press Release (2002)127: Heads of State and Government participating in the meeting of the North Atlantic Council in Prague, 21 November.

NATO. (2007a) *NATO and the fight against terrorism. Response to 11 September*, Brussels: NATO at www.nato.int/issues/terrorism/evolve02.html.

NATO. (2007b) *Partnership for Peace, Annex E, Improving Training and Education in Partnership for Peace*, Brussels: NATO. Available at www.nato.int/pfp/docu/ d990615f.htm.

NATO. (2007c) *PfP Consortium: Historical Background*, https://consortium.pims.org/ historical-background: PfP Consortium of Defense Academies and Security Studies Institutes: accessed 19 September 2007.

NATO. (2007d) *PfP Consortium: Summary*, https://consortium.pims.org/pfp-con sortium-of-defense-academies-and-security-studies-institutes-summary:    accessed June 26, 2008.

NATO. (2007e) *Science for Peace and Security: Calendar*, NATO: Science for Peace and Security (SPS): available at: http://www.nato.int/science/calendar/calendar 2007. htm, accessed 19 September 2007.

NATO. (2007f) *Science for Peace and Security: Introduction*, NATO: Science for Peace and Security (SPS): available at: http://www.nato.int/science/about_sps/introduction. htm, Accessed 26 June 2008.

NATO. (2007g) *Science for Peace and Security: Publications*, NATO: Science for Peace and Security (SPS): available at: http://www.nato.int/science/publication/html/ sts_series.htm, accessed 19 September 2007.

NATO. (2008) *NATO Defence Expenditures since 1963*, http://nato.int/issues/defence_ expenditures/index.html: NATO, accessed 14 April 2008.

NDC. (2011) *60th Anniversary Chronicle Book, 1951–2011*, Rome: NATO Defense College.

NE. (2004) *Europe and its think tanks: a promise to be fulfilled. An analysis of think tanks specialised in European Policy Issues in the enlarged European Union*, Paris: Notre Europe: Etudes and Recherches.

Neumann, Iver B. (1999) *The Uses of the Other. 'The East' in European Identity Formation*, Minneapolis: University of Minnesota Press.

Neumann, Iver B. (2002) Returning Practice to the linguistic turn: The case of diplomacy. *Millennium: Journal of International Studies* 31: 627–653.

Newsom, David D. (1995) Foreign Policy and Academia. *Foreign Policy* 101: 52–67.

Nierenberg, WA (2001) NATO science programs: origins and influence. *Technology in Society* 23: 361–374.

Nye, Joseph S. (1999) Redefining NATO's mission in the Information Age. *NATO Review* 47: 12–15.

Nye, Joseph S. (2004) *Soft Power. The Means to Success in the World of Politics*, New York: Public Affairs.

Onuf, Nicholas. (1995) Levels. *European Journal of International Relations* 1: 35–58.

Oren, Ido. (2000) Is Culture Independent of National Security? How America's National Security Concerns Shaped 'Political Culture' Research. *European Journal of International Relations* 6: 543–573.

OSCE. (2007) *The OSCE Handbook. The Organization for Security and Co-Operation in Europe*, Vienna: OSCE Press and Public Information Section.

Patomäki, Heikki and Wight, Colin. (2000) After Postpositivism? The Promises of Critical Realism. *International Studies Quarterly* 44: 213–237.

Pedrazzini, Fausto. (2004) From Science Fellowships to Reintegration Grants: Evolving Priorities. *Science* June 25. Available at: http://sciencecareers.sciencemag.org/career_maga zine/previous_issues/articles/2004_2006_2025/ndoi.16846093732556032576, accessed April 2014.

Pels, Dick. (1995) Knowledge politics and anti-politics: Toward a critical appraisal of Bourdieu's concept of intellectual autonomy. *Theory and Society* 24: 79–104.

Peters, Guy. (1998) Policy Networks: myth, metaphor and reality. In: Marsh, D. (ed.) *Comparing Policy Networks*, Buckingham and Philadelphia: Open University Press, 21–33.

Petersen, Karen Lund. (2011) *Corporate Risk and National Security Redefined*, London and New York: Routledge.

Pipes, Daniel. (2002) Who is the Enemy?, Commentary, January.

Pop, L. (2007) Time & Crisis. Framing Success & Failure in Romania's Post-Communist Transformations. *Review of International Studies* 33: 395–413.

Pouliot, Vincent. (2004) Toward a Bourdieusian Constructivism in IR: Outline of a theory of practice of security communities. Paper presented to the Fifth pan-European Conference, Standing Group on International Relations, 9–11 September. The Hague, Netherlands.

Pouliot, Vincent. (2006) The Alive and Well transatlantic security community: a theoretical reply to Michael Cox. *European Journal of International Relations* 12: 119–127.

Pouliot, Vincent. (2007) Pacification Without Collective Identification: Russia and the Transatlantic Security Community in the Post-Cold War Era. *Journal of Peace Research* 44: 605–622.

Pouliot, Vincent. (2008) The Logic of Practicality: A Theory of Practice of Security Communities. *International Organization* 62: 257–288.

Pouliot, Vincent. (2010) *International Security in Practice: the Politics of NATO-Russia Diplomacy*, Cambridge and New York: Cambridge University Press.

Rasmussen, Mikkel Vedby. (2001) Reflective Security: NATO and International Risk Society. *Millennium* 30: 285–309.

Rasmussen, Mikkel Vedby. (2003) *The West, Civil Society and the Construction of Peace*, Basingstoke: Palgrave Macmillan.

Ray, Admiral Norman. (1997) The Enlargement of NATO. *Conference on 'Central and Eastern Europe and Euro-Atlantic Security'*, April 24–26, Slovenia.

Ray, James Lee and Russett Bruce. (1996) The future as arbiter of theoretical controversies: predictions, explanations and the end of the Cold War. *British Journal of Political Science* 26: 441–470.

Reckwitz, Andreas. (2002) Toward a Theory of Social Practices. A Development in Culturalist Theorizing. *European Journal of Social Theory* 5: 243–263.

Risse-Kappen, Thomas. (1994) Ideas Do Not Float Freely: Transnational Coalitions, Domestic Structures, and the End of the Cold War. *International Organization* 48: 185–214.

Risse-Kappen, Thomas. (1995) *Cooperation among Democracies. The European Influence on U.S. Foreign Policy*, Princeton and Chichester: Princeton University Press.

Risse-Kappen, Thomas. (1996) Collective Identity in a Democratic Community: The Case of NATO. In: Katzenstein, P.J. (ed.) *The Culture of National Security – Norms and Identity in World Politics*, New York: Columbia University Press, 357–400.

Risse, Thomas. (2000) Let's argue! Communicative Action in World Politics. *International Organization* 54: 1–39.

Robertson, Lord George. (2001a) An attack on us all: NATO's Response to Terrorism, National Press Club, Washington, DC: Remarks by NATO Secretary General at the Atlantic Council of the United States, 10 October 2001.

Robertson, Lord George. (2001b) *The Future of Partnership* , Brussels, Belgium: Speech by NATO Secretary General, Lord Robertson at the EAPC Conference in the NATO HQ, 26 October.

Robertson, Lord George. (2001c) *The Future of the Transatlantic Link* , Lisbon, Portugal: Speech by NATO Secretary General, 24 October.

Robertson, Lord George. (2001d) Press Conference, taped recording is available at, http://www.nato.int/issues/terrorism/chronology/html: accessed 13 May 2008.

Robertson, Lord George. (2002a) NATO after September 11, New York: Speech by Lord Robertson, Secretary General of NATO, to the Pilgrims of the United States, 31 January.

Robertson, Lord George. (2002b) NATO: Enlarging and redefining itself , London: Speech by NATO Secretary General to Chatham House, 18 February.

Robin, Ron. (2001) *The Making of the Cold War Enemy. Culture and Politics in the Military-Intellectual Complex*, Princeton, NJ and Oxford: Princeton University Press.

Sagan, Scott D. and Waltz, Kenneth N. (1995) *The Spread of Nuclear Weapons*, New York: W.W. Norton.

Salter, Mark B. (2007) On Exactitute in Disciplinary Science: A Response to the Network Manifesto. *Security Dialogue* 38: 113–122.

Schatzki, Theodore R., Cetina, Karin Knorr, Savigny, Eike Von, *et al.* (2001) *The Practice Turn in Contemporary Theory*, London and New York: Routledge.

Schiermeier, Quirin. (2003) NATO reform promises more publicity for less science. *Nature* 422: 248.

Schimmelfennig, F. (1998) NATO Enlargement: A Constructivist Explanation. *Security Studies* 8: 198–234.

Schinkel, Willem. (2003) Pierre Bourdieu's Political Turn? *Theory, Culture & Society* 20: 69–93.

Schubert, J. Daniel. (1995) From a Politics of Transgression Toward an Ethic of Reflexivity. *American Behavioral Scientist* 38: 1003–1017.

Schuwirth, Rainer. (2002) Hitting the Helsinki Headline Goal. *NATO Review*: 1–3 (web edition).

Senn, Martin and Elhardt, Christoph. (2013) Bourdieu and the bomb: Power, Language, and the doxic battle over the value of nuclear weapons. *European Journal of International Relations* doi: 10.1177/1354066113476117.

Shapin, Steven and Schaffer, Simon. (2011) *Leviathan and the Air-Pump. Hobbes, Boyle, and the Experimental Life,* Princeton: Princeton University Press.

Shea, Jamie. (2004) NATO-EU Relations, Video lecture available at http://www.nato.int/multi/video/lectures/index.html, accessed 10 October 2007.

Sherrington, Philippa. (2000) Shaping the Policy Agenda: Think Tank Activity in the European Union. *Global Society* 14: 173–189.

Singer, David J. (1972) The correlates of war project. Interim report and rationale. *World Politics* 24: 243–270.

Singer, David J. (1960) International Conflict. Three Levels of Analysis. *World Politics* 12: 453–461.

Singer, David J. (1969) The level of analysis problem in international relations. In: Rosenau, J.N. (ed.) *International Politics and Foreign Policy: A reader in research and theory,* London: Free Press, 20–29.

Singer, Max and Wildavsky Aaron. (1993) *The Real World Order: Zones of Peace, Zones of Turmoil,* Chatham: Chatham House Publishers.

Siverson, Randolph M. (2000) A Glass Half-Full? No, but Perhaps a Glass Filling: The Contributions of International Political Research to Policy. *Political Science and Politics* 33: 59–64.

Sloan, Stanley R. (2005) *NATO, the European Union, and the Atlantic Community,* Oxford: Rowman and Littlefield.

Smith, Steve. (1997) Power and truth: a reply to William Wallace. *Review of International Studies* 23: 507–516.

Smith, Steve. (2004) Singing our World into Existence: International Relations Theory and September 11. *International Studies Quarterly* 48: 499–515.

Snyder, Glenn H. (1984) The Security Dilemma in Alliance Politics. *World Politics* 36: 461–495.

Solana, Javier. (1996) NATO in transition. *Perceptions. Journal of International Affairs* 1: 1–5 (download version at http://www.sam.gov.tr/perceptions/Volume1/March-May1996/NATOINTRANSITION.pdf).

Solana, Javier. (1997) NATO Beyond Enlargement , London: Remarks by the Secretary General of NATO to the UK Atlantic Council, 19 November.

Solana, Javier. (1999a) An Alliance Fit for the 21st Century. *NATO Review* 3: 3–4.

Solana, Javier. (1999b) Growing the Alliance. *The Economist* 350: 23–28.

Solana, Javier. (1999c) Press Statement: NATO Press Release (1999) 041, March 25, Brussels.

Spiegel, Gabrielle M. (2005) *Practicing History. New Directions in Historical Writing after the Linguistic Turn,* New York: Routledge.

Spoerle-Strohmenger, Petra. (2003) *Struggling hard for solutions to the conflict in Iraq,* Munich: Munich Conference on Security Policy.

Stone, Diane. (1996) *Capturing the political imagination. Think tanks and the policy process,* London and Portland, OR: Frank Cass.

Stone, Diane. (2000) Think Tank Transnationalisation and Non-Profit Analysis, Advice and Advocacy. *Global Society* 14: 153–172.

Stone, Diane and Denham, Andrew. (2004) *Think tank traditions. Policy research and the politics of ideas*, Manchester and New York: Manchester University Press.

Stone, Diane, Denham, Andrew and Garnett, Mark. (1998) *Think Tanks of the World: Global Perspectives on Ideas, Policy and Governance*, Manchester: Manchester University Press.

Stone, Richard. (2002) NATO Ordered to Cut Science Program. *Science* 298: 946–947.

Strandsbjerg, Jeppe. (2012) Cartopolitics, Geopolitics and Boundaries in the Arctic. *Geopolitics* 17: 818–842.

Swartz, David L. (1997) *Culture and Power. The Sociology of Pierre Bourdieu*, Chicago, IL and London: University of Chicago Press.

Swartz, David L. (2008) Bringing Bourdieu's master concepts into organizational analysis. *Theory and Society* 37: 45–52.

Swartz, David L. and Zolberg, Vera L. (2004) *After Bourdieu. Influence, Critique, Elaboration*, Dordrecht: Kluwer International Publishers.

Sylvester, Christine. (2007) Anatomy of a Footnote. *Security Dialogue* 38.

Terriff, Terry. (2003) The CJTF Concept and the Limits of European Autonomy. In: Howorth J and Keeler J.T.S (eds) *Defending Europe: The EU, NATO and the quest for European Autonomy*, New York and Houndsmills: Palgrave Macmillan, 39–59.

Toews, John E. (1987) Intellectual History after the Linguistic Turn: The Autonomy of Meaning and the Irreducibility of Experience. *The American Historical Review* 92: 879–907.

Toje, Asle. (2005) The 2003 European Union Security Strategy: A Critical Appraisal. *European Foreign Affairs Review* 10: 117–133.

Treaty of Brussels. (1948) The Treaty of Brussels, WEU, Brussels: Signed by United Kingdom, France, Belgium, Luxembourg, and the Netherlands, 17 March.

Ullmann, John E. (1993) Converting Defence Facilities. *Society* 30: 23–31.

Ullrich, Heidi. (2004) European Union think tanks: generating ideas, analysis and debate. In: Stone, D. and Denham, A. (eds) *Think tank traditions. Policy research and the politics of ideas*, Manchester and New York: Manchester University Press, 51–71.

van Ham, Peter. (2001) Europe's Postmodern Identity: A Critical Appraisal. *International Politics* 38: 229–252.

Villumsen, Trine. (2007) Think tanks in Europe: Shaping ideas of security. *Militært Tidsskrift* 136: 143–160.

Villumsen, Trine. (2008) *Theory as practice and capital NATO in a Bourdieusian field of security in Europe towards a sociological approach to IR*, Copenhagen: University of Copenhagen, PhD Series 2008/4..

Villumsen, Trine and Büger, Christian. (2010) Security Expertise after Securitization: Coping with Dilemmas of Engaging with Practice. Annual Conference of the International Studies Association (ISA), 17–20 February 2010. New Orleans.

Wacquant, Loic J.D. (1998) Foreword. In: Bourdieu, P. (ed.) *The State Nobility*, Cambridge and Oxford: Polity Press, ix–xxii.

Walker, R.B.J. (1993) *Inside/Outside: International Relations as Political Theory*, Cambridge: Cambridge University Press.

Walker, R.B.J. (2007) Security, Critique, Europe. *Security Dialogue* 38: 95–103.

Wallace, William. (1994) Between Two Worlds: Think tanks and foreign policy. In: Hill, C. and Beshoff, P. (eds) *Two Worlds of International Relations. Academics,*

*Practitioners and the Trade in Ideas*, London: Routledge and London School of Economics, 139–164.

Wallace, William. (1996) Truth and Power, monks and technocrats: theory and practice in international relations. *Review of International Studies* 22: 301–321.

Wallace, William. (2004) Afterword: soft power, global agendas. In: Stone, D. and Denham, A. (eds) *Think tank traditions. Policy research and the politics of ideas*, Manchester and New York: Manchester University Press, 281–290.

Wallander, Celeste A. (2000) Institutional Assets and Adaptability: NATO After the Cold War. *International Organization* 54: 705–735.

Wallander, Celeste and Keohane Robert O. (1999) Risk, Threat, and Security Institutions. In: Haftendorn, H., Keohane, R., Wallander, C., *et al.* (eds) *Imperfect Unions: Security Institutions over Time and Space*, Oxford: Oxford University Press, 21–47.

Walt, Stephen M. (1987) *The Origins of Alliances*, Ithaca, NY: Cornell University Press.

Walt, Stephen M. (1991) The Renaissance of Security Studies. *International Studies Quarterly* 35: 211–239.

Waltz, Kenneth. (1959) *Man, the State and War: A Theoretical Analysis*, New York: Columbia University Press.

Waltz, Kenneth N. (1979) *Theory of International Politics*, New York: Random House.

Waltz, Kenneth N. (1981) *The Spread of Nuclear Weapons: More may be better*. Adelphi Paper 171.

Waltz, Kenneth N. (1993a) The Emerging Structure of International Politics. *International Security* 18: 44–79.

Waltz, Kenneth N. (1993b) The New World Order. *Millennium* 22: 187–195.

Waltz, Kenneth N. (2000) Structural Realism after the Cold War. *International Security* 25: 5–41.

Waltz, Kenneth N. (2001) NATO Expansion: A Realist's View. In: Rachaus, R.W. (ed.) *Explaining NATO Enlargement*, London and Portland: Frank Cass, 23–38.

Weaver, R Kent. (1989) The changing world of think tanks. *PS, Political Science & Politics* 22: 563.

Wendt, Alexander. (1992) Anarchy is What States Make of It: The Social Construction of Power Politics. *International Organization* 46: 391–425.

WEU. (1954) *Paris Agreement: The Modified Brussels Treaty*, Brussels, Belgium: Western European Union.

WEU. (1992) *Petersberg Declaration*, Bonn: Western European Union Council of Ministers, 19 June 1992.

WEU. (2000) *WEU Today*, Brussels: WEU Secretariat General.

White, Brian. (2001) *Understanding European Foreign Policy*, Houndsmills, Basingstoke and New York: Palgrave.

Whiting, Allen S. (1972) The Scholar and the Policy-Maker. *World Politics*, spring: 229–247.

Whitman, R. (1999) *Amsterdam's unfinished business? The Blair government's initiative and the future of the Western European Union*. ISS-WEU Occasional Paper 7.

Widmaier, Wesley W. (2004) Theory as Factor and the Theorist as an Actor: The 'Pragmatist Constructivist' Lessons of John Dewey and John Kenneth Galbraith. *International Studies Review* 6: 427–445.

Williams, Michael C. (1997) The Institutions of Security: Elements of a Theory of Security. *Cooperation and Conflict* 32: 287–307.

Williams, Michael C. (1999) The Practices of Security: Critical Contributions. *Cooperation and Conflict* 34: 341–344.

Williams, Michael C. (2001) The Discipline of the Democratic Peace: Kant, Liberalism and the Social Construction of Security Communities. *Cooperation and Conflict* 7: 525–533.

Williams, Michael C. (2007) *Culture and Security. Symbolic power and the politics of international security*, London and New York: Routledge.

Williams, Michael C. and Neumann Iver B. (2000) From Alliance to Security Community: NATO, Russia, and the Power of Identity. *Millennium* 29: 357–387.

Williams, Nigel. (1997) Cold war thaw leads to turmoil in NATO science. *Science* 278: 795.

Wyn Jones, Richard. (2001) *Critical Security and World Politics*, Boulder, CO: Lynne Rienner.

Wæver, Ole. (1995a) Securitization and Desecuritization. In: Lipschutz, R.D. (ed.) *On Security*, New York: Columbia University Press, 46–86.

Wæver, Ole. (1995b) What is security? – the securityness of security. In: Hansen, B. (ed.) *European Security 2000*. Copenhagen: Copenhagen Political Studies Press, 222.

Wæver, Ole. (1996) *The rise and fall of the inter-paradigm debate*, Cambridge: Cambridge University Press, 149–185.

Wæver, Ole. (1997) Concepts of Security, University of Copenhagen, unpublished PhD Dissertation.

Wæver, Ole. (1999) Securitizing Sectors? Reply to Eriksson. *Cooperation and Conflict* 34: 334–340.

Wæver, Ole. (2004) Aberystwyth, Paris, Copenhagen. New 'schools' in security theory and their origins between core and periphery, Montreal: Paper presented at the annual meeting of the International Studies Association, 17–20 March.

Wæver, Ole. (2007) Still a Discipline After All These Debates? In: Dunne, T., Kurki, M. and Smith, S. (eds) *International Relations Theories: Discipline and Diversity*, Oxford and New York: Oxford University Press, 288–308.

Wæver, Ole. (2012) Aberystwyth, Paris, Copenhagen: the Europeanness of New "Schools" of Security Theory in an American Field. In: Tickner, A.B. and Blaney, D.L. (eds) *Thinking International Relations Differently*, Abingdon: Routledge, 48–71.

Wæver, Ole and Buzan, Barry. (2007) After the Return to Theory: The Past, Present, and Future of Security Studies. In: Collins, A. (ed.) *Contemporary Security Studies*, Oxford: Oxford University Press, 383–402.

Zehfuss, M. (2001) Constructivism and Identity: A Dangerous Liaison. *European Journal of International Relations* 7: 315–348.

Zelikow, Philip. (1994) Foreign Policy Engineering: From Theory to Practice and Back Again. *International Security* 18: 143–171.

Zizek, Slavoj. (2004) NATO as the Left Hand of God? In: Cheng, S. (ed.) *Law, Justice, and Power*, Stanford, CA: Stanford University Press, 25–45.

# Index

Note: Page numbers in **boldface** indicate tables.